Jackson Browne

Jackson Browne

His Life and Music

MARK BEGO

CITADEL PRESS
Kensington Publishing Corp.
www.kensingtonbooks.com

CITADEL PRESS BOOKS are published by

Kensington Publishing Corp.
850 Third Avenue
New York, NY 10022

All Kensington titles, imprints, and distributed lines are available at special quantity discounts for bulk purchases for sales promotions, premiums, fund-raising, educational, or institutional use. Special book excerpts or customized printings can also be created to fit specific needs. For details, write or phone the office of the Kensington special sales manager: Kensington Publishing Corp., 850 Third Avenue, New York, NY 10022, attn: Special Sales Department; phone 1-800-221-2647.

CITADEL PRESS and the Citadel logo are reg. U.S. Pat. & TM Off.

Book design by Rachel Reiss

First printing: May 2005

10 9 8 7 6 5 4 3 2 1

Printed in the United States of America

Library of Congress Control Number: 2004116401

ISBN 0-8065-2642-4

To my dear friend Ann Watt

Thank you for my new New York adventure!

Contents

Acknowledgments

Bob and Mary Bego
Angela Bowie
Trippy Cunningham
James Fitzgerald
Susan Gilbert
Chris Gilman
Randy Jones
Marcy MacDonald
Zach Martin
Susan Mittelkauf
Barbra Nagel
Photofest
Peter Pierri
Jeremie Ruby-Strauss
Jed Ryan
David Salidor
Shea Scullin
Barbara Shelley
Bob Shuman
Andy Skurow
Star File Photos
Ann Watt
Mary Wilson

Jackson Browne

Twenty-first Century Everyman

IT IS OCTOBER 30, 2003, AT THE PALACE THEATER in Stamford, Connecticut. At exactly 7:30 P.M. a relaxed and confident Jackson Browne strides out on center stage to a thunderous round of applause. He is wearing a pair of gray jeans and a button-down green paisley shirt. At the age of fifty-five, he still has the same boyish looks, and the straight shoulder-length haircut that graced his very first album cover, over thirty years ago. In an era in which several of his folk/rock singing contemporaries are starting to look their age—and even beyond— Browne appears appealingly ageless.

There is only one chair set up center stage tonight, and behind it, eleven different acoustic guitars upright on individual stands, tuned and ready to be played. Beside the chair, there is an electric keyboard, for the occasional switch from guitar. With the exception of a large area rug on which his chair is resting, the stage is unadorned.

For his first number, he is surrounded by beams of tranquil sapphire blue light. Amid the sea of blue, Browne stands out clearly and comfortably in the glow of a white spotlight.

Launching into "I'm Alive," his first song, Jackson sings it like it is an anthem of survival. It instantly hits a harmonious chord with the mainly baby boomer crowd who has gathered here to be entertained and enlightened.

His voice is a little more gravely than when he released his debut album in 1972, but it is still clear, and filled with conviction. This is no "pretender," this is pure unadulterated Jackson Browne, bare bones, singing his songs of love, or loss, or disappointments, and—occasionally—of more lofty and socially conscious issues.

It is just Jackson, casually dressed, yet emotionally naked. He sits alone: a troubadour and his songs.

Tonight there is no band. There is no opening act. There are no guest stars. It is just Jackson, casually dressed, yet emotionally naked. He sits alone: a troubadour and his songs.

As he comes to the end of "I'm Alive," he acknowledges his messy mid-1990s' breakup with actress Daryl Hannah by commenting, "I started writing this song in the middle of a crisis, but the crisis is over."

Only occasionally does he make eye contact with his audience. And when he does, it is often to banter back and forth with enthusiastic fans who shout out between-song requests and who make pronouncements like he was not only an old friend, but also as though we were all seated in someone's living room.

As several voices shout out the titles of beloved recordings by Jackson, he tunes his guitar and shouts back, "I'll probably sing those songs, but probably not when you yell out for them." Just as in his entire career, this evening it is Jackson who calls all the shots. Throughout the nearly three-hour concert this particular night, he covers five decades of his songwriting, including "These Days" from the '60s, "Running on Empty" from the '70s, "Tender Is the Night" from the '80s, "Too Many Angels" from the '90s, and "The Naked Ride Home" from the 2000s.

He is good natured, but he runs a tight ship. When an overenthusiastic fan defies the ban on personal cameras, and a flashbulb suddenly illuminates the stage, Jackson makes his displeasure instantly known. Like a teacher reprimanding a misbehaving student, he verbally scolds the camera owner.

Although he projects somewhat of a serious attitude from the stage, Browne does manage to get in a few lighthearted jokes. When one of several audience members yells out for the song "Rosie," a

"For some of us, the night's just not complete without 'Rosie.'"

supposed ode to masturbation, Jackson quips, "For some of us, the night's just not complete without 'Rosie.'"

Between songs he says to the audience, "I hope you have a real nice Halloween, and a safe Halloween. I still don't know what to be."

An exuberant woman in the audience yells out to him, "Be at my house."

Browne laughs and replies, "It could happen."

At one point during the show he tunes one guitar, then switches to the keyboard, and then picks up a different guitar before finally sitting back down satisfied with his instrument choice. The set this evening comprises 90 percent of the album cuts and nonhits from his thirteen LPs. He doesn't perform obvious songs like his biggest chart hit "Somebody's Baby," or the song he wrote for the Eagles, "Take It Easy." Instead, he picks and chooses what he wants to sing and play, when he wants to sing and play it. There doesn't seem to be a set playlist. He sings songs like his somber "Love's Dark and Silent Gate," the contemplative "Fountain of Sorrow," and his lamenting "Late for the Sky." The audience obviously loves him just the way he is: unpredictable and sincere.

An amazingly unique performer, Jackson is still very much that same young singer who once played in Greenwich Village folk hangouts on Bleecker Street in the 1960s, and who shaped his onstage persona at The Troubadour in Los Angeles in the 1970s. When he finishes his set, he waves to the crowd and announces, "I wanna thank you for coming out here to see me sing."[1] Brought back by the enthusiastic reception he receives, he comes out for a couple of encore numbers. With the exception of one brief intermission, it has been the ultimate evening with the famed California troubadour. By the time he finally leaves the stage for the last time, it is 10:30 P.M.

This evening, it was "Jackson Browne *Truly* Unplugged." And the sold-out crowd loved him for it.

Jackson Browne has always been a performer who doesn't hesitate to put artistic integrity before money-making concerns. His career has never been shaped by hit singles or highly commercial concerns. He has never won a Grammy Award. He has never had a Number 1 song. Only one of his albums, *Hold Out*, hit the top of the charts. He was never lured into rap, new wave, or disco. And he has never made a startling or abrupt career move to reinvent himself. Even his biggest chart hit, "Somebody's Baby," is one of the least favorite of his songs. Yet, he remains one of the rock age's most beloved, enduring, and consistent stars.

With fourteen best-selling albums—many of them multimillion sellers— Jackson has been at the helm of one of the longest lasting and most impactful musical recording careers of the last forty years. His music has had its distinctly different phases. There was his brooding and sensitive period as personified by his much-covered hit "These Days." Then there was his druggy rocker age as represented by "Cocaine" and "Running on Empty." Next came his government-blasting highly political period as shown on the albums *No Nukes*, *Lives in the Balance*, and *World in Motion*. It was followed by his highly introspective and critically acclaimed survivor's anthem of an album *I'm Alive* in the 1990s.

Most people don't realize that his career has the depth and scope that it does. Few recall that he was one of the original members of the Nitty Gritty Dirt Band. Or that as a teenager he went across country to end up as one of the background musicians for Andy Warhol protégée and cult rock diva Nico.

> Few recall that he was one of the original members of the Nitty Gritty Dirt Band.

When he moved back to Los Angeles, he honed his skills at weekly showcase and "open mic" nights at The Troubadour, alongside Linda Ronstadt, Ry Cooder, John David Souther, as well as Glenn Frey and Don Henley of the Eagles. When his original singer/songwriter demo was sent to a potential manager, the manager—David Geffen—tossed it into the wastebasket. Fortunately, it was fished out by Geffen's secretary.

Jackson's first mainstream New York City solo stage debut came at the Fillmore East as Laura Nyro's opening act. His first wave of success came from being a songwriter, not a performer. His self-titled album was released in 1972, the same year that the Eagles turned his cowriting composition "Take It Easy" into their first chart hit. By the time he was twenty-four, Jackson's songs had already been recorded by the Byrds, Tom Rush, Jennifer Warnes, Bonnie Raitt, Johnny Rivers, and Linda Ronstadt. That same year, his own debut single, "Doctor My Eyes" became his first in a long string of hits for Browne himself.

"Take It Easy" has the distinction of being the opening cut of the biggest selling album in the United States: *The Eagles: Their Greatest Hits*. He was the hot new songwriter of the era, and even the Jackson Five recorded "Doctor My Eyes" and made it into a Top 10 hit in England.

What followed for Jackson Browne was the richest and most creatively fulfilling period of his life. *For Everyman* (1973), *Late for the Sky* (1974), *The Pretender* (1976), and *Running on Empty* (1977) all became million-selling albums, yielding such hits as "Rock Me on the Water," "The Pretender," "Here Come Those Tears Again," "Running on Empty," and "Stay."

In 1979, together with such close friends as Bonnie Raitt, John Hall, Graham Nash, and the Doobie Brothers, Jackson was one of the organizers and stars of the MUSE concerts held in Madison Square Garden. Their antinuclear power organization made headlines and tipped off a decade of politically based albums and songs for Browne. He took on the Reagan-led politics in Nicaragua with his *Lives in the Balance* album (1986) and the U.S. government's stance on homelessness in *World in Motion* (1989). Along the way, he became outspoken in his verbal social consciousness and lost a good percentage of his fan base because of this.

Still, the fact that he had a viable platform from which to expound his political views outweighed any degree of fan disenchantment. During this same era, he joined Amnesty International's Conspiracy of Hope Tour. In 1988, he was the only Caucasian American artist to be invited to a tribute to Nelson Mandela in London's Wembley Stadium.

It wasn't until his own home life began to erode that he once again turned his pen toward more personal issues. Throughout his life, he has had a spotty track record in the personal relationship department. His first wife committed suicide in the mid-1970s. His second wife—who was only a teenager when their relationship began—left him soon after their wedding. Finally, in the early 1990s he began a live-in affair with actress Daryl Hannah. When a highly publicized physical fight "allegedly" occurred between the duo, the press was quick to note that Hannah emerged from the brawl with a black eye. The press jumped to the conclusion that he physically abused her, while his friends claimed he merely defended himself. Again, his list of supporters was subdivided. Even Joni Mitchell wrote a song condemning his actions.

Like at other times in his life when he was faced with emotional turmoil, he turned his frustrations into deeply personal music. The result was the best album he had recorded since the 1970s, the 1993 classic *I'm Alive*.

Like at other times in his life when he was faced with emotional turmoil, he turned his frustrations into deeply personal music.

Since that time, he has continued to record albums full of highly evocative music including *Looking East* (1996) and *The Next Voice You Hear* (1997), his first "greatest hits" collection. He has continued to make several unpredictable career moves. In the mid-1990s, he performed at Lincoln Center in an all-star concert version of *The Wizard of Oz*, with Jewel as Dorothy and Natalie

Cole as Glinda the Good Witch. The role of the Scarecrow was played by Jackson.

As the twenty-first century dawned, it was still Browne's political sensibilities that often provided him with direction. In 2002, he released his thirteenth album, *The Naked Ride Home*, which continued to play on the same harmonic strong points that have characterized his entire career. Then in 2004, Browne was inducted into the Rock and Roll Hall of Fame, throwing the spotlight on his entire body of work.

In spite of all of the songs that Jackson has written about his life, his experiences, and his insights, there is still much that is not known about him. For instance, what is it that makes Jackson Browne tick? In *Time* magazine, Jay Cocks once claimed, "Browne never wears much armor—vulnerability is a great part of his appeal both as a writer and performer."[2]

Although his initial fame was based on his highly personal songs from the 1970s, this did not make everyone his fan. In *Musician* magazine, British rock star Elvis Costello once referred to the long-haired California troubadour's autobiographical, brooding, and poetic singing style as being from the " 'Fuck me, I'm sensitive' Jackson Browne school of seduction."[3]

What drives Browne to use his own life as material for songs? According to him, "The truth is, I don't even know what I do, and I don't quite know how it's supposed to be done. My songs are the residue of my life. When everything else is done, the songs are what's left. Generally, it tends to be sort of looking in the rearview mirror. The songs are about a time that is past or a resolve about the present that in some way relates to the past."[4]

> My songs are the residue of my life. When everything else is done, the songs are what's left.

In addition to being one of the organizers of the historic MUSE concerts, he was arrested while protesting the Diablo Canyon nuclear plant. He has performed at benefit after benefit to raise money for the supporters of the late Karen Silkwood, the politician Jerry Brown, "Sun City," the Children's Defense Fund, and whatever cause that takes his soul.

At what point in his life did he decide to use his songwriting skills to expound on his political beliefs? According to him, "Music really does change the world every time you listen to it. Put on your earphones and you are transported."[5]

While he has been accused of using his position on the concert stage as a soapbox for his own views, he replies, "People who think artists should not be political would leave war to the generals, and politics to the 'professional' politicians. To me, that's the opposite of a democracy. A democracy implies that we have the participation of everybody."[6]

Throughout his career, Jackson Browne has sold over 15 million albums, and his music has deeply touched fans around the world. Still, many more questions remain unanswered. Questions like: How is it that he was actually born in Germany? Is it true that he was named after a character in a movie? What was his family life like when he was growing up? Why did his relationship with his father fall apart? What drove his first wife to commit suicide? What have his experiences been like as a single father? Who is the "Red Neck Friend" he sings about in that particular song? How important was cocaine in his life in the 1970s, and what made him want to kick his substance abuse problems? What fuels his deep and sincere interest in political issues? What were the facts behind his breakup with Daryl Hannah? Is the song "Rosie" really about masturbation? What is his relationship with the Eagles, Bonnie Raitt, and Crosby, Stills & Nash? How does he feel about his induction into the Rock and Roll Hall of Fame? To find the answers to these questions, one has to delve all the way back—to his growing up years in Orange County, California, and beyond...

> Jackson Browne has sold over 15 million albums, and his music has deeply touched fans around the world.

CHAPTER 1

Clyde Jackson Browne

To fully understand Jackson Browne, you have to know something about his family background. Although Jackson did come out of the whole California music scene, he was in fact born in Europe, right after World War II. His natural quest for knowledge was primarily shaped by both of his parents, by his sister and brother, and—even though he never met him— by his paternal grandfather. His grandpa Clyde was a freethinker, and he, too, used his influential position in the community to voice his highly liberal and humanistic opinions. He set the tone within the family to think for one's self and to speak up—whether your message was popular or not.

> His natural quest for knowledge was primarily shaped by both of his parents, by his sister and brother, and—even though he never met him—by his paternal grandfather.

Clyde Browne is said to be the kind of man who marched to the beat of his own drum. Born in 1872, he was a printer by trade in the Los Angeles suburb of Highland Park. He loved poetry, and as a printer he was able to publish his own volume of poems. Clyde rhapsodized in his poems about local sites and items of inspiration, including one called "The Old Pear Trees." He also authored his own regular column in the local weekly newspaper. In his column, he reported news, and in the section "Clyde Browne Remarks" within the column, he could write about whatever he wanted and express his own opinions on any number of subjects.

He was someone who loved adventure. At one point in his life, he set off in a boat for a Pacific Ocean sea voyage with a couple of his printer buddies. Their tour was set to last three months. However, when Browne failed to arrive home at the appointed date, his wife, Grace, notified the authorities. Clyde and crew were fine, however they had shipwrecked the boat onto a small island off the coast of California, south of Los Angeles.

In addition, Clyde was also a gifted musician. He could adeptly play keyboards—including the pipe organ—the mandolin, and several other instruments. Politically, he was a staunch Democrat. A liberal thinker, he strongly advocated women's suffrage.

Clyde also had his own images of grandeur. It was his dream to build a house that would be something of a monument in which he could live. With that basic goal, he set about to design and construct a stone and adobe mansion to be called Abbey San Encino. Working with a pair of friends, Browne made deals for his building materials, finding all kinds of bargains on used roofing tiles and discarded bricks. Since this was the era of Prohibition, he came across one of his best deals when a local hotel was forced to dismantle its bar. It seemed that the bar had several exquisite stained glass windows, and Clyde was able to get them for a fraction of their worth. The windows became an impressive feature of the mansion.

Jackson Browne later said of Grandpa Clyde, "I grew up in the house that my grandfather built outside of Los Angeles, in the countryside. He built it by hand, one stone on top of the other. The house had a chapel with a pipe organ. He was part of a generation of people in L.A. who were spiritualists and poets; I think Southern California in general drew those kinds of people. I grew up with those kinds of values."[1]

> "I grew up in the house that my grandfather built outside of Los Angeles, in the countryside. He built it by hand, one stone on top of the other."

By 1922, seven years after Clyde had started the project, he was still hard at work on Abbey San Encino. There was adobe to treat, masonry to set, tile setting and plastering needing to be done, and copper chimney aprons to construct. The work seemed endless. Finally, in 1925 the structure was completed, and the Browne family took up permanent residence there.

The Browne family consisted of Clyde and Grace and their son, Clyde Jack Browne. While he was still a child, young Clyde became the "littlest apprentice" to his dad and was sent off on rock gathering expeditions. Since they were going to live in an abbey, what more fitting playtime fantasy to have than pretending to be a knight in shining armor? Little "Jack" had his own suit of armor. The helmet was fashioned from a tin can, a trash can lid made the perfect shield, and a stick replicated the sword.

As a teenager, Jack Browne was an active and popular student at Franklin High School. He sang with the glee club, performed in school plays, was a cheerleader, and managed the football team.

From an early age, Jack began to glean his father's proficiency for musical instruments. His instrumental scope encompassed the French horn, the piano, the guitar, the tuba, the clarinet, and the huge pipe organ at Abbey San Encino. His huge interest in jazz music made joining the high school's Almanac Jazz Orchestra a natural move. His tenure with the jazz ensemble even led to a gig at the Hollywood hot spot, the Mocambo.

Unable to decide which career course he liked the best—printing or music—he simply continued in both. He worked in his father's print shop by day, and played in local piano bars or picked up gigs at dance halls by night.

According to Jack, during this era he had a chance meeting with young Mickey Rooney and Judy Garland. They asked him if he could write some music for them, as they were the costars of the popular Andy Hardy series of films. He was interested in their offer, until he found out that he would be required to do the work "on speculation." He told Rooney and Garland, "I'm a professional. As such I must be paid for my work."[2] He later admitted that he regretted that decision, because he could have ended up with a career writing music for films.

While Clyde was building the mansion, he also constructed a wooden house on the same property for the family to live in. In later years, Clyde rented out the house to several people. More often than not, it was local artists who called the wooden structure "home."

Clyde was able to reside in his beloved Abbey San Encino for over fifteen years. However, when he died, his son Jack closed the family print shop, sold the printing equipment, and enlisted in the military. It would be nearly ten years before he saw the mansion again.

In the army, Jack was stationed in Seward, Alaska. While there, he met and fell in love with Beatrice Amanda Dahl. They had met at a USO military dance, where Jack was playing in the band. When Jack was transferred for duty in Germany, Bea managed to land a job as an army typist and joined him in Europe, where they were married.

Jack was fortunately not on the battlefield, but instead—due to his printer's experience—was the production manager and copy editor of the military newspaper *Stars and Stripes*. When the war ended, he opted to remain in Germany with Bea to start a family. In less than four years, three children were born to Jack and Bea Browne.

A daughter, Roberta, was born in 1946 in Nuremberg. The family nicknamed her "Berbie." The second child, Clyde, was born in Heidelberg on October 9, 1948. As a child, he was known as "Jackie," but the music world would later come to know him as "Jackson Browne." The third child, Edward Severin, was born in Frankfurt in 1949.

> As a child, he was known as "Jackie," but the music world would later come to know him as "Jackson Browne."

Time magazine later revealed where the name "Jackson" came from. According to that publication, "His father was also something of a jokester (the name 'Jackson' was partly inspired by a gag in a [Bing] Crosby/[Bob] Hope/[Dorothy] Lamour *Road* excursion) and [he was] a reasonably hot Dixieland jazz player."[3] In fact, one of Jack Browne's prime claims to fame was that while in Germany he once played with the French jazz guitar legend Django Reinhardt.

Born in 1910 in Liberchies, Belgium, Reinhardt was the son of an impoverished gypsy family who eventually moved to the vicinity near the fortifications that surround old Paris, close to the Choisy Gate. He was given his first guitar at the age of twelve, and he immediately showed that he possessed an instinctive musical ability. Playing in the local bars and clubs in Paris, he began to make a name for himself. At the age of eighteen he and his wife, Sophie, lived in a cavern. The cavern was filled with celluloid artificial flowers that his wife sold in the marketplace. When Django dropped a lit candle on the highly flammable flowers, they went up in flames. In seconds, the room was engulfed in blazing plastic. Wrapped up in blankets, the pair narrowly escaped from the fire, but Django sustained severe burns on his left hand and on the right side of his body, especially his leg.

Doctors wanted to amputate his badly burned right leg, but he refused to allow it. As he convalesced for months, someone bought him a guitar. His left hand had been so damaged that only two of his fingers still had full mobility. Determined to live with his new physical limitations, Django came up with a whole new way of playing music with the functional fingers he still had. A band comprising fourteen players—including Django, violin player Stephane Grappelli,

Roger Chaput, and Louis Vola—were hired to play music at the Hotel Cambridge during teatime. He built up a following there. Finally, in 1934 Reinhardt found fame as the star of the Quintet of the Hot Club of France. When Ultraphone Records recorded the quintet's first songs, "Dinah," "Tiger Rag," "Oh Lady Be Good," and "I Saw Stars," they became a huge musical sensation. The quintet went on to produce hundreds of recordings that are still popular with jazz aficionados on both sides of the Atlantic. He remained a jazz star until his death in 1953. There is still a tiny bar in the northern part of Paris in which Reinhardt once played. The walls of the bar are covered with pictures of Reinhardt, and the music of that legend is kept alive by his fans and musicians who emulate his unique playing style.

When Jack Browne had the privilege of playing with Reinhardt one day at a USO-sponsored tour of U.S. army bases in postwar Germany, it had a profound effect on him. It made him want to really pursue the musical career he had once dreamed of having. As a souvenir of having played piano with Django, a friend took a black-and-white photograph of the pair making music together. Jack had Reinhardt autograph the photo for him on which he inscribed, "Pour Jaks: En Souvenir du Chatau Meaux–Django Reinhardt." The photo became a prize possession of Jack Browne's.

> When Jack Browne had the privilege of playing with Reinhardt one day at a USO-sponsored tour of U.S. army bases in postwar Germany, it had a profound effect on him.

By 1951, Jack Browne was ready to pack up his family, return to the United States, and concentrate on music. The five members of the Browne family took up residence in Abbey San Encino, which had been waiting for them all these years.

Back in the Los Angeles area, Jack wasted little time. He ended up recording some songs in the early 1950s for television with gospel great Mahalia Jackson. And with trombone player Jack Teagarden he recorded several of his own songs on acetate. One of the songs was a jazz variation on a Dear John letter, called "Dear Jackson."

When neither of these projects yielded a musical career, Jack returned to the printing business. However, on Sundays he continued to play Dixieland jazz onstage with the Hot Jazz Society of Glendale. Often, he would host jazz jam sessions in his home.

Beatrice began tidying up the mansion. Flowers were planted around the circular driveway and the patio was fixed up. Young Jackson, Eddie, and Berbie loved playing in the large yard. It had tall trees to climb and a hill perfect for riding a large piece of cardboard down, as though it was a toboggan on a snowy slope. Jackson especially loved playing cowboy, complete with a scarf and a favorite cowboy hat.

One evening in 1954, Bea went outside to call Eddie into the house for the family's 6:00 P.M. dinner. Hearing his mother call him, Eddie jumped on his bicycle and pulled out of a blind alley, only to be struck by an oncoming car. He ended up with a fractured jaw, pelvis, and ribs and a cracked skull. He was in a coma for two weeks. The five-year-old boy survived, after having a plate put in his head. Thereafter, his physical activities were severely limited.

Around this same period of time, young Jackson decided that what he most wanted to be when he grew up was an artist. Since there were over a dozen cats that lived on their property, it was felines that were his favorite subject for drawings and paintings.

> Young Jackson decided that what he most wanted to be when he grew up was an artist.

Looking back on his growing up years, Jackson Browne later said, "If you ask me what kind of childhood I had, I'd say, 'Normal.' "[4]

Jack Browne began to encourage his children to get involved in his love of jazz music. Berbie wanted to focus on the piano. Eddie was asked by his father what instrument he wanted to play. When he told his father that what he wanted most was an accordion, like the one he saw Myron Floren playing on the *Lawrence Welk Show*, Jack was a bit dismayed. Eddie very quickly went through the accordion, the saxophone, and then the drums. Jackson was the most disciplined of the three, taking up the cornet and playing in the Garvanza Elementary School orchestra.

Jackson recalled, "I used to sit around . . . and [my father] would play me these records, and I'd copy the licks . . . Red Nichols, Louis Armstrong. I had Louis Armstrong solos down to the note, or so I thought. . . . It was probably more like a *Reader's Digest* version of his solos. The problem was . . . that I missed the whole point—I didn't understand what jazz was all about. . . . I never understood that jazz was a system of people digging one another . . . and I didn't understand until I was in a band myself."[5]

Looking back on this era, Jackson remembered, "My father was a jazz musician, and he had a lot of horns. He had a whole collection of horns. He used

> My father used to have these enormous jam sessions, and there would be like 50 people standing around here laughing and drinking and playing Dixieland

to call us in to play. We'd be playing in the neighborhood, and my father would get on the front porch with a Sousaphone or a French horn, and play the theme to *Dragnet*. And these kids would say, 'Your dad's calling you home.' It was a little odd, but everybody in the family made music. My father used to have these enormous jam sessions, and there would be like 50 people standing around here laughing and drinking and playing Dixieland, and just this uproarious crowd of people—having fun and making music. My father would always say, 'You should play an instrument because it's really a lot of fun and you get to go places and do things and see things that you wouldn't get to do ordinarily.' "[6]

However, by the time that Jackson was nine years old he noted that his father had become more and more devoted to his work. As an extracurricular activity, Jackson joined a group of young boys who called themselves the Thunderbirds. Organized by John Menesees, a local Highland Park man, the Thunderbirds learned Indian skills, as it was a Boy Scout–like youth group. Since Menesees claimed he was part Native American, it seemed like the perfect activity in which to get involved. When he joined the group, Jackson was given the Indian tribal name of Quick Fox.

There were camping trips to attend, survival tips to learn, and baseball games to play. One of the most fascinating activities that Menesees got his young tribesmen involved in was a trip to the Hopi Nation in northeastern Arizona. Spending a week in the Indian mesas residing with and learning from real Native Americans was a big thrill for young Jackson.

He later explained, "From the time I was 8 till about 12, I was mentored by a man, John Menesees, whose interest was Native American culture and their current plight. So we went to Hopi land and met all these wonderful elders. I found people who were living in this austere environment where they'd literally pray their corn up and drive 10 miles to get a drum of water and bring it back for bathing and for cooking and irrigation. I became acquainted with their ecology and their choices and how they survived, and the tenuous balance they kept between survival and not surviving."[7]

On the Indian reservations, Jackson was able to see firsthand the living conditions of most Native Americans. And he was able to see the shameless way that the U.S. government literally screwed the Indians out of their land. When

Jackson went back to school, he found that he now was armed with "a version of history that was not being represented in school," he recalled.[8]

For a while, Jackson found being one of the Thunderbirds to be a lot of fun. And along the way, it instilled in him a great sense of independence.

However, no longer bamboozled by the perspective of U.S. history that was presented to him in school, Jackson Browne began to mouth off in class. This was the beginning of Jackson becoming the freethinking person he would become famous for embodying.

In the time since Grandpa Clyde had built Abbey San Encino, the neighborhood in Highland Park was becoming a bit rougher. By 1960, there were increasingly more negative activities for the Browne kids to get involved in, which had the potential for getting them into trouble. It was around the age of eleven that Jackson started to feel that he had outgrown the Thunderbirds.

It wasn't long before Jackson started hanging out with a group of young juvenile delinquents. Proving that he had a temper and was not to be pushed around, he settled an argument with a neighbor boy by hitting him over the head with a bottle.

> It wasn't long before Jackson started hanging out with a group of young juvenile delinquents.

One day, Eddie, who was in the fifth grade, was crossing a grocery store parking lot on his way home from school when he found himself being pushed around by a local group of young hoodlums. When he got home, he told his older brother about the incident. Jackson took out a copy of his *Luther Burbank Junior High School Yearbook* and asked Eddie if he could identify any of his assailants. When Eddie pointed out one of them in the book, Jackson told Eddie that he would not have to worry about being bothered by him again.

Jackson never told his brother what kind of a confrontation had occurred between him and his younger brother's assailant, but the next day the young hood went up to Eddie and apologized to him for the incident.

On another occasion, Jackson and a friend were caught by a local policeman puffing on cigarettes a block from the Browne house. Jackson recalled, "We [Berbie, Eddie, and Jackson] were starting to become delinquents, carrying chains. This cop caught us smoking. I was 12. He told us to put 'em out and this guy with me gives him some lip. So it was, 'Empty out all your pockets.' A mini-arsenal. And it's only a block from my house. My father drives by and wants to know what's going on. Evidently it was a pack of cigarettes that I lifted, but they found all these chains and one or two of his really beautiful straight-edge razors from Germany."[9]

Bea and Jack Browne became more and more aware that their beloved neighborhood was on a downward slide and becoming rougher. Although they loved living in the mansion, a decision was made to move out of the area, for the sake of their three young children.

"So we moved," Jackson explained. "My sister is a whole 'nother story—the razor blade and the ratted hair and all that. So they moved [the family] to Orange County and put us in this real sterile tract community."[10]

At the time, Bea was working as a substitute teacher in the Los Angeles school system. In a decisive move, Jack closed down the print shop and rented out Abbey San Encino. To get their children in a safer atmosphere, the Brownes relocated their family to Fullerton, in Orange County, California. The neighborhood that they moved to is an area known as Sunny Hills. And the house they purchased was on a tree-lined suburban cul-de-sac.

It was 1961, and the family was now ensconced in the middle-class suburbs. According to Eddie, "Sunny Hills didn't have the inner-city realities of struggle and survival. No gangs, no winos in the park, not a lot of dope."[11]

Berbie was not happy about the family's move, because she didn't want to leave her friends in Highland Park. So, when the family moved to Orange County, Berbie was allowed to live with the family of one of her friends and stay in the old neighborhood.

Eventually, "Jackie" preferred to be addressed by his middle name, "Jackson," and Eddie also preferred to be called by his middle name, "Severin." It wasn't long before Jackson made friends with Eric Brown, a neighborhood boy his age. Eric came from a nice middle-class family and was a well-mannered young man. While Jackson never dared to bring any of his Highland Park friends home with him, Eric often visited the Browne household.

Other changes were underway as well. Jack Browne, like his wife, took a job as a teacher. He became an English teacher at the local Sunny Hills High School. Although they missed Berbie's day-to-day presence, the move to Orange County proved to be a positive move for the family. Jackson especially seemed to be turning his energies toward more positive and creative pursuits. In the spring of 1962, Bea was thrilled when Jackson presented her with a poem he had written. Since his mother was an English teacher, he wanted a critique on his writing, as he had his eye on winning a poetry writing contest at his new school, Wilshire Junior High. Not only did he end up winning first prize, but his poem was also printed in the school newspaper.

Too slight of build to be of interest to either the football team or the basketball team, Jackson turned his focus to creative pursuits. "I got into music 'cause I couldn't get into driving a GTO like some of the kids had. I just didn't have any money to dress. I would have done anything to wear a fucking varsity jacket. But I couldn't hang in there long enough. I ran some track and I did a little wrestling. That's what the skinny geeky kids do. And I blew it. The thing is, I was getting good at wrestling. And that's a fair sport. They put you with someone your own size. But football, man . . . all my friends went out for football and like an asshole, I went out for football. And it was terrible. You're just fucking beating each other on the head and shoulders all afternoon. I cut practice all the time and they threw me out. They wouldn't let me go out for wrestling because they caught me cutting football, isn't that a bitch? No fucking flexibility, so then I was an outlaw, right? A desperado. From then on, music was left."[12]

Severin, too, turned his interests to more creative ventures, becoming fascinated with the new wave of surfer rock and roll which had recently become popular. In 1962, the Beach Boys released their first hits, and the California beach scene was suddenly the focus of a whole new genre of pop music. Severin became fixated on becoming a rock star.

Jackson, on the other hand, turned his adolescent musical taste to another popular idiom: folk music. The year 1962 also marked the record chart debut of a new group of folk music stars, particularly Peter, Paul, and Mary and their hits "Lemon Tree" and "If I Had a Hammer."

When Berbie resumed living with the Browne family, in their new home in Orange County, she brought with her a love for folk music as well. One night, after attending a performance by a local folk duo, Joe and Eddie, Berbie invited the pair to come home with her. What ensued was a late night hootenanny music session, reminiscent of Jack Browne's jazz gatherings back in Highland Park.

It was high school–age Berbie Browne who brought to her family circle two of her fellow students. One was a member of the senior class, Steve Noonan, and another was the school's debate team star, Greg Copeland. Both Noonan and Copeland became involved in singing folk protest songs and organizing hootenannies in which Berbie became involved. At lunchtime gatherings, it was Berbie who became adept at playing a pair of spoons as a percussion instrument.

The duo of Copeland and Noonan began writing their own protest songs. Copeland contributed the lyrics and Noonan wrote the music for their first joint composition, "The Ballad of Rosa Parks." It was a folk ode in support of Rosa Parks, a black woman who made headlines for standing up against southern segregation laws by refusing to give up her seat in the front of a public bus in Alabama to a white person. She became a strong and inspiring symbol for not accepting racial prejudice, so she was the perfect inspiration for the changing political climate of the early 1960s.

Berbie had begun to date Steve Noonan, and on occasion she invited him to come home with her. It was there that he first met Jackson, who at the time was a sophomore at the same high school. Although Jackson and Steve would not become close friends for several months, theirs was later to become a significant friendship. Both Steve Noonan and Greg Copeland, separately, would eventually become Jackson Browne's first two songwriting partners.

One of Jackson's friends was Steven Solberg, who was an artist, and a year older. Browne looked up to Solberg and loved his Salvador Dali–inspired painting style. Steven was a bit of an anticonformist, because he wore the sleeves of his shirts rolled up and carried himself as something of a rebel.

A local hangout was a coffeehouse that Steve Noonan's father, Alan, owned. The coffeehouse, which was called The Aware, opened in the summer of 1964. It became a place where patrons were encouraged to show up with a guitar and to hang out. The Aware was also the hangout of three teen musicians: Jeff Hanna, Bruce Kunkel, and Jimmie Fadden. The trio eventually formed their own group, the Nitty Gritty Dirt Band.

More sweeping changes came about within the Browne household, when— after two years as an English and journalism teacher at Sunny Hills High School—Jack Browne was fired. Apparently, he was too much of a freethinker for the conservative academic atmosphere of the school.

In late 1964, when Jackson was fourteen years old, his parents separated. Jack Browne moved to Placentia and took a job as a technical writer for a company in the aerospace field, while Bea and the children moved a mile east to a three-bedroom house. It was nowhere as lush and tree lined as the previous family home had been, but it was a spacious house for parties and entertaining. The house became a music-making haven for the growing circle of Jackson's and Berbie's friends.

In a 1993 issue of *GQ* magazine, feature writer Rob Tannenbaum, reported, "His father, an English and journalism teacher, was an alcoholic." In the same paragraph, Jackson himself claimed, "The word 'dysfunction' gets thrown around a lot, but I don't think this was a particularly 'functional' family."[13]

It was the first era in which mind-altering substances were finding their way into the mainstream of American suburbia. One of the first things to show up in Jackson's circle of friends was marijuana. Looking back on this era, Browne recalled, "I really romanticize those times. The beach towns, the clubs. Somebody had always rented a big house in which there'd be 18 people sleeping, a party every night, and no shortage of wine or guitars. . . . I remember the first time I smoked pot, lying on this couch in Newport Beach, listening to Ray Charles and watching the sunset through the window. Thought it was the most beautiful thing I'd ever seen. I'm lucky I didn't burn my little eyes out."[14]

One of the things that Jackson remembers the most from this period of his life is the music. According to him, "The first music that I heard that I really went crazy for was Bob Dylan's. Songs like 'Talking World War III Blues' or 'The Lonesome Death of Hattie Carroll' and 'Blowin' in the Wind.' It was 1963–4. I come from that period of time, the early '60s was when I started playing the guitar. Of course, I heard Woody Guthrie and Pete Seeger, too, and The Staples, and Sonny Terry, and Brownie McGhee. A lot of blues artists. But Bob Dylan, Bob Dylan, Bob Dylan!"[15]

> "The first music that I heard that I really went crazy for was Bob Dylan's. Songs like 'Talking World War III Blues' or 'The Lonesome Death of Hattie Carroll' and 'Blowin' in the Wind.'

Jackson's taste in music, and his desire to infuse his songwriting with meaning and purpose, came directly from his idolizing Bob Dylan. "He showed me what could be done with a simple tune if the lyrics were right," Browne claimed.[16]

The first time that Jackson saw Dylan was at a Joan Baez concert. She brought him out on stage during her show at the Hollywood Bowl. Browne was instantly knocked out by Dylan, and he went out and bought Dylan's first three albums: *Bob Dylan* (1962), *The Freewheelin' Bob Dylan* (1963), and *The Times They Are A-Changin'* (1964).

"He's always been a preacher. That's something I didn't know then," says Jackson. "I mean, he's been a political singer. He's been a nihilist. He's been a foggy voice in a completely wasted scape. Bob Dylan is always incredible. It used to be that I would get the Bob Dylan album, and I would breathe it for six months or a year or until he put out the next one. Around the time I started making my own music, I stopped following him that closely. If, when I die, they open my brain and do a cross section, like the rings of a tree or something, they will find several years in there where there's nothing but Bob Dylan. I don't need for Bob Dylan to become one thing or another. What he is is a constant—a constant mystery, always a surprise."[17]

Listening to the music that was being made by visionary artists expanded his horizons. "The fact is that most of these songs—especially Dylan's songs—exist on multiple levels," Browne explained. "So it's possible to love a song for many years before you really hear what he might be doing with it. Look at 'Like a Rolling Stone.' I mean, I was 16 or 17 when that song first came out. I loved it. I took in every syllable, every inflection, and got so much from it. I really think you make more than you get. So much of what he was talking about changed for me. The imagery of that song is so penetrating; it's so non-specific, but it's exact. There's something really wondrous about it."[18]

Jackson was hooked on the idea of making music. According to him, "By the time I was 15, I was hanging out with Steve Noonan and Greg Copeland; that got me writing too. Greg Copeland was the poet laureate of the school; Noonan played bluegrass before school in the morning; they'd rip off a bass fiddle from the music department. Everybody always talks about how plastic Orange County is, but it's not. I mean all those blond-haired surfers who were into flashing a bare ass at the old Atchison, Topeka & Santa Fe are total blues fanatics and mushroom freaks. Silver surfers. I don't think L.A. was any more a legitimate music scene than Orange County."[19]

In 1964, at the age of sixteen, Jackson Browne saw the Rolling Stones in concert, and it was a life-altering experience. According to him, "You automatically associate a song with what you were going through at the time. You go see The Stones when you're sixteen, and you see these panties go sailing through the air. Ruffled pantaloons were the big thing among surfer girls in Orange County when I was fifteen or sixteen, and somebody wrapped their panties around an ashtray so they had weight, and they flew through the air and hit Keith. The girl I was with was just losing her mind, and I thought, 'That would be a good job to have.' Certain experiences become cardinal points in your compass."[20]

Being exposed to both folk music and rock music, which one fascinated him the most? According to Jackson, he thought it was folk music that would be the longest lasting genre, and that it was rock and roll that would eventually fade away. "But it's that old 'doo-ron-ron' [of rock music] that's had the longest-lasting effect on me as a musician and a songwriter," he explained.[21]

One of Jackson's new friends at the time was Roger Dutton, who arrived on the scene in 1965. From nearby Idyllwild, Roger had just been kicked out of high school. It seemed that he wanted to keep his shoulder-length blonde hair, and the high school saw it differently. Before long, he was living in a spare bedroom at Bea Browne's spacious house. Inspired by Dutton's own long blonde locks, and fresh from having seen the Beatles in their debut film *A Hard Day's Night*, Jackson let his own brown hair grow long.

Jackson spent part of the summer in San Francisco with Berbie and their friends Steve Noonan and Greg Copeland. Steve Noonan recalled going to Bay Area hootenannies with all of them participating on stage. He also remembered Jackson's shyness, "I really loved to be in front of people. And Jackson wasn't that way at all. I can remember him kind of standing behind everybody, sort of looking to make sure no one's looking at him. 'Cause he was much shyer and much less in command. It wasn't natural for him to be a jump-out performer."[22]

Meanwhile, in 1965 another creative influence arrived in Jackson Browne's circle of friends: the notorious psychedelic drug LSD. Uncertain if he wanted to get involved in LSD or not, the first time he was given a tab of "acid" he gave it to his artist buddy Steve Solberg. When Solberg not only lived through the experience, but raved about it, Jackson decided that it was cool to venture out on a "trip."

Not long afterward, Jackson and Roger Dutton dropped acid and ventured out for a walk in Newport Beach—stoned out of their minds. Spotted wandering the streets in a daze, Jackson and Roger were stopped by police officers and put in the back of a patrol car. Cushioned from reality by a healthy acid buzz, the stoned duo thought they were simply being offered a ride when the cops announced that they were going "downtown." Convinced that the kids were ultimately harmless, the cops eventually set them free.

One of the first songs that Jackson Browne wrote during this era is "Lavender Windows." In the song, he sings of sitting in a room that is a swirl of colors including olive green pillows, ebony floors, burgundy doors, and lavender windows. In another of his compositions, he wrote about his buddy Steve Solberg in "The Painter." As if some part of a rainbow-colored paisley-patterned dream, it was the dawn of the psychedelic era of the 1960s, and Jackson Browne was right in the middle of it, steeped in music and colors, and a rich pallette of new experiences to draw on and write songs.

CHAPTER 2

The Balladeer

THE YEAR 1965 WAS A MAGICAL TIME to be growing up in Orange County, California. Surf music was huge, and the Beach Boys' "Help Me Rhonda" was a major summer hit. The Byrds were also suddenly huge, as they scored a chart-topper with their version of Bob Dylan's "Mr. Tambourine Man" and their interpretation of Pete Seeger's "Turn! Turn! Turn!" The success of the Byrds was based on using the sensitive lyrics of Dylan and combining his songs with the creamy harmonies of David Crosby, Chris Hillman, and Roger McGuinn—whose voices blended well with all of the melodic success of the Beatles. According to Dylan, "The Byrds are able to do things most people don't even know about!"[1] Meanwhile, the pop/folk group the Mamas and the Papas took a similar harmonic formula as they rhapsodized romantically about the West Coast scene and threw the spotlight on the entire "Gold Rush State" in their smash hit "California Dreamin'."

While Jackson Browne's first forays into songwriting were blossoming, so was his romantic life. According to his classmates and friends, teenage Browne soon found that girls loved guys with guitars. Steve Solberg recalls, "Jackson was always sort of girl-crazy. He went through a lot of young girls." And his sister, Carol Solberg, was later to confirm from personal experience that the young balladeer was quite the sixteen-year-old Lothario. "A lot of girls thought he was pretty great. And, he was aware of it, *oh yes*."[2]

Another girl he dated during this time period was Marianne Luther. On one of their dates, they went out to see the movie *Baby the Rain Must Fall* at the local drive-in theater. He drove his Volkswagen van, and while parked there, he took out his guitar and serenaded her. The song he sang for her was one of his own compositions, the romantic ballad "Marianne." In the song, he told his date that her voice was as beautiful as guitar music and that she had a heart like a "shaft of light." Although she was impressed, their affair didn't last. She ended up returning to her old boyfriend, and according to Jackson, he was emotionally crushed. However, the pain of heartbreak can make for some great songwriting explorations—as Jackson was to demonstrate several times in his career.

Who were Jackson's musical heroes when he was growing up? "My real hero is my little brother, who taught me to play piano. He loved The Byrds, and I remember hearing The Byrds coming through my bedroom wall at all hours," he claims.[3]

According to Browne, another one of his true musical heroes was "my friend Greg Copeland, who I wrote 'The Fairest of the Seasons' with. He's a hero of mine because he never wanted to get rich."[4] The fact that Copeland just wanted to write songs and sing them, and harbored no monetary aspirations, was something that Browne most admired. This same love of music for music's sake is something that has stayed with him all of his career. He makes career decisions for their integrity, and not their potential popularity.

Does Jackson have any regrets about his teenage years? "I think back now on that time and I wish I had been in a band in high school. . . . One of my best friends, Eric Brow, he loved The Righteous Brothers, and he used to stand on his bed and just howl. Eric wound up joining a group. And, another guy from our class was the guitar player. They played at all the school dances, and I wish I'd done that."[5]

In the fall of 1965, Jackson Browne entered his senior year at Sunny Hills High School. That same autumn, a new local folk club opened up in the nearby town of Tustin. It was called The Paradox. It was the remodeled reincarnation of the Mon Ami coffeehouse, owned by Bob Sheffer and Hank Fisher, who were both big folk music buffs. Sheffer in fact was one-third of a local folk singing trio. They would serve their coffee and espresso drinks and chocolate chip cookies baked by their wives. The Paradox provided a laid-back local hangout for the music-making circles Jackson gravitated toward.

Steve Noonan recalls, "The Paradox is the story of two thirtyish guys who wanted to have a place. They weren't really hip; I don't think they even got stoned at the time, although everybody else who hung around there did. The point is, they were willing to have a club where people could hang around, even if they were ten years older than anyone. They created an environment for people to be artistic."[6]

On Thursday nights at 7:00 P.M., hopeful singers could sign up for a three-song on-stage gig. Among the yet-to-be-stars who performed at these Thursday "open mic" nights at The Paradox were Jennifer Warnes, Mary McCaslin, Penny Nichols, Kathy Smith, Jimmy Spheeris, and Tim Buckley, who performed as a member of the Harlequin Three.

Actually, the first time that one of Jackson's compositions was heard at The Paradox was sung by someone else. Bob Sheffer remembers, "There was a girl there…Janet. She was only about fourteen, but she could really sing. She sang one of his songs, 'She's a Flying Thing,' and I said, 'Gee, that's a good song!' And that's how I found out about Jackson. He was really quiet. Just nice. No wisecracks. Really a great young man."[7]

> Actually, the first time that one of Jackson's compositions was heard at The Paradox was sung by someone else.

On one occasion, this girl sang one of his compositions, but she did not perform the song the way he envisioned it being sung. Instead of really listening to the lyrics, she chose to present the song with a superficial country and western slant. Jackson reportedly was not amused. Bob Sheffer comments, "It was the first time I had seen Jackson angry. That kind of clued me in that he was really serious, and he didn't like people not understanding him."[8]

Apparently, at first young Jackson was really nervous about getting up on stage. However, the owners of The Paradox knew that he had talent; all he had to do was add a little bit of self-confidence to the equation. Hank Fisher recalls, "Just as he was about to go up, he tried to back out. He said, 'I don't want to do it.' I told him, 'Oh yes you do.' At six-foot-two I was considerably bigger, so I just kind of intimidated him."[9]

Although Jackson Browne was clever enough and musically developed enough to write songs like "These Days" and "Shadow Dream Song" by his senior year in

> Although Jackson Browne was clever enough and musically developed enough to write songs like "These Days" and "Shadow Dream Song" by his senior year in high school, he still knew deep down inside that singing wasn't necessarily his strong point.

high school, he still knew deep down inside that singing wasn't necessarily his strong point. It wasn't that he couldn't sing, but he lacked the self-confidence to sing with authority on stage. There was only one way to solve the problem: he had to simply do it, and he would progressively get better.

Bob Sheffer explains, "Jackson sang really soft. His voice frankly was not that strong. There wasn't too much eye contact. He seemed nervous...although I immediately sensed this was something he really wanted to do. Maybe 'shy' fits better; there was a sort of gentleness. But even in not coming on in the traditional show business way—i.e., showing a lot of confidence—he seemed to project a very subtle power. You could tell he was presenting something serious."[10]

Jackson's father, Jack Browne, moved to Japan in December 1965, and for a long period of time Jackson didn't see him. Jack had gone back to work for *Stars and Stripes*, this time in Tokyo. Sadly, for most of his adult years, Jackson's father was not to be a present or active participant in his life.

In 1993, Jackson looked back on his lifelong disappointing relationship with his father and said that Jack Browne had died in the mid-1980s. He reported at that time that his father's death had been "five or six or seven...he might've died ten years ago. I should know the date, but...when he died, I didn't stop my tour to come back [to Los Angeles] or anything."[11]

In a rather interesting move, Jackson Browne became a member of the Nitty Gritty Dirt Band in early 1966. Also in the band at that time were Jimmie Fadden and Jeff Hanna. This was an important step for him, because it would enable him to perform on stage without being the central focus of the set. With all of the California surfer bands that were around at the time, the music that the Nitty Gritty Dirt Band played was decidedly more of a blend of ragtime and rock and roll. With instruments like a banjo and a washboard, the band's sound and concept were just off-the-wall enough to form a unique niche all their own.

When the Nitty Gritty Dirt Band played at a band contest at The Paradox, they were not only a hit, they also won first prize! This won them their first paying gig at a club called The Golden Bear, in nearby Huntington Beach. They were to become the opening act for the Sir Douglas Quintet. The band was a big hit, and they were asked to be the opening act for the Lovin' Spoonful. Two of the songs that Jackson Browne wrote in 1966 were a ragtime number called "Melissa," which the Nitty Gritty Dirt Band added to their repertoire, and "These Days."

Looking back at this time in his life, it was all a big adventure for Jackson. According to him, "I graduated high school in '66 and hung around Hollywood and Orange County for about six months."[12]

In the summer of 1966, shortly after his high school graduation, Jackson decided to quit the band to concentrate on his own music. He was replaced in the Nitty Gritty Dirt Band by John McEuen, who was another talented musician who hung out at The Paradox. According to Browne, he wasn't interested in making ragtime-styled music and being part of a band; instead, he wanted to make it as a solo act.

It was in August 1966 that the name "Jackson Browne" first appeared on the marquee of The Paradox. He was now officially on his way to etching out his own musical identity. It was the song "These Days" that seemed to hit a great chord with audiences, and from that day forward, it was to be a part of his stage act.

Although at the time Jackson's brother, Severin, was also interested in a career in music, when the opportunity presented itself, he decided to take off on an Asian adventure. In August, Severin left for Japan, where he would spend two years living with his father, Jack. He left his brother back in Orange County to chase his own dreams of a career in show business.

During this period, Jackson was dating the singer/songwriter Pamela Polland. While on a trip to Hollywood to visit Polland, Browne was inspired by Jimmie Fadden to write the song "Shadow Dream Song" in her honor. Pamela had her own songwriting career, and together with Rick Stanley she became part of the duo Gentle Soul.

Gentle Soul had a management deal in place, when all of a sudden Rick Stanley quit the group and left Pamela dangling. Desperate to find a singer, she asked Jackson Brown to be part of her group. He accepted her offer, and for two weeks he was the second singing half of Gentle Soul. When Rick Stanley showed up and asked if he could rejoin the group, Jackson was reportedly "relieved" to turn his attention back to his solo career. However, since he had helped her out in a pinch, she decided to do what she could to be of help to him.

Just like his tenure in Gentle Soul, Jackson's romance with Pamela was also short lived. However, they were to remain good friends. Gentle Soul at one point was the opening act for José Feliciano when the blind singer was booked at The Golden Bear. Pamela put in a good word about Jackson to record company insider Billy James, who at the time was a publicity writer for the Los Angeles office of Columbia Records. Pamela told Billy great things about Jackson's songwriting skills, and Billy agreed to meet with Jackson one night at The Golden Bear.

Billy liked what he heard, and through him, he landed Jackson a demo recording session at the company. Not long afterward, James quit Columbia Records and assisted in opening the first Los Angeles office of Elektra Records. At the time, Elektra was the label with whom folk singers Judy Collins and Tom Rush recorded. The latest act Elektra had signed to the label was an up-and-coming group called the Doors.

Thanks to a deal that Billy James put together, a month before his eighteenth birthday, on October 9, 1966, Jackson Browne was signed to be a staff writer for Elektra's publishing company, Nina Music. He was paid $500 as a signing advance.

"The summer I was out of high school I got busted for pot," Jackson recalls.

While his songwriting career was taking off, there were some adolescent mishaps along the way, and some lessons in life to be learned. "The summer I was out of high school I got busted for pot," Jackson recalls. "But I got out of it because I paid a lawyer to tell the judge that I was a nice boy and that this was the first and last time I would ever be in trouble. I had this $500 publishing advance from Elektra's publishing company, Nina Music, and it all was used to buy off some smarmy judge who had the same twinkle in his eyes as my lawyer. There were 200 black and Chicano kids in court that day and it was an inescapable fact that they were all going to 'the slammer,' while the other three or four clean-cut kids like me, whose parents had paid a lawyer to stand up and say how 'upright' we were—well, you just knew we weren't going to jail. I mean, I was glad not to be going to jail, but it was pretty obvious that whoever had the bread was gonna be all right."[13]

In the October 28, 1966, issue of *Time* magazine, in the article "The New

Troubadours," several of the new California folk/rockers were mentioned, including the Mamas and the Papas, Simon and Garfunkel, and the Lovin' Spoonful. It also quoted four lines of a yet-to-be-recorded new folk song of the genre. It turned out to be lyrics from Browne's "Shadow Dream Song." Although he was not mentioned in the article by name, the seventeen-year-old Jackson was already being written about.

Meanwhile, Greg Copeland, who had been spending a lot of time in San Francisco, decided it behooved him to see more of the world. All he needed was a compatriot for the adventure. He found the perfect cohort in Adam Saylor. The son of a doctor, Adam briefly went to college, but soon found it was not for him. When he and Copeland cooked up a travel itinerary, they decided to first go to the port city of Veracruz, Mexico. From Veracruz the plan was to charm their way onto a Europe-bound boat and travel to that continent. When that didn't work out, they returned to Los Angeles. Their new plan was to drive to New York City and then fly to Europe. Shortly before leaving Los Angeles, they decided to ask Jackson Browne if he wanted to come along with them to Europe. He thought about it and agreed that he would ride along to New York City, but would pass on the European leg of the tour. Since Steve Noonan had moved to New York City, there was sure to be a sofa to crash on once he got there.

Jackson recalls, "In January of '67, some of my friends and me drove across the United States in a Rambler station wagon. It was the dead of winter and it took us less than four days. We never stopped, we just barreled straight through. I remember listening to the Clay-Liston fight while we were driving across the Texas panhandle. My hair was down to my shoulders and I had people genuinely mistaking me for a girl in places like Missouri. We'd stop for gas, and I'd ask for the restroom and this old guy dressed like a sack of potatoes says, 'Right over there, dearie.' Being from Orange County, where people were normally hostile to anyone who looked like a freak, I was used to it. But this old guy had really directed me to the women's restroom. When I came back and asked him for the key to the men's room, he got real embarrassed. He really did think I was a girl."[14]

Jackson remembers having a great time on that trip across the country, "I really admired those guys. I went with them, but I didn't have the bread to go to Europe. I was just 17. Also, New York was such a number!"[15]

Steve Noonan's convenient move to New York City's Lower East Side by this point did mean that his sofa turned out to be Jackson's residence for much of the time he spent in Manhattan. It was like Alice's trip to Wonderland, to be a West Coast teenager in the Big Apple—especially during this era.

It was 1967, the year of the famous Summer of Love, the Beatles' *Sgt. Pepper's Lonely Hearts Club Band*, the Detroit and Newark riots, the Monterey Pop Festival, and the films *Valley of the Dolls* and *To Sir with Love*. Jackson remembers, "In New York, I lived for a while on the Lower East Side. New York was such a fascinating place. I was there in the spring of '67 for the first 'be-in.' They had a be-in in New York and a be-in in San Francisco and a love-in in Los Angeles, and it all happened on the same day. It was some sort of synergy going on, people heading for these places with this wild understanding happening between everyone. It was really amazing."[16]

> "In New York, I lived for a while on the Lower East Side. New York was such a fascinating place. I was there in the spring of '67 for the first 'be-in.'"

One of the first people Jackson met when he got to New York City was Nancy Demey, who was the secretary to Jac Holzman at Elektra Records. She later recalled, "I think we were at Steve Noonan's apartment. Steve was there, Tim Buckley, and Jackson . . . he was so young, innocent, and warm hearted." She also recalled, "This was when we heard that [smoking] banana peels got you high. So Jackson, Tim, Steve, and I scraped off the inside of bananas, roasted them, and smoked them. 'Are you high?' 'Are *you* high?' And I can remember Jackson being funny about that. I think he was the one who realized we weren't high."[17]

There were all kinds of new and exciting things to do and see in New York City. One night they all got into the trippy club The Electric Circus and danced amid the flashing strobe lights and all of the madness.

Jackson played his first East Coast concert with Steve Noonan and Tim Buckley at the State University of New York. A Sunday afternoon event, several hundred people came to listen to the West Coast blend of folk/rock music that day. There were also several people tripping on acid and openly smoking marijuana. One of the people who was tripping that day was Tim Buckley, with whom Jackson had become friends.

Meanwhile, back in the city, while hanging out with his folk singing buddies, Browne was offered his first Manhattan club gig—as part of singer Nico's band. The way it unfolded, says Jackson, is that "Tim Buckley was in New York at the time and I went to see him play at this place called The Dom."[18]

Jackson recalls that The Dom was a hot place to hang out, "Dom was 'mod'

Meanwhile, back in the city, while hanging out with his folk singing buddies, Browne was offered his first Manhattan club gig—as part of singer Nico's band.

spelled backwards, and there was always this carnival of people around. Andy Warhol with his entourage, a film loop of Lou Reed eating a Hershey bar, Nico sitting at one end of the bar in this Dietrich pose singing these incredible songs, and Tim Buckley as opening act."[19]

Nico was the occasional lead singer for the Velvet Underground, who in March of that year had just released their debut album *The Velvet Underground with Nico*, produced by Andy Warhol. In addition to her position in the group, Nico was also working on a solo career. Her incredibly dry and monotone singing voice, along with her heavy German accent, made her a unique vocal curiosity.

Browne recalls, "It was sort of contingent on [me] playing the electric guitar, because Andy and Paul Morrissey wanted to be modern. He [Warhol] wanted Nico to sit [on stage] in a plexiglass box, and sing inside there. And, she wasn't having it!"[20]

"I had a gigantic crush on Nico," Jackson admits. "She was so fucking beautiful. She fucked me around, really, goddam, man, she was just...and I had seen these 20-foot-high posters of her for the three weeks I'd been in New York and then I went down and saw her—it was even my first time in a bar, I think, 'cause I'd just turned 18—and a week later I got a call: would I like to be her guitar player? I went over and got my brains fucked loose."[21] That was not only the beginning of Browne being Nico's guitar player, it was the beginning of another of his painfully disappointing love affairs.

According to Jackson, "When I got hired to play, Nico was being accompanied by various members of The Velvet Underground. They'd trade off. Lou Reed would back her one night, John Cale the next, and so on. And she was getting crazy about not having the same guy backing her every night. So she asked Tim to do it and he said, 'no.' Then she asked me. First thing they asked me was whether I could play an electric guitar. I said, 'yes,' but I didn't have one. They said if I could get one, I could have the job. So I borrowed a friend's."[22] With that, he was suddenly Nico's new guitar player, while having an affair with Nico as well.

Although, in retrospect, the idea of seeing Jackson and Nico in a club in Manhattan would be a dream teaming, Browne is quick to dispel any illusions about his success, "Nobody came to The Dom to see me. Nobody came to see Nico. They came because Andy Warhol's name was in neon outside."[23]

"Nobody came to The Dom to see me. Nobody came to see Nico. They came because Andy Warhol's name was in neon outside."

Jackson recalls the ambiance of The Dom and the music that he heard there. He recounts of his specific recollections, "The songs on the jukebox at the Dom, where I played accompanying Nico: [The Beatles'] 'Penny Lane,' 'Strawberry Fields,' [Ike and Tina Turner's] 'River Deep, Mountain High.' The Dom was Andy Warhol's club most nights, but then there was one night that it was a black disco, and so the jukebox had some great R&B. And The Velvet's stuff."[24]

He also claims, "And then I remember hearing 'A Day in the Life' on the radio. It was off a Beatles acetate, before the *Sgt. Pepper* album even came out. Nothing before had prepared me for this incredible song. It was a milestone, and it changed everything."[25]

Like all singer/songwriters, certain songs and certain performers become touchstones of inspiration. For Jackson, which songs from this era struck inspirational notes in his creative consciousness? According to him, "Stuff like 'Everyday People' [Sly and the Family Stone]—that really high note. And 'Walk away Renee' [the Left Banke], when they say, 'The empty sidewalks on my block are not the same.' I remember the first time I heard a record that reminded me of the past. I was eighteen, and somebody put on *Another Side of Bob Dylan*—I was flooded with memories."[26]

In May 1967, the Nitty Gritty Dirt Band became the first group to record Jackson Browne's songs. Both "Melissa" and "Holding" appeared on their self-titled debut album.

While he was in New York City, two very important things happened for Jackson. The first was recording demos of his compositions for Nina Music, and the second was supplying songs for Nico's debut solo album. Not only did she cover three of his songs, he played guitar on the trio of tracks: "These Days," "It's Been Raining Here in Long Beach," and "Shadow Dream Song." Her first album, *Chelsea Girl*, was released in July of that year.

Astonishingly enough, when it came time to record his demos, Jackson already had thirty songs he had written, both solo and with collaborators: "Fourth and Main," "Bound for Colorado," "We Can Be," "And I See," "Ah, but Sometimes," "Marianne," "Tumble Down," "You Don't Need a Cloud," "Lavender Bassman," "She's a Flying Thing," "It's Been Raining Here in Long Beach," "You'll Get It in the Mail Today," "Shadow Dream Song," "The Light from Your Smile," "Gonna See a Man About a Daydream" (lyrics by Greg Copeland), "Time Travel Fantasy" (lyrics by Pamela Polland), "The Fairest of Seasons" (lyrics by Greg Copeland), "Sing My Songs to Me," "Lavender Windows," "The Painter," "Holding," "Somewhere There's a Feather," "I've Been Out Walking (These Days)," "Funny You Should Ask," "Love Me, Lovely," "You've Forgotten," "Someday Morning," "Cast off All My Fears," "In My Time," and "Melissa." Reportedly, one hundred copies were pressed onto vinyl and sent to various record companies for consideration by artists and producers.

One of the most memorable things that happened while hanging out with Nico at The Dom was that Jackson got to meet another songwriter that he highly revered: Leonard Cohen. It was Cohen who had penned the haunting Judy Collins hit "Suzanne." Browne recalls of meeting Leonard, "That was real important. He used to come in because he was real infatuated with Nico, and he would sit there and write poems on the front table and just sit there and look at her. He'd write these perfect poems on little pieces of paper. He'd just knock them out in between songs and read them to us and get very dreamy. He was an old-fashioned poet, which was the only kind I knew there was. I was real impressed with him. I was no fixture at all in that scene. I made no impression on it."[27] Still, it created one of the most indelible memories of his first New York City adventure.

When a *Rolling Stone* profile by Richard Meltzer was later published about this era, he wrote that cute and eighteen-year-old Jackson Browne not only caught the eyes of the girls, but the guys also found him pretty hot. In Meltzer's words, Jackson was "one hell of a prototype sex symbol for the gay rock underground."[28]

> In Meltzer's words, Jackson was "one hell of a prototype sex symbol for the gay rock underground."

Browne later explained, "What R. Meltzer said in that article—that I became the object of many lustful old faggots—was not professional. Because I really didn't know what was going on. I mean, I realized it later, just remembering scenes of what people said to me. But it was like candy or something. I knew what a fag was, you understand, and I knew that when this outrageous trans-vestite came up and said he was Nico's little sister... 'I'm Renee Ricard and I make movies with Andy.'...I knew what it was. It scared me. I kept my distance." [29]

And then there was Lou Reed, who at the time was a member of the Velvet Underground. Jackson recalls attending the Central Park love-in that spring, "Lou Reed, who always had this incredible menacing scowl on his face, wouldn't say more than one or two syllables because that was how Andy [Warhol] was[as well].... Lou Reed is a sweetheart underneath. We got to rapping and he turned out to be this great person. And the way he described it, you realized there was a place for all that inside of him. He loved seeing Central Park full of people all just...high and loving each other. I mean, you don't think about that when you think of all those Warhol people."[30]

During all of these adventures, the teaming of laid-back California teenager Jackson Browne with cool, sophisticated, avant-garde Warhol icon Nico was the most legendary aspect of his 1967 East Coast adventure.

However, in reality his tenure as a guitarist to the Germanic rock chanteuse lasted less than two months. Jackson expressed his frustrations to his friends in New York. According to Steve Noonan, "I got the impression [from Browne] that, 'Hey, I'm really good, and I'm playing back-up for this girl who can't sing in tune sometimes.' "[31] Although he realized that in terms of musical talent he was stronger than she was, he was still in love with her, even though she wasn't interested in a relationship.

Reportedly, Nico went to the point of complaining about her personal life on stage. At one point, she referred to Browne as a "creep" and accused him of making obscene phone calls to her.

"It was much later," he recalls, "a month later, before I realized that the whole thing was just like this fling [in Nico's mind]. I really cared about her in spite of the fact that I was real disap-pointed. I mean, I dug her."[32]

Although Nico broke his heart, Jackson's first trip to New York City had been a big success. He had landed a paying gig—$150 a week—playing at The Dom. He appeared on Nico's album playing his own compositions. He recorded his own songwriting demo while in town. And he was still only eighteen years old. When he decided to return to Los Angeles, he had saved enough money for the plane ticket.

According to him, "I ended up leaving New York shortly after the spring."[33] When Jackson Browne went back to Los Angeles, he moved in with his mother. Bea had rented an apartment in Silver Lake, not far from Highland Park. The song "From Silver Lake," which appears on his debut album, was written during this time period, about a perspective from this very location.

He then went to Monterey, California, with friends to catch the huge music festival that was held there June 16, 17, and 18, 1967. Among the pop/rock legends to headline the Monterey Pop Festival included the Mamas and the Papas, Big Brother & the Holding Company with Janis Joplin, the Jefferson Airplane, the Jimi Hendrix Experience, the Who, the Byrds, Laura Nyro, Otis Redding, the Grateful Dead, the Steve Miller Band, Buffalo Springfield, Johnny Rivers, Quicksilver Messenger Service, Eric Burdon and the Animals, Moby Grape, and Simon & Garfunkel.

According to Micky Dolenz of the Monkees, "This was the beginning of The Summer of Love. There were love-ins, laugh-ins, and in the middle of June, there was only one place to be: The Monterey Pop Festival. The Festival was to be the social, musical, spiritual, chemical, event of the year."[34]

All firsthand accounts seem to proclaim that it was an inspiring experience for everyone involved. For nineteen-year-old Jackson Browne, it strengthened his drive to become a stage performer, as well as a songwriter.

There was also a bittersweet quality to attending the Monterey Pop Festival. Creatively, it was very inspiring. However, knowing that his former love, Nico, was also there—and on the arm of Brian Jones of the Rolling Stones—was emotionally upsetting to him. Meanwhile, back in Orange County, Steve Copeland had returned from his creative sojourn in Europe and was sharing an apartment with Pamela Polland in nearby Echo Park. They lived in a duplex apartment, and in the other apartment lived Glenn Frey, an aspiring singer/songwriter from Royal Oak, Michigan. At the time, Frey was one-half of a singing duo that went by the name of Longbranch Pennywhistle. His singing partner was the Texas native John David Souther.

Two of Jackson's other compatriots, Steven Solberg and Roger Dutton, shared a "cold water flat" in a funky stretch of Pico Street in Los Angeles. According to author Rich Wiseman in the book *Jackson Browne: The Story of a Holdout*, "Dutton...says he was shooting Methedrine regularly at the time."[35]

At this point, Billy James and his wife, Judy, were also key people in

Jackson's life. Not only did James land him the demo deal at Elektra, but also his house was always open to their circle of singer/songwriter friends. Several of these struggling singers would show up around dinner time, where there would always be a free meal and some creative camaraderie. Browne often came over to the James's house to hang out, talk about music, and write songs late into the night.

In the fall of 1967, Jackson Browne gave his very first press interview to a teenage writer for the publication *Cheetah*. Larry Dietz, the editor of the magazine, had heard a lot about young Jackson from Billy, so he assigned his teenage writer, Tom Nolan, to interview the up-and-coming songwriter.

One of the songs that was discussed in the short-lived pop music magazine was a new song of Jackson's called "Birds of St. Marks." According to Browne, "That's a song I wrote about Nico. And, that's all I'm prepared to say about that song."[36] He was still sensitive about being Nico's jilted lover.

What he did reveal in the January 1968 issue of *Cheetah* magazine was that he was now determined to record his own songs. "Right now all I'm thinking about is making an album," proclaimed Browne, "and all I want is somebody to invest the money in me so I can do that. I'm getting sort of impatient now, because I think I'm ready. Now in six months I'll know I wasn't ready, just like I know I wasn't when I thought I was—six months ago. But that can go on forever, you know. You're never really ready."[37]

Speaking of his songwriting subject matter, he revealed, "I've written a few good songs...nothing really heavy yet. Though...I think I'm headed that way...I'm not trying to be different; I'm just trying to be real. Trying to write what's around me, inside of me."[38]

> Speaking of his songwriting subject matter, he revealed, "I've written a few good songs...nothing really heavy yet. Though...I think I'm headed that way...I'm not trying to be different; I'm just trying to be real. Trying to write what's around me, inside of me."

The Nitty Gritty Dirt Band released *Ricochet*, their second album, in November 1967. On it were their versions of Jackson Browne's compositions "It's Been Raining Here in Long Beach" and "Shadow Dream Song."

In January 1968, a singing group called the Hour Glass released their self-titled debut album and covered Jackson's song "Cast off All My Fears." And, in March 1968, Elektra Records released the album *The Circle Game* by Tom Rush. On the album, Rush chose songs by three of the brightest and most aspiring new folk songwriters around: Joni Mitchell ("The Circle Game"), James Taylor (George Harrison's "Something in the Way She Moves" and "Sunshine Sunshine"), and Jackson Browne ("Shadow Dream Song.")

Later that year, Jackson was mentioned for the first time in *Rolling Stone* magazine. In a column that was called "John J. Rock," the magazine heralded: "New face to look for is that of Jackson Browne, a young Southern Californian. . . . Browne's old acetates include a few truly mind-boggling melodies."[39]

Through hanging out at a Hollywood club called The Hullabaloo, Jackson got to know the musicians in the band the Allman Brothers. He turned them on to one of his favorite late-night eateries, the local Greenblatt's Deli, where they would hang out together and talk about music. He became quite chummy with guitar legend Duane Allman. Duane told Jackson that he ought to buy an electric guitar. When Browne informed him that he couldn't afford one, Duane gave him one of his.

In the early part of 1968, Jackson Browne returned to New York City. When he had performed at the State University of New York in Stony Brook the previous year, he had met and befriended rock journalist Richard Meltzer. Richard became a big fan of Jackson's music. A friend of Meltzer's, Sandy Pearlman, was concurrently booking talent and staging rock shows at the Anderson Theater in Greenwich Village. It was Meltzer and Pearlman who thought it would be a great idea for Jackson to be fronted by an East Coast band.

Jackson explains, "I was all set to have this group, The Soft White Underbelly, as my back-up band. I spent a week trying to figure out some arrangements to my songs that would fit this band, and it didn't matter, because they later became Blue Oyster Cult. They were great musicians, they really were. And they played my songs really well. I'm afraid I was the least proficient musician among them."[40]

The rehearsals were problematic, and the show—and the series of concerts—at the Anderson Theater ended up being canceled. He later stated, "We had a lot of fun jamming around, but when it came down to arranging songs . . . it didn't work out . . . we had very little in common musically."[41] Had it worked out, who

Had it worked out, who knows, Jackson Browne's fame might have been as part of the heavy metal band Blue Oyster Cult, instead of as a solo singer.

knows, Jackson Browne's fame might have been as part of the heavy metal band Blue Oyster Cult, instead of as a solo singer.

While he was back on the East Coast during 1968, Jackson did manage to perform one concert appearance. Returning to Stony Brook, he was booked as the opening act for Judy Collins. Jackson recalls that this was his first real in-the-spotlight kind of a show. As he finished his set, he turned to leave the stage, but was so blinded by the spotlight that he wandered into the front row of the audience instead of exiting into the wings. He then had to get back up onstage to make his exit.

In March 1968, Elektra Records released Steve Noonan's debut album. Included on the LP were five songs penned by Jackson Browne: "The Painter," "She's a Flying Thing," "Tumble Down," "Shadow Dream Song," and "Trusting Is a Harder Thing" (cowritten with Noonan).

That same year, Pamela Polland's album with the group Gentle Soul was released by Columbia Records. It was produced by Terry Melcher, who is best known for being the son of screen actress Doris Day. During this period, Terry was very active in the music business, producing several of the biggest hits by the Byrds and a number of other folk/rock acts. Unfortunately, the Gentle Soul album went nowhere.

During the summer of 1968, Jackson gravitated toward the Laurel Canyon area of Los Angeles. The roadway of Laurel Canyon stretches from Sunset Boulevard in the West Hollywood area, up the Hollywood Hills, across Mulholland Drive, and into the valley. On the Hollywood side of the mountain-crossing roadway are several roadways and houses that seem to hang off the hills. Partially because of its proximity to the Sunset Strip, Laurel Canyon suddenly became a hotbed of yet-to-be-discovered musical talent. There was a lot of creative cross-pollination between the talents there in the late 1960s and early 1970s.

Describing the communal scene in the Laurel Canyon area in a cover story on Linda Ronstadt, *Time* magazine explained, "Colonies of rock musicians were forming in the Los Angeles subdivisions of Laurel Canyon, Echo Park and Venice. Glenn Frey drifted in from Royal Oak, Michigan. Don Henley was a North Texas State English major before he decided to move west. They eventually formed the supergroup The Eagles. Before long everyone knew Jackson Browne and Bonnie Raitt, who had grown up around L.A. Neil Young, Joni Mitchell, and Stephen Stills lived near the top of Laurel Canyon, Frank Zappa in an old Tom Mix house a short walk away."[42] Also in the area at the time were Micky Dolenz and Peter Tork of the Monkees, Carole King, Lee Michaels, and the Turtles.

Explaining the communal feeling of the Los Angeles music scene at the time, Linda Ronstadt recalled, "We were all learning about drugs, philosophy, and music. Everything was exciting."[43]

Remembering the living situation in Los Angeles during this era, Jackson claims that he is "flooded with memories" about the era and about the music that he heard over and over during that

> Linda Ronstadt recalled, "We were all learning about drugs, philosophy, and music. Everything was exciting."

period of time. He fondly recalls, "Oh, certain friends and a house where we all used to hang out. There were these older girls—one would have a job and a house where everybody could party. I don't listen to music the same way anymore. If you live communally, sharing a house, records are being played all the time. I'll never hear a record as often as I heard [Bob Dylan's] *Highway 61 Revisited* [1965] or Van Morrison's *Blowin' Your Mind* [1967], because every time it stopped playing, somebody would just turn it back on."[44]

In the 1990s, Jackson would recall, "There was a house in the Hollywood Hills that was owned by Peter Tork. He had all this money from being in The Monkees, and he was a freak. I saw Hendryx play in the pool house, with Peter's girlfriend, Ren, playing drums, naked. It was wild! At that particular house, there was an abundance of beautiful women. Everyone slept with everybody, and nobody wore any clothes. It was ... paradise. I really feel bad that that world's gone, irretrievably, because I really had a great time."[45]

It was one big orgy of sex, drugs, and rock & roll. Jackson says, "These beautiful chicks from Peter Tork's house, they kept coming over with these big bowls of fruit and dope and shit. They'd fuck us in the pool. We'd wake up and see this beautiful 16-year-old flower child who only knew how to say 'fave rave,' with a bowl of fruit, get you incredibly high and take you downstairs and go swimming."[46]

> "These beautiful chicks from Peter Tork's house, they kept coming over with these big bowls of fruit and dope."

According to Browne, he did a lot of hanging out at Peter Tork's house. Two other frequent guests at chez Tork were David Crosby, who had just left the Byrds, and Stephen Stills, who had recently departed Buffalo Springfield.

David Crosby had left the Byrds in October 1967 after a dispute with his band mates. In his temporary sabbatical from active recording, he bought a boat called *The Mayan*, and for a long period of his life he lived on it. According to him, "I got *The Mayan* for $22,500, which I borrowed from Peter Tork, who was flush with Monkees money. It's the best spent money I ever spent. *The Mayan* stands for the good things in my life: health, sanity, and freedom—all the positive values."[47]

Someone else who resided in the Laurel Canyon area was the promoter Barry Friedman. Jackson met him, and Friedman took upon himself the challenge of figuring out how to properly exploit Browne's obvious talents. The previous year, Jackson's huge musical idol, Bob Dylan, had taken some time off and moved to the Woodstock, New York, area. While there, he met up with a group of musicians who were recording tracks in the basement of a large pink house. When Dylan decided to record some tracks with this basement band, the sessions yielded the most successful bootleg album of all times: *The Great White Wonder*. The following year, in 1968, The Band released their own album, *Music from Big Pink*.

Suddenly, the spotlight was thrust on the idea of musicians sequestering themselves in a rural setting and coming out with a brilliant album. Barry Friedman came up with the idea of sending a trio of musicians—Jackson Browne, Los Angeles–born Ned Doheny, and Ohio native Jack Wilce—to a woodsy locale. They were to help each other create enough music for three solo projects. The idea itself went under the heading of the Los Angeles Fantasy Orchestra.

Jackson recalls that Jac Holtzman, the head of Elektra Records, was very interested in the idea of this recording process. "We were saying 'We want to make a record, in a house, in the country,'" he says. "Jac went for the idea that we would have a repertory recording company, a loose aggregation of musicians that all responded to each other—the band, or the rock community, however large a circle you want to draw. We were all interested in making our own albums, and we were all going to play on each other's records."[48]

Ned Doheny recalls his audition for Barry Friedman, "I hooked up a little amplifier, played some Eric Clapton stuff, and was hired. At that time Barry was looking for somebody to play with someone named Jackson Browne, who I thought must be a huge black man. Imagine my surprise when I met him in Laurel Canyon and he was a small white person in his teens."[49]

The spot for sequesterment was the Paxton Lodge. Located in Paxton, California, it was 150 miles northeast of Sacramento, situated in the Pulmas National Forest.

According to Browne, "The fact of the matter was that when we got there, we thought of anything but recording. It was so beautiful up there...swimming in the river, sitting around in the sunshine getting high....We just couldn't seem to achieve what we'd set out to do."[50]

Severin Browne had just returned from his two-year trip to Japan to visit their father. He decided to hitchhike up to the Paxton Lodge to visit his older brother. However, when he got there he found Jackson to be very distant. According to Severin, "There was a distance between us because we hadn't seen each other in a long time. And also because I just happened on him. He might have been on acid for all I know. He was pretty freaked out. There were a lot of strange, strange vibes that I picked up."[51]

In addition, there was no inspiration for writing love songs, since they were out in the wilderness and no women were present. Then a trio of girls was imported to the Paxton Lounge, and it all turned into one big sexual free-for-all. According to Jackson, "There was this one chick who was fucking *brainless*. We had to tell her what a douche was: 'Janis, would you please tell Connie what a douche bag is? Please hurry, because...it's getting bad.' You, know, she'd fuck like four of us without douching and a week later, *man*."[52] Hey, it was the "free love" era of the 1960s!

Not only did Browne, Doheny, and Wilce not come up with their anticipated solo albums, there was also the idea of each of them contributing tracks to one single collaborative disc—as a group.

Among the bantered around ideas for a group name, both Still Birth and Baby Browning were under consideration. However, the project was never to see the light of day. It, too, was "still born."

Jackson later complained, "I've never been able to collaborate with others. Another person with an idea is a problem for me. I'll be thinking of something, and then another person will say, 'Hey, how about this?' And I won't even know what they're saying because I've been off in my head thinking something else."[53]

When the trio turned in their tapes for the proposed project at the beginning of 1969, Elektra rejected it. In fact, they hated it so much that they pulled the plug on Jackson both as an artist and as a songwriter. They were finished promoting him and his songs.

"Each of us was let go," Browne recalls, "and given our publishing back. We all went down together, and Jac [Holtzman] was out a lot of money—the lease on the lodge, months of food and drink and gasoline, the cost of building the studio and renting the remote truck, on and on."[54]

He left northern California and returned to Los Angeles. "It was humbling to be back on the street and not have a record deal. I hung around my art school friends down at Pico and Vermont. I hit The Troubadour, the Monday night hoots. I'd show up and play, maybe sit around a bit, but I didn't want to hang out. I wanted to be taken seriously. My stopping smoking dope had a lot to do with my becoming a serious musician. For many others, and lots of my best friends, it is not a factor in their musicianship. But for me, I think I had a huge identity crisis. It was after Paxton, after two or three years of walking barefoot around Laurel Canyon and sleeping in people's living rooms and smoking the best dope on the planet at the time. I had this huge self-conscious flash. It was in Paul Rothchild's house." With that, he thought to himself, "'Who the fuck are you really? What are you doing? All these incredibly accomplished people here—Paul is one of the absolute best producers in rock & roll, [John] Haeny is like this miracle engineer. And what do you do, some kind of hanger-on or something? This is bullshit! I haven't done anything apart from sitting here getting loaded. What am I to these people? They're nice to me, they think well of me, and they'll get me high. And, so what!? Who am I? And, what am I going to do in this life?' [It was] a terrible paranoid flash. It made it really hard for me to continue getting high the way I had been, which was to stay blitzed. Smoking a lot of dope is a way to avoid coming to terms with work. So Paxton was actually a very instructive time."[55]

After he had returned to Los Angeles, Jackson started dating Janice Kenner. When he met her, she was modeling clothes on *The Lloyd Thaxton Show*. Browne was very vocal about being hurt when she broke up with him. It seemed that so many things in his life were suddenly turning sour.

Another bit of bad news came to Jackson Browne's circle when word came back from the Orient. Jackson's friend Adam Saylor, who had toured around the globe with Greg Copeland, had continued his journeying into Asia. Adam's journey ended when he took a plunge from a third-story window of a

> "I hit The Troubadour, the Monday night hoots. I'd show up and play, maybe sit around a bit, but I didn't want to hang out. I wanted to be taken seriously."

hotel in Bombay, India. It was never ascertained whether his fall was a suicide or an accident. Regardless of the circumstances, Jackson was heartbroken when he heard this news. To voice his frustration and sense of loss, he sat down and wrote the lyrics to "Song for Adam." Another equally touching and moody song he penned during this period was "My Opening Farewell."

Looking back on his friendship with Adam, Jackson later explained, "He was this friend of Greg Copeland who had this great character. Although he was very salty and sarcastic by the end of a month hanging out with him, we all really cared about each other. Greg and Adam went to Europe and wound up in Tangier and eventually India. I wanted to go, but I didn't have the money to do it. Adam was this biology freak, and people were down on him because once he took somebody's cat apart."[56]

Jackson began to question what he was doing with his life at the time. According to Pamela Polland, he told her that he was so frustrated with the music business, he was contemplating quitting it and becoming a police officer. "He was very serious about it," she later claimed. "He was really considering becoming a policeman. And that was an amazing thing for him to say in 1969, 'cause the cops were 'pigs' in 1969; they were the enemy, right?"[57]

In addition to dealing with his career frustrations, beaking up with his girlfriend, and coping with Adam Saylor's death, he received his notice to report to the local draft board. The Vietnam War was raging at the time, and he was a prime candidate to be drafted.

What was he going to do? He sure as hell didn't want to get drafted! To the rescue came his old friend Roger Dutton. It seemed that Dutton himself dodged the draft by tainting his blood with enough drugs to make him undesirable to the military. If it worked for him, why wouldn't it work for Jackson?

According to Roger, "We started filling him up with Methedrine. About the third day we were kind of worried about him, because he wasn't getting crazy. But on that day he walks out of the house—it's the evening—and he comes back inside and goes: 'There's a flying saucer out there.' 'This is good,' we think."[58] Well, the following morning, when Jackson reported at his local draft board, he was indeed too "chemically enhanced" to be deemed a desirable soldier.

Browne recalls, "Every club had a different night of the week when they had an open mike. So you could go from hoot to hoot, and get to know a whole bunch of music—folk music, even though it was happening in the middle of

> "Every club had a different night of the week when they had an open mike. So you could go from hoot to hoot, and get to know a whole bunch of music—folk music, even though it was happening in the middle of The Beatles and [The Rolling] Stones."

The Beatles and [The Rolling] Stones. Ry Cooder and David Lindley came out of the folk scene at the Ash Grove, where they'd have Sonny Terry and Brownie McGhee, people like that. [Linda] Ronstadt and me and guys in The Eagles like Bernie Leadon came out of the Troubadour on Monday nights. You see, you'd go to hear the greats play at the Ash Grove, but the owner wasn't going to hire you. He'd send you up to the Troubadour, which was considered a bastion of commercial folk music—Hoyt Axton and The Smothers Brothers, which was not really folk. To me, The Smothers Brothers were heroes: They were funny, and lost their show by criticizing the Vietnam War."[59]

In 1969, at the age of twenty, Jackson decided that hanging out at The Troubadour was going to be the answer to relaunching his career. At least he would hang out there until he came up with a solution to his dilemma. "A lot of people hung out at the Troubadour, but I used to be wary about it. I wanted to be taken seriously, and I would show up with my guitar, and I would sing and I wouldn't sing, but I couldn't really hang there in the bar."[60]

Recalling the scene back then, Browne explains, "The Troubadour was the big thing then, but I'll tell you something, I don't really think there was ever [a] songwriter's scene around The Troubadour. It was like Bob Dylan said, 'You probably call it folk music, but it's not.' It wasn't folk music at The Troubadour, and nobody thought of it as folk. People came in with a full band. They'd come and they'd get record deals and they'd go. A lot of them were real corny. And, flashy too. If you hung out there long enough, you could almost chart someone's progress. You'd see them one day by themselves, and the next day with two or three people they'd be forming a band. Like J. D. Souther and Glenn Frey began playing there as a duo, and eventually you'd hear J.D. go up there by himself. And then a couple of weeks later Glenn would be in rehearsal with these other guys and they'd become The Eagles."[61]

By concentrating his efforts on the showcase nights at The Troubadour, Jackson Browne was going to further hone his performing talents, as well as find several new lifelong friends there. Now, all he had to do was to overcome his shyness for performing and get himself off the bar stool and up on stage.

CHAPTER 3

Saturate Before Using

IN 1969—TO PARAPHRASE JACKSON'S IDOL Bob Dylan—the times were definitely "a-changin'" in a lot of big ways. *Hair* was celebrating its first full year on Broadway, and it was the year of the biggest rock festival ever: Woodstock. The Beatles' *Abbey Road* was the rock album of the year, and harmonious folk/rock was taken to new heights as David Crosby, Graham Nash, and Stephen Stills joined forces to become known as Crosby, Stills & Nash.

It was also the year of one of the most horrendous murders in Hollywood history: masterminded by Charles Manson, an insane would-be folk singer. The bizarre thing was that not a lot of people recall how Manson and his "family" of followers were actually trying to land a recording deal. In fact, Manson had met with producer Terry Melcher and was courting Melcher to sign him to a record deal.

Jackson had heard about the whole "free-love" and "free-sex" atmosphere around the Manson camp. And, at the time, growing out of the whole "peace/love/dove" aura of the era, it actually sounded fascinating to Browne.

However, he later stated, "When people talk about the '60s—it's impossible to talk about the '60s. It means so many things, so many things, so many things were going on. It's all subjective. For instance, I had heard about Charles Manson. And this guy, Mike Deasey, had been out there once trying to record Charles Manson and all those people. He suggested that there was a lot of tribal unity there, but very sexually free. For someone who was—I think I was nineteen at the time—I thought, 'Yeah, let's go out there.' It sounded great to me. Then Terry Melcher said, 'Well, no, actually, you better not, because it's a little strange, it's a little odd.' And Mike Deasey—who was a guitar player and a really nice guy—said, 'Don't mess with it.' When I say it sounded great, I mean, in the depths of my ignorance it sounded great."[1]

When things turned sour between Manson and Melcher, Manson vowed to get revenge. His twisted idea of revenge was to brutally murder the people who had just moved into the house in the Hollywood Hills that Melcher had owned. The people who had just moved into the house were film director Roman Polanski and his pregnant actress-wife Sharon Tate. Polanski was not in Los Angeles at the time, but Tate and a group of her friends were, and they met a brutal end at the hands of the Manson clan. The infamous murders shocked the world. And to think that Jackson Browne, in all of his innocence, nearly got involved in the whole Manson musical scene. Fortunately for him, Melcher had steered him out of harm's way.

When the original *Lillian Roxon's Rock Encyclopedia* was published in 1969, it proved that Jackson already had an audience awaiting his debut album. According to *Roxon*, "'Some things take a long time to happen,' said Danny Fields on WFMU when queried on the progress of young Californian singer/ writer Jackson Browne. Browne's poem/songs appear on Steve Noonan's album and also on Nico's first solo album. (He was in New York Playing for Nico at The Dom in 1967.) And it's clear from them that when he does happen, when he's good and ready, the wait will be worth it."[2] Talk about a prophetic vote of confidence!

Meanwhile, Jackson Browne was turning his energies to the showcase nights at The Troubadour on Santa Monica Boulevard. It was often filled with young hopefuls, as well as record company executives on the lookout for the "next big" singing sensation. Jim Croce, the late folk singer, once said of the scene at the club, "The Troubadour was one of the most unique and respected places to play. There would be Cadillacs and Porsches parked outside, and inside it was one big wild party. People would be doing drugs and trying to get picked up, while young talent was being revealed on its stage. There was no club that was more influential during the '60s and '70s for promoting new talent than The Troubadour. If you were lucky enough to get a gig there then you had a shot at getting discovered and getting signed to a recording contract."[3]

> "There was no club that was more influential during the '60s and '70s for promoting new talent than The Troubadour. If you were lucky enough to get a gig there then you had a shot at getting discovered and getting signed to a recording contract."

Jackson explains, "The real rock & roll scene started happening around The Troubadour, and people would showcase. They would call it a 'hoot,' but you would go up there [on stage] and you'd sing four songs and it was like an 'open mic' type thing, and people started gravitating to that scene."[4]

There were also several characters who used to hang out there. Jackson remembers hanging out and chatting to many of them, "There was this one writer who used to be a doorman at The Troubadour. One time he said to me, 'You ever wonder how Humphrey Bogart became Humphrey Bogart? Like, he probably had an uncle who talked that way.' These are the people who really enrich your life."[5]

From the very beginning, the sensitive songs that Jackson wrote, and the way he performed them on stage, was somehow magical. However, even he knew that his onstage singing wasn't always his strongest point. He needed to build confidence in himself and to crystalize his own singing style and lyric phrasing. The Troubadour open mic "Hoot Nights" were the perfect way to polish and develop his singing skills.

Don Henley recalls of Browne's performances at The Troubadour, "His lyrics were some of the first lyrics I had heard that dealt with the kinds of subject matter that he dealt with. The way he dealt with them, they were poetic, but they were also very straightforward, and I think Jackson certainly had some influence on me, and on Glenn [Frey], and maybe J. D. [Souther]."[6]

Troubadour owner Doug Weston had been watching Jackson Browne for a while and noted that he was becoming stronger and stronger as a performer. In September 1969, Linda Ronstadt was about to headline a week at the club, and an opening act was needed. It was Doug who offered Browne the gig. Needless to say, it was just the boost that his fledgling career needed.

"I felt that his songs were introspective and at the same time had a maturity beyond his years," Weston recalled. "[He wrote] penetrating songs that dealt with real things, the things involved in growing up. Jackson had a personal charisma, even onstage. Charisma can be of all kinds. With him it was that particular combination of charm and shyness. His shyness was appealing, attractive."[7]

Opening Ronstadt's set was the perfect showcase for twenty-year-old Jackson. Linda, who was two years older, had al-

> Opening Ronstadt's set was the perfect showcase for twenty-year-old Jackson. Linda, who was two years older, had already had a huge hit—"Different Drum"—with her former group, The Stone Poneys.

ready had a huge hit—"Different Drum"—with her former group, The Stone Poneys. Her debut album, *Hand Sewn, Hand Grown*, had just been released by Capitol Records in March 1969.

She had debuted as a solo act earlier that year at The Whisky a Go Go on Sunset Strip at the time her album was released. When its country/rock sound failed to click, she, too, took to hanging out at The Troubadour—taking the stage as a headliner.

Linda recounts, "That's where I met Bernie Leadon and where I met Glenn Frey, who was in a group called Longbranch Pennywhistle with my boyfriend at that time, John David Souther."[8]

To say that the performers stuck up for each other at The Troubadour was something of an understatement. One night, Linda was watching Jackson Browne's set on stage while a drunk patron kept making distracting comments. She ended up picking a fight with the loud-mouthed man. "I hauled off and punched him right in the mouth," she claims. "I mean I really hit him. And he went back and into the wall and would've gone down if the wall wasn't there. And, of course that made it worse!"[9]

Ronstadt recalls the sense of camaraderie that existed between the performers at The Troubadour during this era, "Jackson and J.D., they pulled each other through some awful times. They encouraged each other about their writings, became each other's fans. And the women—there were very few of us, and we were really oddballs. We really didn't know how to act, or what to do, or how we were supposed to be. We didn't know whether we were supposed to be real earth mamas like Maria Muldaur, you know, with a baby under her arm and a fiddle in her hand . . . or what."[10]

Linda Ronstadt's headlining engagement at The Troubadour in September 1969 drew a large circle of music industry insiders. Among the celebrities in the crowd on opening night was David Crosby. Crosby had a Top 10 album at that time with Crosby, Stills & Nash. And the trio had just rocked the world with their appearance the previous month at Woodstock.

David Crosby had been a member of one of Jackson Browne's favorite groups—the Byrds—he was a singing star with Crosby, Stills & Nash, and he was also a record producer. He had produced Joni Mitchell's highly literate first album, *Joni Mitchell: Songs for a Seagull*, in 1968. He had also been dating Joni during that time.

Jackson was completely blown away by the fact that Crosby had been in the audience. Not only had he been there through Browne's set, he was also greatly impressed. In fact, following Browne's set, Crosby told Jackson backstage that he wanted to be the producer of Browne's first album.

Months later, David Crosby bragged to *Rolling Stone* magazine of this new singer whom he was interested in producing an album for: Jackson Browne. Crosby said, "The cat just sings rings around most people, and he's got songs that'll make your hair stand on end."[11] In spite of the backstage promise from Crosby, the proposed album production deal was never to be made. But the compliment was flattering just the same.

In the autumn of 1969, Jackson Browne signed a nonexclusive music co-publishing deal with Criterion Music, in hopes that they would help market his music. He had a new song he had written, "Jamaica Say You Will." In February 1970, he recorded an acetate demo of this new song, with John David Souther on drums and Glenn Frey and Ned Doheny backing him.

At the time, it was easy to follow patterns in the music business. For instance, Joni Mitchell, Laura Nyro, and Crosby, Stills & Nash were all managed by one person: twenty-eight-year-old rock manager David Geffen. In a very clever and aggressive move, Jackson packaged up an eight-by-ten-inch glossy black-and-white photo of himself, a copy of "Jamaica Say You Will," and an impassioned letter that began, "I am writing to you out of respect for the artists you represent..."[12]

The package was delivered to David Geffen's office, located on Sunset Boulevard. Geffen received the package, opened it up, glanced at it, looked at the photo, and tossed everything into the wastebasket. After he had left the office, his secretary emptied the wastebasket and immediately caught a glimpse of young Jackson Browne. Liking what she saw, she fished out the

Jackson was completely blown away by the fact that Crosby had been in the audience. Not only had he been there through Browne's set, he was also greatly impressed. In fact, following Browne's set, Crosby told Jackson backstage that he wanted to be the producer of Browne's first album.

Geffen received the package, opened it up, glanced at it, looked at the photo, and tossed everything into the wastebasket. After he had left the office, his secretary emptied the wastebasket and immediately caught a glimpse of young Jackson Browne.

demo and the letter. She took the package home, listened to the acetate recording, and loved the song and the singer she heard.

The next day, she brought the letter, the acetate, and the photo back to the
office and presented them to her boss, telling him that she thought Jackson
was very good and that he should at least listen to the acetate. On her insistence, he did exactly that and was instantly impressed with the performance
and song he heard.

He was so impressed by it that he picked up the phone to call Jackson immediately. Unfortunately, Browne had left town. Jackson later recounted, "I
went to Colorado. From there I was gonna go to New Mexico and check out
the communes. You can make bricks or something. There's all kinds of things
to do, 'cause it was getting really depressing here [in Los Angeles]. And I came
back, it turned out he had been trying to get a hold of me."[13]

When Jackson returned to Los Angeles, he called Geffen back, and an audition
was set up. Browne provided David Geffen with a one-man show, and David
loved what he heard and saw. Shortly thereafter, it was announced that David
Geffen was to be his new manager.

When the suggestion of immediately recording an album came up, Geffen
told Jackson that they would wait a while and stick to developing his songwriting and performing before they took that step. Browne himself knew that
he had been getting stronger and stronger as a stage performer. Now, with the
knowledge that he had a high-powered manager behind him, his self-
confidence was bolstered even further. Geffen handed Browne $300 and told
him to have a good summer and that they would be back in touch.

With that, Jackson set about getting a release from Billy James, his former
manager. Knowing that Geffen could do more for Jackson's career than he
could, James issued an official release.

James recalls, "I wasn't able to move him as fast as he was ready to move. I
don't do deals all that well."[14]

The next task at hand was to gain a release of the twenty-two Jackson
Browne songs that had been signed over to Criterion Music. Also, three of
Jackson's newest compositions—"Jamaica Say You Will," "Song for Adam,"
and "My Opening Farewell"—were caught up in the Criterion deal.

Geffen felt that he could make Jackson a substantial amount of money by
selling his song catalog to a music publisher. However, Criterion wasn't about
to let it go, especially now that someone else wanted it.

As a sign that interest was heating up in the industry over Jackson Browne, Mickey Goldsen at Criterion Music began to receive phone calls from Vanguard and Columbia Records. It seemed that talent scouts for those labels were actively inquiring about Browne's recording plans. Jackson followed Geffen's advice and told Goldsen that he had other plans in the works. Geffen did indeed have big plans for Jackson.

During the summer of 1970, Jackson started hanging out with the cast of musicians who made up Joe Cocker's famous *Mad Dogs and Englishmen* tour of the United States. Alongside Rita Coolidge, Pamela Polland was one of ten members of "the choir" featured on Cocker's show. It was one of Browne's highlights that summer. Through his association with the Joe Cocker tour, he got to know Denny Cordell, Cocker's producer and manager.

During this period, Geffen invited Jackson to move into his house on Alto Cedro Drive. David gave him money for food and clothes. He couldn't have his new star not dressing in a starlike fashion. On a couple of occasions, Jackson invited his buddies John David Souther and Glenn Frey over for a swim. The trio ended up skinny-dipping in David's swimming pool.

> During this period, Geffen invited Jackson to move into his house on Alto Cedro Drive. David gave him money for food and clothes. He couldn't have his new star not dressing in a starlike fashion.

It was a whole new lifestyle for Jackson Browne. He would hang out at Geffen's mansion in the Beverly Glen area of Los Angeles, adjacent to Beverly Hills. Jackson would swim in the pool there, write songs, play music, and even showcase his talent before other songwriting stars such as Jimmy Webb and Laura Nyro. Geffen was clearly grooming him for pop music stardom.

When Geffen felt that Jackson was ready for a record deal, he made appointments with the top people at the New York–based record labels. First on the list was Clive Davis, who at the time was the head of Columbia Records— which was also Bob Dylan's label.

In Davis's office, Geffen had Browne take his guitar out and sing his new composition, "Doctor My Eyes." However, in the middle of Browne's performance, Clive's secretary came in and whispered something to him. Apologizing, Davis told Geffen and Browne that he had to take this call and that he would be right back. Geffen went crazy with anger. How could he be treated this way?

"Pack up your guitar," Geffen instructed the young balladeer.

"What?" said a startled Browne.

"Pack up your guitar, we're leaving," Geffen insisted.

"We don't have to do that," said Browne.

"Just do what I tell you," he instructed his client.[15] And with that, they left.

The next appointment was with Ahmet Ertegun of Atlantic Records. In terms of enthusiasm, his audition in Ertegun's office failed to yield the offer of a record deal.

When Geffen pressured Ertegun to sign Browne, claiming, "You'll make a lot of money," Ertegun said, "You know what David, I have a lot of money. Why don't you start a record company and then you'll have a lot of money?"[16]

Right then and there, Geffen told Ertegun that if he gave him his own distribution and manufacturing deal, he would split the profits fifty-fifty, and start his own record label. Ertegun agreed, and so was born Asylum Records. It was the perfect deal for Geffen. He wouldn't have to lay out any money, and he would sign Jackson as his first recording act.

Next, it was Geffen's plan to put Jackson Browne on tour with one of his other star attractions, Laura Nyro. At the time, Nyro was just experiencing her first wave of success as a songwriter and performer. She had released three separate albums, each filled with excitingly original hit songs. Actually, it was other performers who were scoring the hits with her songs, but she was becoming something of a sensation as well.

> Next, it was Geffen's plan to put Jackson Browne on tour with one of his other star attractions, Laura Nyro.

Her debut album by Verve/Forecast Records in 1966, *More Than a New Discovery*, contained the original versions of the songs "Stoney End" (Barbra Streisand), "And When I Die" (Blood, Sweat & Tears)," and "Wedding Bell Blues" (the Fifth Dimension). (It was rereleased on Columbia Records in 1973 under the title *The First Songs*.) Her second album, *Eli and the Thirteenth Confession* (1968), contained "Eli's Coming" (Three Dog Night), "Sweet Blindness" (the Fifth Dimension), and "Stoned Soul Picnic" (the Fifth Dimension, the Supremes, and the Four Tops). And her third album, *New York Tendaberry* (1969), featured "Time and Love" (the Fifth Dimension, LaBelle, Barbra Streisand, and the Supremes) and "Save the Country" (the Fifth Dimension).

This was also the era in which Carole King was *the* huge singer/songwriter sensation. Her Number 1 *Tapestry* album soundly put the spotlight on her, after years of providing hits for everyone else. Laura Nyro's fame in many ways paralleled King's in the business. And it was David Geffen who was guiding Nyro's career along those same lines.

According to inside sources, David Geffen was determined to make Jackson Browne a star in a big way. One of his first plans in 1970 was to put Browne on tour with Nyro. As it turned out, it would be the perfect showcase for him.

In Los Angeles, the show was at the Dorothy Chandler Pavilion, which is located in Los Angeles's Music Center. Instead of an audience of somewhere in the vicinity of 300 people, like he was used to at The Troubadour, here he sang in front of a crowd of 3,000.

According to Michele Kort, in her book *Soul Picnic: The Music and Passion of Laura Nyro*, "Browne would become not only her opening act but—according to several of Laura's close friends—her lover."[17]

Music critic Robert Hillburn wrote of Jackson in the *Los Angeles Times*, "Both his gentle, hopeful material and manner are reminiscent of James Taylor, but he is still in the development stage. His songs are more promising than rewarding at this point."[18]

The show continued on to New York City, where Laura Nyro and Jackson Browne headlined The Fillmore East in the Village. Rock & roll feature writer Susan Mittelkauf vividly recalls seeing Browne on the bill the night of December 24, 1970, "I went to see Laura Nyro, and because it was Christmas Eve, and everyone was in a very mellow holiday mood. Although he was 22 years old, he looked to be about 18. It was just Jackson on the stage that night, strumming his guitar, and no band. I had never heard of Jackson Browne at that point, but I liked him right away. And even though I was not there to see him—it was Laura that I was dying to see—I was very taken by his show. She was blue-eyed soul, and he was very folky, so musically it was a perfect fit. I was very impressed with his songs and I immediately liked him right away. It was obvious that night that a vastly successful future was already in the cards for him."[19]

In the December 25, 1970, issue of the *New York Times*, reviewer Mike Jahn claimed of the singer/songwriter's solo Manhattan stage debut, "Jackson Browne is a 22-year-old Californian whose gifts as a songwriter have been noticed for some time.... He has shoulder-length hair, is rather soft spoken and given to absent-minded rambling between songs.... Mr. Browne certainly is worthwhile as a songwriter. At his Wednesday evening performance he played only slow ballads, sticking to a traditional format of songs.... It seems obvious that Jackson Browne has a promising career ahead of him."[20]

During the same East Coast visit, Jackson Browne was also on a double bill with another promising female singer: Bonnie Raitt. Theirs would be a lifelong bond of friendship. Just like Jackson, at this point in her career Raitt was still working on putting her first album together. Her first LP would hit the marketplace the following year—just as Browne's would.

> During the same East Coast visit, Jackson Browne was also on a double bill with another promising female singer: Bonnie Raitt. Theirs would be a lifelong bond of friendship.

Raitt, who was a year younger than Jackson, was the daughter of Broadway star John Raitt (*Carousel, Oklahoma, The Pajama Game*). An avid fan of folk music in the early 1960s, she was a great guitar player. In 1967, she started college at Radcliffe, where she majored in African studies, and it wasn't long before she started playing her own brand of blues/rock in coffee houses in the Boston area. Her boyfriend, Dick Waterman, was a musician and a music promoter. When he introduced Raitt to such blues masters as Son House, Fred McDowell, and Otis Rush, it had a profound effect on her and her music.

She and Jackson were both at the same stage in their young careers, and they hit it off instantly. The gig was at Syracuse University, at a club on campus called The Jabberwocky. Fortunately, a tape was made of that show. On the tape Jackson was captured at his most innocent. As he tuned his guitar between the ten songs he sang that night, Browne started onstage chats with his audience.

He spoke that night about David Geffen's thoughts about creating a whole new record label to release his new album on, "We thought of so many names, and the lawyers kept saying we couldn't use them. 'Apple.' 'Capitol.' My manager's such a square, he was thinking 'Integrity Records.'"[21]

Introducing the song "From Silver Lake," Browne claimed it was about his two friends Greg Copeland and Adam Saylor, "This is a song I wrote for some friends of mine who were living in Long Beach, California. I see no one's started to gag so no one knows about Long Beach. It's like San Diego—it's got a lot of sailors.... So the two of them, Greg and Adam, they went to Mexico...."

But that legendary banana boat from Mexico to Spain never did materialize, and they decided they'd come back and drive from Long Beach to New York. And that's what they did."[22]

Before he launched into "My Opening Farewell," Jackson said, "I figure the crowd's at the state of drunkenness where they're feeling pissed and things start flying." And during that night's second show, he told the crowd, "Bonnie said a real outasite thing. She came backstage and said, 'Man, those people are strange. They got to be drunker than we are.'"[23]

Prior to singing his last song he claimed, "This here song I wrote for someone who hasn't quite materialized yet. It's called 'Looking into You' and I'd like to sing it for you, seeing that this particular person hasn't come up yet." However, he was a little miffed that people in the audience continued to talk instead of paying attention to him. "And I want to really sing it well," he claimed, "so shut the fuck up! All right? 'Cause I'm going to do this one more and I want to do it well . . . because I want to do something well."[24] After he performed his song, he received a big round of applause.

Jackson's tour with Laura Nyro then moved on to Europe. It came to a conclusion in London at Festival Hall in early 1971. When Browne's tour with Laura ended, so did their affair. It was fun while it lasted, but their involvement was brief. However, sources close to Nyro claimed that she was very much in love with him at the time.

According to David Geffen, "It was never a great big relationship, frankly. Maybe it was for her. I don't remember it being a cause of tremendous pain. Jackson was very pretty, not at all the kind of guy she was usually interested in. She liked Sonny Bono! Jackson Browne was classically good looking, 'matinee-idol' good looking."[25]

While he was in London, Jackson reconnected with Denny Cordell, Joe Cocker's manager and producer. Not only had he produced the *Mad Dogs and Englishmen* album (with Leon Russell), but he had also worked with Procol Harum and singer/songwriter Leon Russell. And he had his own label, Shelter Records. Jackson just so happened to be looking for a producer.

> When Browne's tour with Laura ended, so did their affair. It was fun while it lasted, but their involvement was brief. However, sources close to Nyro claimed that she was very much in love with him at the time.

Jackson felt at the time that Cordell was the right man for the job. Cordell would produce, and David Geffen's record label would release it. In London, Browne recorded a handful of tracks with Cordell at the helm. Several of the players from the *Mad Dogs and Englishmen* tour and album were on Jackson's British tracks including drummer Jim Keltner, Chris Stainton playing piano and guitar, and Leon Russell playing the piano on "Jamaica Say You Will." One of the guest players on the tracks was guitar wizard Albert Lee.

Just like Browne had told the crowd at The Jabberwocky in Syracuse that night in 1970, David Geffen—after he couldn't find the kind of deal he wanted—did start his own record label, with Jackson Browne as the first act he signed. It was now officially called Asylum Records, and it would be part of a distribution deal with Elektra Records, which was owned by the same parent company as Atlantic Records.

David Geffen recalls, "I couldn't find a record company that was interested in Jackson. I figured I'd better put my money where my mouth is, so I started Asylum Records."[26] It was reported that by the time Jackson's first album hit the stores, Geffen had already advanced Jackson $100,000.

At the time of these sessions, Cordell was harboring hope that Jackson would end up signing with Shelter. When he got news that Jackson would sign with Asylum Records, he lost interest in the sessions. Jackson and Cordell decided to just pull the plug on the tracks they had laid down.

Meanwhile, in September 1971, David Geffen struck a deal for his next artists at Asylum Records. The deal was solidified at Geffen's house. There sat Glenn Frey, Don Henley, Jackson Browne, John David Souther, Ned Doheny, and David—all naked in his sauna. Geffen sent the group of Frey, Henley, Randy Meisner, and Bernie Leadon to Colorado to write songs for their debut album, and they were also assigned the task of coming up with a name for their quartet. They ultimately decided on "the Eagles." Taking them under his wings like he had Jackson, Geffen also footed the bill to groom them a bit. In the process, he sent the group to his own dentist to get their teeth fixed.

In late 1971, Browne went into Crystal Sound Studios in Los Angeles with producer/engineer Richard Sanford Orshoff and began recording the tracks that would ultimately comprise his debut album. Albert Lee would play the electric guitar on "A Child in These Hills" and "Under the Falling Sky." David Crosby provided harmony vocals. Jimmie Fadden of the Nitty Gritty Dirt

Band played the "mouth harp" (harmonica). And Leah Kunkel sang the "countersong" on the track "From Silver Lake."

Speaking of the sessions for his debut album, Jackson recalls, "I chose a lot of these songs by who played on them. Jesse Ed Davis plays lead guitar on this one. He was kind of a guitar god. He had played with Taj Mahal, Bob Dylan, John Lennon, Leon Russell. I called him and he came in to play and was sort of...in a hurry. Jesse died of a heroin overdose, and I don't know what he was using at the time, but he came in and just wanted to play and get out—and he wanted to get paid cash. So there was that vibe going on. I played him a different song at first, and he said, 'I don't hear myself playing on this. You got anything else?' So I played him 'Doctor My Eyes,' and he said, 'Okay, I can play on this,' and he was so brilliant—he just tuned up, played a couple of licks and said, 'Okay, take it to the solo.' He was a great player—I never saw him do anything the same way twice."[27]

Albert Lee recalls of those sessions, "Jackson had taken charge by that point. He knew what he wanted, but he was relying on Richard to help him out in the control room. In my experience in working with artists doing their first record, they are totally out of their depths, really. They're just at the mercy of the guys who are producing them, the engineers. But Jackson seemed to know what he wanted."[28]

It had originally been Geffen's idea to have David Crosby sing harmony vocals on "Doctor My Eyes." He knew that it would aid in making Jackson's album instantly radio friendly when it was released. Jackson loved the idea, since Crosby had become a genuine friend of his. Crosby's voice on the song truly enhanced its importance.

However, the recording process of the *Jackson Browne* album wasn't all smooth sailing. At one point, Browne and Geffen got into a huge fight over a particular idea that David had come up with. Since Carole King's *Tapestry* album had become the biggest commercial hit of the year, Geffen wanted Jackson to record a duet with Carole.

"I don't know Carole King," Jackson said.

"That's okay," said David. "Just invite her to play on a record with you. She'll do it."

"But I don't know her!" Jackson argued. "You want me to invite her to sing on my album because now she's got a big record? That's not music. That's commerce. It's bullshit."[29]

Reportedly, the two did not talk to each other for several days. Finally, they patched up their differences. But the fact remained that Jackson stood his ground on the issue of recording a song with Carole King just to sell albums.

"It was 1971, I was waiting to go on tour and didn't have a place to live, so David [Crosby] let me stay on his boat," Jackson later recalled. He also claimed that living with highly paranoid Crosby was filled with many complications. "One time I drove him to the studio. I was going with him and he had me drive. He criticized my driving the entire time because he says, 'Look, I got a lot of drugs here. You have to drive really legal. You're a person that drives along with his head in the clouds, not thinking about how fast he's going, and I can't do that.' David was a real careful driver and drove his 6.3-liter Mercedes that you couldn't get in America; it has to be snuck in somehow on the gray market; there were only ten of them in the States. So I'm zipping along in this thing, doing about 68 miles per hour, and Crosby's white-knuckling it. 'Listen are you crazy? Stop that! Drive right!' More than just a backseat driver, this was someone with a satchel of the purest Merck, of which I got a little. Crosby wasn't plying me with drugs. Any one of us could go and score our own drugs, except Crosby's dope was always a lot better, the quality was great, and it never occurred to me to say, 'David, I'd like to buy some of what you have there.' "[30]

When the recording of the album was finished, David Geffen was convinced that the songs contained on it were the perfect distillation of what he had envisioned it would be. Browne later told Lou Irwin of *Earth News* that he was tripping on LSD one day, listening to his album on Geffen's turntable, and was shocked to hear himself on record. "I sat there poleaxed, 'Well, God, no. I sound so green.' And I was seeing my young little self coming out of those speakers. And I was embarrassed for myself. I thought I was naked."[31]

The album was finished in enough time to be released in the fall of 1971. However, because that is traditionally the season for superstar albums to be released in time for the Christmas season, a decision was made to hold the *Jackson Browne* album's release until the following calendar year.

One of the important aspects of the album was its cover concept. Since this would be the record-buying public's first view of Browne, it was an important aspect to the package. According to Jackson, "Album covers for me—they were bigger [in size] than they are now [as CDs]—and they were like, I always thought of them like the shield the way Indians would dream up, they would literally dream or imagine or think of that thing that would represent them."[32]

The duo of Gary Burden and his photographer buddy Henry Diltz were brought in to design the cover. They had also done the album covers for the Doors' 1970 *Morrison Hotel* album, the *Crosby, Stills & Nash* album, and the Mamas and the Papas LP *The Papas & the Mamas*. Gary recalls, "David Geffen who managed Jackson, and literally owned the label that Jackson was on—Asylum Records—had called me up and set it up for us to go and meet this young singer/songwriter named Jackson Browne."[33]

Henry Diltz says, "So we went up to the door, knocked on the door, Jackson opened the door, said 'Hi, I'm Jackson.' We introduced ourselves, went in, sat down, opened up a beer, and Jackson said, 'Do you want to hear the album?' And we said, 'Sure,' and he sat down at the piano and just played these amazing songs, these beautiful heartfelt lyrics."[34]

It was Jackson himself who came up with the idea of making the album cover look like a car's canvas radiator cooling bag. As he explains, "We used to spend a lot of time in the desert, and I had this water bag on my wall, and I was having the conversation with Gary—just discussing ideas—I was on the phone with him and I was just staring at this water bag, and I said, 'Well we could make it a water bag.' Our generation knows what a water bag is. It's a canvas bag that you submerge, probably in the tire trough at the gas station and get it wet. So the flax—it was made of flax—and it expands and it holds the water. You literally hang it on the front of your car, so when you passed through the Mojave Desert, the water sort of evaporates as it goes through the radiator grill, and helps the car stay cool."[35]

Gary agreed to the concept and explains, "So we decided to make the album cover look like that. And, I made it as authentic as possible. On the real bag it says 'Saturate before Using' meaning get it wet, and it would be effective."[36]

The final product had a black-and-white portrait photo of Jackson Browne, with the gray tones dropped out—taken by Henry—and silkscreened onto one of the automobile radiator bags. His name—the title of the album—appears in an arc over his head in large brown letters. On the actual canvas bags, the words "Saturate before Using" were printed on the top of the bag. Gary decided to keep those words on his artwork, to add authenticity to the cover concept. When Gary Burden showed Jackson the finished product, with the words "Saturate before Using" intact at the top, the singer was skeptical.

Gary recalls, "So, Jackson said, 'I'm really afraid that if you put that on there, people are going to think that that's title of my album.' And I said, 'No way, man. There's no way they would think that's part of it.' "[37]

Although the album is officially entitled *Jackson Browne*, many people assumed that the title was actually "Saturate Before Using." In fact, over a decade later, when the album was released on CD, the spine and disc label both carried the words "Saturate Before Using" as the album's assumed actual title.

> Although the album is officially entitled *Jackson Browne,* many people assumed that the title was actually "Saturate Before Using."

The *Jackson Browne* album was finally released in January 1972. A full-page advertisement in *Rolling Stone* magazine in their January 17 issue used the Henry Diltz cover portrait of the singer/songwriter. The headline on the ad read, "Jackson Browne. If the name looks familiar it should." According to the ad copy, "It's a name you've read a lot on albums by people like Tom Rush, The Byrds, Three Dog Night . . . they've all recognized his songs because they were quick to recognize Jackson's great talent with words and music. Jackson Browne has finally recorded an album of his own. And it proves the time-tested adage: 'Nobody can sing a song like its composer.' "[38]

The *Jackson Browne* album is by the far the most rudimentary of the singer/songwriter's LPs. Undoubtedly, the songs on this particular disc most closely replicate what hearing him in a nightclub setting—circa 1971—was like. However, unlike his stage act there was a band behind him and singers to perform harmony vocals. The fact that Jackson had the capacity to just sit alone on stage and sing his songs to the audience—naked to the world except for his voice and his guitar playing—was a talent he has not lost. In his stage show, he didn't need a drummer or a chorus of voices behind him. His great strength has always been the fact that he could, and can, perform an entire concert all alone. That is the sign of a true troubadour.

However, when it came time to record his album, there was a need for more layers of sound to accompany him. At this point, he still didn't have a band of his own. The sound on the *Jackson Browne* album is much fuller, and it set the tone for the classic "Jackson Browne sound" that has characterized his entire career.

The sound on the *Jackson Browne* album is much fuller, and it set the tone for the classic "Jackson Browne sound" that has characterized his entire career.

For instance, Jeff Hanna's harmonica break in the first cut of "Jamaica Say You Will" took the song to a different dimension, by providing a harmonic tail-end section instead of just having the song go into a guitar-led fade. "Jamaica" remains one of Browne's finest straight love ballads. Singing a song about a girl named "Jamaica," he croons to the daughter of a ship's captain.

In "A Child in These Hills," Jackson sings with a childlike sense of discovery about his life in the Hollywood Hills and away from the house of his father. Celebrating his complicated life in Laurel Canyon, the song is Browne at his most innocent. Jeff Hanna's harmonica gives the song a nice bluegrass/rock sound to it. "A Child in These Hills" is one of the songs on which Albert Lee lent his tasty electric guitar playing.

"Song for Adam" tackles the young and tragic death of Jackson's friend Adam Saylor. It is odd how we often think more about friends when they are deceased than while they are sitting right next to us. How easy it is to wonder how two people can go through the same experiences, know the same people, do the same things, and yet one survives and one perishes. These are the thoughts that Browne ponders on in this touching and pensive song. David Campbell's viola gives this beautiful and emotional ballad the right touch of appropriate sadness.

"Doctor My Eyes" was reportedly heavily retooled to turn it into the album's sure-fired hit single. Lyrically, it is about seeking help from a "doctor" to explain the effects of seeing too many things—both evil and good. Apparently, the original version of the song had a chorus about seeing an "Angel of Darkness" hovering. That was removed to make the ultimate song more rocking and upbeat. With great percolating drum and conga work from Russell Kunkel and the thumping bass playing of Leland Sklar, this remains one of the most satisfying and self-assured of all of Jackson Browne's songs. In addition, the harmony vocals of David Crosby took the sound to still another level. This song was meant to be the album's stand-out radio friendly hit, and it worked brilliantly.

One of the catchiest aspects of "Doctor My Eyes" is the unique double beating of the piano keys. Of that bouncing piano key sound, Jackson later said, " 'Doctor My Eyes' was based on this piano thing, which I basically lifted off of my friend Pamela Polland, who lived in this same apartment complex we all lived in. She had a piano that basically had a . . . it was an upright piano, and it had this one key that when you hit it, it sort of flopped twice."[39]

"From Silver Lake" is a song of "good-byes," a somber and mournful song. Midway through the recording, under Jackson's voice, a female singer sings a counterverse. That voice belongs to Leah Kunkel, who was not only the sister to Mama Cass, she was also married to Russell Kunkel. Her vocal adds a haunting quality to the slow and sentimental song about afternoons of smoke, wine, and pleasure and saying "good-bye" to a "brother" who doesn't intend to come back.

"Something Fine" is a lazy song about laying around and presumably getting high and contemplating the meaning of life. Jackson sings of leaving a pile of newspapers outside his door, while the world outside is clambering for him to interact with it. He sings of smiling at the mention of "Morocco," and other such pipe dreams, and obtaining a "taste" of something "fine."

> "Something Fine" is a lazy song about laying around and presumably getting high and contemplating the meaning of life.

Although the message is thin as cigarette paper, there is something somehow charming and engaging in his autobiographical style. In the song, he sings of a simple life that he knows, in the quest of his big break. "Something Fine" is an interesting time capsule in Jackson's life. Soon, his life would drastically change, and the days of lazily having a smoke and contemplating the meaning of life would come to an end.

"Under the Falling Sky" is an upbeat jam session of a love song. And "Looking into You" is a pensive look back at his life. He speaks of going back to the house he grew up in, presumably Abbey San Encino. This slow ballad perfectly showcased Jackson in the highest gear of his sentimental storyteller mode. He is singing this song to a lover, into whose eyes he is gazing longingly.

"Rock Me on the Water" has a very Eagles-sounding chorus backing that harmonically supports Jackson's voice very nicely. Singing about being soothed by the sisters of the sun, this song builds very nicely and is one of the best performances on the album.

Jackson Browne ends with a song of love and defeat called "My Opening

Farewell." A slow and touching ballad about an old woman and an invalid man, Jackson proves he can pull at the heartstrings, while spinning a delicate and touching tale of devotion and memories. The chorus about there being a train that leaves either way, every day, is especially moving.

One of the strongest aspects of Jackson's album was the fact that he was supported by some of the most adept backing musicians in the business. Albert Lee, David Crosby, and Jimmy Fadden gave the album a gleaming sort of insider's star appeal. Bass player Leland Sklar was to become well known for his work with James Taylor, and eventually drummer Russell Kunkel would go on to work with Linda Ronstadt and several other singing stars. Craig Doerge, who played the piano on "Rock Me on the Water," would be a recurring fixture on several Browne albums.

Reviewing the *Jackson Browne* album in the *Washington Post*, writer Alex Ward proclaimed, "Not so long ago I was convinced that hearing just one more folkie-turned-soft rocker would drive me right around the bend, but Jackson Browne makes it a downright pleasure to swallow that assumption."[40]

In *Rolling Stone* magazine, Bud Scoppa raved about the album glowingly. According to him, "It's not often that a single album is sufficient to place a new performer among the first rank of recording artists. Jackson Browne's long-awaited debut album chimes in its author with the resounding authority of *Astral Weeks* [by Van Morrison] . . . *Gasoline Alley* [by Rod Stewart] or . . . *After the Goldrush* [by Neil Young]. Its awesome excellence causes one to wonder why, with Browne's reputation as an important songwriter established as far back as 1968, this album was so long in coming. . . . *Jackson Browne* is more than worth the years it took to be hatched!"[41]

Billboard magazine asserted, "Finally the long-awaited and much heralded first album from Jackson Browne, and it is indeed a work of beauty and charm."[42]

The *Jackson Browne* album didn't exactly set the world on fire the minute it was released. It entered the *Billboard* magazine chart at Number 198 the week of March 18, 1972. However, his first single release from it, "Doctor My Eyes," premiered on the "Hot 100" singles chart in that same issue of the industry publication, at Number 80. By the week of May 6, 1972, it hit its peak at Number 8 in the United States. Voila! His first single was suddenly a Top 10 hit!

> The *Jackson Browne* album didn't exactly set the world on fire the minute it was released.

Jackson later credited David Crosby's contribution to the record's success by proclaiming, "When I made a record, he sang on it and that was impressive. It was a very high recommendation that David would sing on someone's record. I have no doubt that the fact that David and Graham [Nash] sang on 'Doctor My Eyes' was what got it played [on the radio] . . . it was unusual that they would do that."[43]

Based on the success of "Doctor My Eyes," the *Jackson Browne* album made it all the way to Number 58. The singer/songwriter was officially on his way to fulfilling his dreams of being a full-fledged recording artist on his own. The critical acclaim that he won in the press made him *the* new troubadour on the scene to watch. Now it was time to go out and meet his public—on both sides of the Atlantic.

CHAPTER 4

For Everyman

ONCE THE *JACKSON BROWNE* ALBUM hit the stores, the troubadour immediately began another high-profile concert tour, with another of David Geffen's artists: Joni Mitchell. The four-month trek was to take the duo on several stops throughout the United States and Europe.

It was not only the beginning of Jackson's most successful push into the mainstream of the music business, it was also the beginning of his love affair with Joni. Thanks to the huge success of both her *Ladies of the Canyon* album (1970) and her touching lyric masterpiece LP *Blue* (1971), she was the hot newcomer female singer/songwriter of the era. Judy Collins's recording of Joni's "Both Sides Now" put Joni on the map in 1968. She was also legendary for her close, personal relationship with Crosby, Stills & Nash. When they enthusiastically told her about the music festival they had just played, she wrote the song "Woodstock" for and about them.

When Browne was later asked if it was a hindrance being the opening act for the most successful woman of her genre, he argued that it was a blessing. "No, no, it was incredible.... That was what they call a 'break,' because I don't think I could have attempted to play for a better audience...more suited to me," claimed Jackson.[1] The fact that he and Joni were lovers at the time only intensified the whole affair.

One of the most memorable dates on this tour was playing at Carnegie Hall, as the opening act for Joni Mitchell. This was an honor that was not lost on Jackson. The following night, he had his own out-of-town gig. It was a return to the East Coast stronghold of his popularity: Stony Brook, New York.

On the stage that night at Stony Brook, Jackson spoke of his having played at Carnegie Hall the previous evening, "I'm not telling you that to impress you or anything. When you play in a big city everybody from the record company comes around and greases you to make you feel that you're on the job: 'You sold five records yesterday, kid.' So the only way to get through that is to anni-hilate yourself and see how long you remain standing. That's what I did. Woke up this morning at 11 with all the lights on," he claimed.[2]

Rambling on, he said, "I like working in places this size 'cause I tend to mum-ble a lot. In big concert halls you don't realize it, 'cause you can't see anything. You can't even see the front row, and there'll be people sitting at a 90-degree angle above you. People in the back going, 'Speak up! You're mumbling!' And I'll say [mumbling]—'Well, mumbling's my thing.' "[3]

Jackson toured with Joni for four months, beginning in February 1972. After the tour ended in England in the summer, Browne was able to visit Albert Lee, who lived just outside of London, in Blackheath. When they made plans to get together, Jackson told Lee that he was going to be bringing a friend along with him. That was fine with him. Lee had no idea at the time that the friend was going to be one of the hottest female singing sensations in the busi-ness: Joni Mitchell.

According to Albert Lee, Jackson seemed to exude more ease and self-confidence. He had a Top 10 hit, a critically acclaimed debut album, and was romantically involved with Joni. Lee noted that day, "He seemed really enam-ored with her."[4]

Jackson's longtime friends were all abuzz about his affair with Joni. Steve Noonan was especially curious. According to him, "I remember saying to Jackson, 'Gee, tell me about Joni Mitchell,' and him saying, 'I don't want to talk about it.' "[5]

> Jackson's longtime friends were all abuzz about his affair with Joni.

Jackson's love affair with Joni Mitchell was to burn out rather quickly. It was over by the fall of 1972. Pamela Polland hypothesized, "With Joni it was again the thing where she embodied all the things that he was in the process of developing. He was also in the process of developing them, but she was ahead of him. She'd certainly been involved in the music business longer. She had more deep-rooted awareness of the busi-ness…a popularity that couldn't be denied, that is attractive in itself, and a strong devotion to her own artistry.… Unfortunately it became conflicting. And then, beyond the conflict, the even more unfortunate thing is that it be-

came too heavy for Jackson to be with someone who was so much more pro-
lific than he. She was creative in so many ways, and it came out of her so easily, that to face his own struggle with his craft, his own slowness with his
craft—to have those two mirrored against each other—I think was very
painful for him."[6]

For whatever reason, Jackson's love affair with Joni Mitchell was brief. Was
the problem that they were too much alike? They came out of the same Laurel
Canyon circle of friends, and they were seeking to capture the same kind of
audience, musically. Perhaps the problem was that they were just too similar.

According to author Tom King in the book *The Operator: David Geffen
Builds, Buys, and Sells the New Hollywood.* "Joni Mitchell's romance with Jackson
Browne was short-lived and had an ugly
ending. Unlike her previous relationships
with Graham Nash and David Crosby, she
was not the one to end this one. Browne
broke it off."[7]

Looking back on his string of love-
affairs-gone-wrong, including his affair
with Joni, Jackson stated, "I got my heart
crushed about eight times in a row. It
would happen every two years or so; I'd forget and fall in love."[8]

> "Joni Mitchell's romance with Jackson Browne was short-lived and had an ugly ending. Unlike her previous relationships with Graham Nash and David Crosby, she was not the one to end this one. Browne broke it off."

In addition to the noise that his own debut album and single were making
on the charts, in 1972 his songs were showing up in other places as well.
Jackson's song "Rock Me on the Water" was covered by Linda Ronstadt on her
third solo album. The song spent three weeks on the *Billboard* record charts in
the United States and made it to Number 85. That album, entitled *Linda
Ronstadt*, also includes three live performances, which were recorded in front
of an audience at The Troubadour: "Rescue Me," "Birds," and "I Fall to Pieces."
She had put together a band for herself for that particular album from the
friendships she had made at The Troubadour, including Glenn Frey, Bernie
Leadon, Don Henley, and Randy Meisner. It was right after they recorded this
album that they would go on to form their own group and call themselves the
Eagles.

Also in 1972, Bonnie Raitt included the song "Under the Falling Sky" on her
second album, *Give It Up.* Between the exposure that his own album had garnered for him, and being represented on Linda's and Bonnie's albums, he was

suddenly the new kid on the block to be listened to and looked to for writing and singing hit songs.

However, the most successful instance of an artist having a hit with a Jackson Browne song that year was by the Eagles. After he was finished getting Jackson Browne's album together, David Geffen turned his attention to the Eagles, the act formerly known as "Linda Ronstadt's band."

Looking for material to put on their debut album, Glenn Frey turned to Jackson. When Browne had been recording his own debut album at Crystal Sound Studios, Glenn stopped by for a visit. While he was there, he heard parts to a song that Browne was working on, but never finished.

During a telephone conversation with Jackson, Glenn asked him if he had finished that particular song. When Jackson informed him that he had not and wasn't planning on putting it on his album anyway, he told Glenn he could take it and finish it if he liked. He did exactly that.

Among the things he added was the whole verse about a girl in Winslow, Arizona. Jackson was happy with the changes that Frey made to the song, so the Eagles went ahead and recorded the song for their self-titled debut album. On July 22, 1972, the song "Take It Easy" peaked at Number 12 on the U.S. record charts in *Billboard*. Another single from the same album, "Witchy Woman," made it to Number 9 on the singles chart, and the album, *The Eagles*, hit Number 22.

It was in June 1972 that Jackson Browne was first written about in a profile in *Rolling Stone*. Richard Meltzer, his old buddy from Stony Brook, was now writing for the national rock & roll publication and talked the editors into the assignment. This was the aforementioned article in which Meltzer wrote that at The Dom Jackson was a sex symbol who appealed to "the gay rock underground."[9] Reportedly, Jackson freaked out when he read that. That wasn't exactly the kind of image he wanted to project.

Meltzer later explained, "His reaction filtered back. He thought the piece made him look too much like a punk."[10] This particular article began a pattern for Jackson. Some years he courted the press to talk to him, and other years he wanted nothing to do with the press.

In September 1972, Jackson Browne went back on the road, this time as the opening act for the Eagles. Throughout this period, he was also busy writing and selecting material for his new album. He had to admit that there was a push at that time for him to write another "Doctor My Eyes"–style radio hit—

immediately. Reportedly, this only fueled the sudden writer's block he felt toward the second album.

An important addition to the Jackson Browne camp during this period was
the multitalented musician David Lindley. Originally, Jackson had met Lindley
when Browne was the opening act at The Troubadour for Linda Ronstadt. Lindley
"sat in" that night at The Troubadour during Jackson's rendition of "These Days."
Jackson recalls, "He played his fiddle and I sang... and it just blew my mind."[11]

Then, when he had worked in London on the aborted Denny Cordell sessions from his "proposed" first album, Lindley had played on the original version of "Song for Adam" in the studio. Meanwhile, Browne and Lindley had
become good friends.

Lindley accompanied Jackson Browne out on the road with the Eagles. It
was Lindley who was to give Browne's concert version of "Take It Easy" a nice
country feeling with his crying fiddle sound. When Browne and the Eagles
played in New York City, Jackson joined the group on stage. The concert took
place in the Felt Forum, the smaller arena in Madison Square Garden.

Finally, in the fall of 1972 Jackson started recording tracks for his second
album. One of the last things that he and Joni Mitchell would collaborate on
was her playing the electric piano on the
recording of "Sing My Songs to Me."
Jackson's affair with Joni officially came
to an end when another young lady suddenly came into his life.

> One of the last things that he and
> Joni Mitchell would collaborate on
> was her playing the electric piano
> on the recording of "Sing My Songs
> to Me."

Jackson Browne's meeting with Phyllis
Major was one quite by chance. He was
hanging out one night at the bar of The Troubadour when he interceded in a
fight between a belligerent unemployed actor and a woman. Jackson lost the
physical fight and wound up on the floor. However, he won the attention of
the woman he had defended: Phyllis Major.

Phyllis had an interesting background story of her own. Her mother was
Nancy Farnsworth, who was a songwriter in the 1950s. After her parents di-
vorced, Phyllis moved with her mother to the Greek island of Hydra. While
living a very bohemian hippielike existence, she met Jackson's lyric idol,
Leonard Cohen. She left Greece for Switzerland with a Frenchman she had
met. She worked for a while in Switzerland as a governess, and eventually
made her way to Paris, where she found work as a model.

One of her best friends on the circuit in the "City of Light" was fellow model Terry Reno. They were both Americans in Paris, both popular models, and both loved rock & roll music. However, their personalities were very different. Terry considered herself a very straight arrow of a person, and Phyllis was one to cast caution to the wind. For instance, Terry had no interest in "dropping acid," and Phyllis loved a good LSD trip.

According to Reno, Phyllis was someone who "was throwing herself into the fire all the time" when it came to new experiences. "She talked of herself being a Capricorn. She said Capricorns have some kind of flirtation with death. I remember hearing about one of her LSD trips where she said she went into the fetus position. . . . She was always searching for those experiences. Real intense."[12]

Phyllis was, however, someone whose extreme highs were counterbalanced by extreme lows. In 1966, she was dating Keith Richards of the Rolling Stones. When their relationship ended, she attempted suicide. Shortly afterward, she moved back to New York City.

She lived with Terry Reno in New York, and while there Phyllis began dating singer and songwriter Bobby Neuwirth, who had worked as Bob Dylan's right-hand man. During this era, she began to dabble in songwriting as well. Two of her songs, cowritten with former Blood, Sweat & Tears member Al Kooper, appeared on his 1971 album *New York City (You're a Woman)*. When she grew tired of New York City, Phyllis ventured out to Los Angeles, where she wandered into the bar at The Troubadour one night.

To make a long story short, Phyllis came home from the Troubadour with Jackson that night, and they began an affair. She ended up moving in with Jackson at Abbey San Encino, and the next thing Browne knew, Phyllis was pregnant. At the age of twenty-four, Jackson was suddenly going to be a father. Jackson never said to anyone that Phyllis was the love of his life, yet he ended up marrying her— basically because she was having his baby.

> To make a long story short, Phyllis came home from the Troubadour with Jackson that night, and they began an affair. She ended up moving in with Jackson at Abbey San Encino, and the next thing Browne knew, Phyllis was pregnant.

This was to signal a huge change in his lifestyle. Living in Abbey San Encino, with his pregnant girlfriend Phyllis, he used the room that was his grandfather Clyde's chapel as a rehearsal studio for his music.

"I've always known I would live there someday," Browne told the *Chicago Tribune* that year. "I have a real appreciation for the bare walls and plants... for family, too. My grandfather was an incredible person...totally unhappy with modern things. He built that house like something out of the past.... And now I'm going to be a father there, in the house where I was a child."[13]

Browne confessed that he suddenly had been stuck for ideas. "When I was just sitting around writing tunes—which is all I'm doing now—but before anybody heard them, it was really easy to write whatever came out of your head and you weren't so hard on yourself. But as soon as you believe someone who comes up to you and says, 'Hey, this tune's great,' and they treat you like a king—complete strangers—it becomes hard."[14]

On Jackson's second album, he was credited as the "producer," and for technical expertise he utilized recording engineer Al Schmitt. According to Schmitt, Jackson was obsessed with getting his vocals just right on every track. He recalls Browne rerecording his vocals on this album over and over again. While he was recording the album, he enlisted the help of the vocal instructor Warren Barigian. He had originally consulted Barigian when the time came to record his first album. But this time around he was obsessed with getting his vocals right. His rerecording exercises would reportedly continue until the last minute on this project.

According to Browne, "Warren can do everything he says he can do. It's great, incredible...already I feel tremendous improvement."[15]

Meanwhile, Jackson was to make several contributions to the Eagles' second album, *Desperado*. The Eagles turned to both Jackson Browne and J. D. Souther for song ideas. Souther recalls, "The first thing we ever tried writing together was the stuff that was on our *Desperado* album. Ned Doheny laid a book about gunfighters on us. It had a chapter in it about the Doolin-Dalton gang. We started talking about it, ranting and raving through the night about the role of the outlaw and using that as a metaphor. We kicked the idea of all of us being in one group around a lot. We always refer to each other as The White Temptations. It would be a lot of fun if we ever found the time.[16]

Jackson is credited as one of the writers on the song "Doolin-Dalton," which opens and finishes the Eagles' 1973 *Desperado* album. He was also one of the writers of another song that was supposed to be on this album, "James Dean." "James Dean" was held for the group's third album, *On the Border* (1974). As such, Jackson Browne was one of the songwriters on the first three Eagles' albums.

In addition to his contribution to *Desperado*'s music, he was also part of the photo session. The cover depicted the four members of the Eagles in cowboy get-ups looking like one of the outlaw gangs of the Wild West of the late 1880s. On the back of the album was a shot of the quartet, and several of their cohorts, bound and lying on the ground, like captured criminals of the cowboy era. On the far left, next to the Eagles and J. D. Souther, is a somewhat obscured Jackson Browne. This was another concept photo session helmed by Gary Burden and photographer Henry Diltz

While Browne was busy taking his time on his own album, he missed the first deadline for the recordings. In fact, there was a concert tour set up to coincide with the projected release date of the album, but when the first concert date arrived, there was still no new release to promote.

With regard to the writer's block that Jackson had fought during the making of the *For Everyman* album, he later said, "You get the impression that you know what it was that they liked about it [the *Jackson Browne* album], and you try to do that again. You just fall into a bunch of pitfalls and it takes a long time [to] get yourself out of them. I think my foremost problem was that it got very important to write heavy songs. I mean, I never thought they were heavy when I wrote them, but gradually I got the impression they were by the way people related to them. That's a bad connection—I'm taking someone else's word for them. That's what fame does. It's a crusher."[17]

He finally was in the position where he had to hire a band with which to tour. There was no other way to replicate onstage the songs he was recording. According to him at the time, "I have the best of both worlds. I have a band. And they do my tunes. But I feel a little weird. I'm an *employer*."[18]

Since David Lindley could play the acoustic guitar, the electric guitar, the slide guitar, the electric fiddle, and several other instruments, when it came time to record his second album, Jackson found several spots on the recording where one or more of those instruments were needed for his songs. In fact, Lindley appears on every single cut of Jackson's album.

A few months before the release of the *For Everyman* album, the August 7, 1973, issue of *Senior Scholastic* featured a story on young Jackson Browne. At that point, he was still "under the radar" to the general public. Although *Senior Scholastic* was sent mainly to teachers, writer Bud Scoppa—who had reviewed the *Jackson Browne* album in *Rolling Stone*—made several strong and insightful points about the budding troubadour. According to Scoppa, "Just a year ago, Jackson Browne came out of seclusion. He brought with him his first album. It was full of some of the prettiest, most po-

> "Just a year ago, Jackson Browne came out of seclusion. He brought with him his first album. It was full of some of the prettiest, most poetic songs I've ever heard."

etic songs I've ever heard. Jackson sang them movingly indicating he's been listening to Dylan and Van Morrison, but he'd worked out a style of his own. And he was getting better all the time."[19]

Scoppa was also very observant about Browne's onstage persona. He proclaimed, "On the first tour after his album came out, he was quite good, but beneath the cocky exterior, Jackson seemed unsure of himself as a performer. A few months later, he'd become one of the most polished, confident, and effective club performers around. And he was still visibly improving from week to week, writing songs, telling stories, picking things up all the time."[20]

It was into this atmosphere of constant improvement that finally, on October 8, 1973, Jackson's *For Everyman* album was released. Like its predecessor, the album contained ten new Browne originals. It opened with his own version of the Eagles' hit "Take It Easy," which he had cowritten with Glenn Frey. For the most part, "Take It Easy" is a direct copy of what the Eagles did with the song, trading Jackson's voice in the lead, and Doug Haywood chiming in for harmony vocals on the chorus lines. Thanks to David Lindley, and the pedal steel guitar work of Sneeky Pete, this has even more of a country twang. Frey needs to be credited for taking a great Jackson Browne song and turning it into a catchy rock classic. It kicked off the album with its liveliest single song. While the Eagles' version clearly has more of a rock and roll beat, Jackson's version gives the song a strong country flavor.

Jackson had several specific ideas about how he wanted the *For Everyman* album sequenced. Three times he made the decision to fade one song into the next one. The first instance of this involves using the fade out of "Take It Easy" as a lead-in to "Our Lady of the Well." Stylistically and thematically, the two songs have nothing to do with each other; it was just an idea Jackson had in his head to do, to make this sound like a more unified and conceived album than his debut effort.

According to Jackson, "Our Lady of the Well" was inspired by a group of friends who moved down to Mexico to escape being drafted into the Vietnam War. He sings of "Maria" and her peaceful life among the people in the sun, people who work the land the way they have always done it. He lyrically sings of drawing a picture of "Our Lady of the Well" and laments about the direction in which "my country" has politically turned—referring to the then raging Vietnam War.

The similarly plotted "Colors of the Sun" finds Jackson wanting to just be left alone to meditate on the reflections in a pool of water. He bids friends good-bye, as he is content with his solo quest to contemplate the meaning of life. Jackson accompanies himself on piano, and Don Henley adds his pleasing harmony vocal to this slow and visionary cut.

For "I Thought I Was a Child," Bill Payne of the group Little Feat leads the song with his piano work. An autobiographical song about being surprised by the arrival of love in his life, this is Browne's big romantic coming-of-age number on the album. He speaks of not knowing which way to run. This song clearly finds its inspiration in suddenly being in a relationship with Phyllis, his pregnant girlfriend. Prior to this, he thought that it was he who was a child, and now he was about to have one of his own.

The most emotionally effective song on this album is Jackson's now-classic "These Days." Browne explains, "It's a song from when I was about 16. It was first recorded by Nico, later by Tom Rush, but it was Gregg Allman's version that made me want to do it. Originally it was a very folky-strummy, flat-picked song. But he slowed it down and played it that slow-walk tempo, with that really soaring, plaintive way of singing. I thought, 'Man, that's the way to sing that song.' So I kind of took his arrangement."[21]

> The most emotionally effective song on this album is Jackson's now-classic "These Days." Browne explains, "It's a song from when I was about 16. It was first recorded by Nico, later by Tom Rush, but it was Gregg Allman's version that made me want to do it."

He had waited until his second album to tackle this much-covered song. At this point, even David Geffen's current girlfriend, Cher, had recorded the song on her *Stars* album. For his own interpretation of "These Days," the number features the lush piano work by David Paich of Toto and Lindley's moody slide guitar.

The song "Red Neck Friend" was Browne's answer to the challenge of being pressured to write a fast-paced radio-friendly hit. This is the only song on the album with a real classic rock & roll sound. The song is an ode to pick-up lines. In the lyrics to this unabashed rocker, he addresses a girl he has met and wants to introduce her to his "red neck friend."

Over the years, people have wondered exactly who or what the inspiration is for this song. Several people assumed that it was his buddy Gregg Allman who was Browne's "red neck friend." However, there was also the recurring rumor that it was just a term that Jackson used for his own sex organ. Which is correct?

It is Steve Noonan who unraveled—or unzipped—this mystery. According to him, "Jackson used to tell me, 'I'm going to take a pee—I'm going to take a friend by the hand.' And I'd go, 'Ha ha ha.' His 'red neck friend,' it was a real sexual connotation."[22] In other words, Jackson's "red neck friend" is just a euphemism for his penis.

When Jackson sings of showing a young girl his "red neck friend" in this song, he does so to a rock/boogie that would make Jerry Lee Lewis and Little Richard proud. Actually, the frenetic piano work on this song is credited to "Rockaday Johnny." "Rockaday Johnny" was a fictitious name for a very well-known rock star, whom Jackson thought would be perfect for this guest piano part of his album. Apparently, the British rock star didn't have a valid U.S. work permit at that exact moment, so he went ahead and recorded his part at Sunset Sound Studio under a pseudonym. The mysterious piano player who is credited as "Rockaday Johnny" is, in reality, Elton John.

The song "The Times You've Come" is full of undeniable sexual double entendre. It is about a sexual relationship—the orgasm and the postorgasm aftermath. Browne sings of lying still in the "ruins of our pleasure," referring to the calm after a sexual storm. Addressing concert audiences, he explained that "The Times You've Come" was one-half of his "sex medley." Bonnie Raitt provides harmony vocals on this ode to orgasm.

After the sex, what comes next? Pregnancy obviously. The fade to the song "The Times You've Come" leads directly into the highly autobiographical "Ready or Not." This is the album's most straight-out-of-his-diary tune. In the context of this electric fiddle-driven song, he sings of defending a girl in a bar and then taking her home for an evening of sex. According to the song, not long afterward her jeans start getting tight, and she notes that she is sick to her stomach every morning. Yup, Jackson got a girl pregnant after a one-night stand. In the lyrics of the song, Jackson asks himself if he is "ready" to get married and become a father. Well, here he was about to go off the deep end and into a full-time relationship. In retrospect, it was not the relationship that he was looking for; rather, it was the relationship that he settled for.

As Cameron Crowe was later to confirm in *Rolling Stone* magazine, "The baby's mother, Phyllis," was "the model, actress star of the bar-fight knock-up adventure, described in Jackson's song 'Ready or Not.' "[23]

The simple ballad "Sing My Songs to Me" is another autobiographical narrative about what Jackson Browne's life had become. He would write the songs, then other people would record and interpret them, and he would hear shadings in their performances that he had not dreamed of when he composed them. He ponders where his dreams go when the morning comes, and wonders if his dreams really hold the answers to his life. A nice, slow contemplative ballad, "Sing My Songs to Me" nicely benefits from the multilayered music of his assembled band, including Greg Mallaber's drums, Mike Utley's organ, and the special guest electric piano work by Joni Mitchell.

The song "For Everyman" was originally written for David Crosby by Jackson Browne. In fact, Browne penned part of the song on Crosby's boat, *The Mayan*, and it features a nice harmony vocal by David. Reportedly, it was Browne's answer to the Crosby, Stills & Nash recording of sailing away to a peaceful Utopia, "Wooden Ships." This song provides a big sweeping finale for a strong and very pleasant album. With themes of sex, solitude,

> The song "For Everyman" was originally written for David Crosby by Jackson Browne. In fact, Browne penned part of the song on Crosby's boat, *The Mayan*.

and redemption, *For Everyman* showed off the growing confidence that Jackson had gained since recording his debut disc. A stronger effort, with more musical layers, Brown was well on his way to defining his own sound—and finding his own voice musically.

On the cover of the *For Everyman* album is a photograph of Jackson Browne, seated in an outdoor courtyard at Abbey San Encino, where he was now back in residence. The photograph by Alan F. Blumenthal is done to look like a tinted sepia portrait from the era in which the mansion was built. It is an incredibly effective image, which perfectly set the tone of this deeply personal album.

The reviews of *For Everyman* were especially glowing. Janet Maslin wrote of

Browne's songwriting skills in the November 30, 1973, issue of *New Times*, "No one else wrote quite so carefully, or so well. And no one else had anything like his gift for singling out universally affecting subject matter, then writing about it in such a private way."[24]

Maslin also reviewed *For Everyman* for *Rolling Stone*, raving about Jackson's "inwardly panoramic songwriting of an apocalyptic bent." She claimed the he was "stunningly eloquent," "incomparably immediate," and that the album was "brilliantly conceived."[25]

In the October 12, 1973, issue of the *New York Times*, writer John Rockwell proclaimed, "Browne has his limits as a performer, even with a solid voice and a deft back-up band behind him—David Lindley, on fiddle and a variety of guitars, was alone worth the price of admission. Browne is more limited in his materials, too, in that he writes his own songs.... But at their best—as in his classic 'Rock Me on the Water'—Browne captures the laid-back nostalgia beloved of contemporary song writers and anybody else around."[26]

In an issue of *Rolling Stone* magazine published in 1998, writer Anthony DeCurtis looks back on this quintessential Jackson Browne album and claims, "Browne is still searching for his true voice on *For Everyman*. Is he the genial rogue of 'Red Neck Friend' or the mystical dreamer of 'Our Lady of the Well'? He will find that voice the following year on his masterpiece, *Late for the Sky*. But on *For Everyman*, he was testing his various talents with obvious joy, because, like his audience, he was just discovering them."[27]

One of the most complimentary notices that *For Everyman* received was from David Crosby himself. In an interview with *Rolling Stone*, Crosby claimed, "He stopped me cold in my tracks. He nailed a certain thing in me, that escapist thing, and he called on something in me...that I really believe in—and that's human possibility."[28]

In an interview with *Rolling Stone*, Crosby claimed, "He stopped me cold in my tracks. He nailed a certain thing in me, that escapist thing, and he called on something in me...that I really believe in—and that's human possibility."

The *For Everyman* album reached Number 43 on the *Billboard* album charts in the United States, which was ten points higher than the *Jackson Browne* album achieved. However, the first single released from the album, "Red Neck Friend," failed to find an audience. The single peaked at Number 85, then disappeared from the charts. A second single off the album was released in early

1974, teaming "Take It Easy" on one side with "Ready or Not" on the other. However, both songs failed to even make the charts. This was to be something of a pattern in Jackson Browne's career. He became known as "an album artist," in which his albums consistently garnered strong reviews and became chart contenders, but his track record for having individual "hit" singles was pretty much "hit or miss."

In October 1973, Scott Runyon, an artist, dancer, and ice skater friend of Jackson Browne and Pamela Pollard's, died when a bathhouse caught fire in Hollywood. A self-professed bisexual, Runyon auditioned for the Ice Capades, and at the age of eighteen was signed to be a dancer on ice. He took Pamela to all the gay dance clubs and they wore matching outfits. His skate/dancing career was cut short when he caught hepatitis, so he bounded back with an interest in photography. Jackson remembered Scott as a true "free spirit." At the time of his death, Runyon had a flamboyant circle of friends. According to Polland, Scott's funeral was a carnival-like celebration of his life with transvestites and women clad only in scarves, "It was like a big LSD freak show...a Fellini movie...and these 'pals-in-art' of his were playing it to the hilt."[29] Pamela remembers Jackson being very withdrawn at Scott's funeral.

It was around the time of Scott Runyon's death, with his first child about to be born, that Jackson began to have self-doubts about his life and his craft. Did he really want to chase this "rock star" dream? Did he really want to be doing this as a career? It was the fall of 1973, and Browne made the two-hour drive down to San Deigo to see a concert by the Allman Brothers. That night the band really rocked. They embodied the kind of energy and life on stage that he felt his own stage show lacked. A light went off in Jackson's head.

> Browne made the two-hour drive down to San Deigo to see a concert by the Allman Brothers. That night the band really rocked. They embodied the kind of energy and life on stage that he felt his own stage show lacked. A light went off in Jackson's head.

What the hell was he thinking? Quit making music? Hell no! Days later, having mulled over the impact that the Allman Brothers had on him that night, he decided to forge ahead with a hell of a lot more enthusiasm. According to Browne, "I was so ashamed of myself for my thoughts [about quitting the business] that I immediately went home and played all night. The next week I rehearsed my band to go on the road, to get on-stage and 'get off.' "[30]

Regarding the many changes that impending fatherhood had on him, Jackson claimed, "It's given me a certain hysterical composure, another kind of sense of humor...I'm hoping people will flash on it. If they look at me the way I look at my favorite artists—watching somebody's life grow and change, knowing a lot about them...through a vicarious sense of living their exploits—then they'll buy the record."[31]

Another major event occurred in 1973, when Jackson met his idol, Bob Dylan, one night at The Roxy in Los Angeles. He was so freaked out by the experience that he didn't know what to do or say. At the time, he was sitting down, having a conversation with a friend. "I'm talking to this guy," he recalls, "then somebody comes from behind and says, 'This is Bob Dylan,' and I turned around and he suddenly looked like a monolith. He looked like [the statues on] Easter Island. He's wearing a fucking fur cap, he's got his shades on, gloves and a coat. I just looked at him, and [said] 'Hi,' and he gave me this sort of imperceptible nod of the head, and I thought, 'Jesus Christ, excuse me.' And I split. I didn't know how to deal with it. There it was—that mouth, that jaw, those eyes, the inscrutable presence. It scared me to death. I went next door and got a drink."[32]

While meeting Dylan did not quite turn into the life-altering experience that he once thought it would be, becoming a father certainly did. Jackson and Phyllis's son, Ethan Zane Browne, was born at 6:40 on the morning of November 3, 1973, at Cedars-Sinai Medical Center, near Beverly Hills. Not only was his career developing and evolving, so was his personal life. Although he still professed "I Thought I Was a Child," at the age of twenty-five, ready or not, Jackson Browne was well on his way to facing grown-up responsibilities.

CHAPTER 5

Late for the Sky

IN EARLY 1974, JACKSON BROWNE SET OUT on his first headlining concert tour. Ironically, his opening act on this tour was Linda Ronstadt. At The Troubadour, years ago, it was he who was opening for her. For the time being, he was the bigger star, with bigger hits. After the tour ended in September of that year, Linda recorded the album that would take her from "star" to "superstar": *Heart Like a Wheel*. However, with his recent Top 10 single "Doctor My Eyes" and two critically acclaimed albums under his belt, for the time being Jackson was the bigger star, and it was Jackson's show.

When he returned to Abbey San Encino, he found that he was able to bring to fruition the dream of his grandfather, Clyde Browne. It was Clyde who always envisioned the mansion to be a gathering point for artists, singers, and dancers. In 1974, Jackson—in his new roles as domestic partner and father—was able to create an artist's colony all his own. There were drugs, food, booze, and music until all hours of the night.

Every weekend there were free-flowing parties at Abbey San Encino, much to the chagrin of the local neighbors. Often, the cops were called to the property to tell Jackson and his fellow revelers to keep the noise down. That was the sure sign of a good party!

In fact, on one occasion the police showed up just before midnight to inform Browne to tone down the noise. However, both officers returned at 12:05—after their shift was over—to join the party!

According to the 1972 hit by the group Dr. Hook and the Medicine Show, you're not a bona fide rock star until you get your picture on the cover of *Rolling Stone*. Well, the honor was bestowed on Jackson Browne on *Rolling Stone*'s May 23, 1974, issue.

In an extensive interview with Cameron Crowe, Browne tried to explain the dichotomy of his life, of his philosophies, and of his singing and songwriting. With regard to the balance between his whole mental apocalypse doom trip, and his party-down laidback side, he explained how he balanced the two. "I think the whole fucking thing is coming down, I think it's all over," he said of the state of the world at the time, in his best prophet-of-doom voice. "There are hundreds of people in the woods of Vancouver and Oregon and New Mexico who make music and entertain themselves but happen to do something else for a living. As David Lindley has been known to say, 'plastic is plastic.' When do I think it's all gonna come down? Seventies, Eighties, Nineties, it doesn't matter. The way things are in the world, the fact that people live in square rooms and they go to bars and shit...you know, I used to think it was lame to go to bars, but now I go to bars. On the other hand, the moment is everything. I can't deny that I'm from Southern California and I dig going to get a beer, I wanna get high, I wanna enjoy it. I don't want to pretend to be a spaceman. Fuck that shit. I'm just what I am and that's however good it is."[1]

In other words, his philosophy was not: The sky is falling, so we should all repent. It was more like: The planet is doomed, so let's party like it's 1999!

He also tried to explain how a swinging bachelor like himself suddenly ended up becoming Mr. Domestic. According to Jackson at the time, "I wanted a baby 'cause I wanted a baby. I play with him all the time; there's something pure about it. Look at all those expressions he got. He's a real kick in the ass."[2]

Oddly enough, after years of courting success, Jackson started to make public statements about being uncomfortable with the stardom he had obtained. He realized that he was now in the business of selling record albums and concert tickets. That was not exactly how he wanted to think of what his life had become.

Citing the song "Big Yellow Taxi" by Joni Mitchell, Jackson said, "You know that line about how you've paved paradise and put up a parking lot? Well, that's all very nice, but the song was recorded for a multimillion-dollar conglomerate that owns half the parking lots in this country. It's economics and I'm caught up in it too."[3]

From as early as 1974, Browne began using his time in the spotlight as an artist to expound on his views about the commercialism of society. He complained to David Resin of *Crawdaddy* magazine, "This fucking world . . . is nothing but toothpaste ads and Scope mouthwash and 'You can get laid if you have a Camaro.' "[4]

As far as his talent, Jackson was still Jackson's own harshest critic. With regard to his singing voice on his first two albums, he claimed, "I don't want to put down the way I sing . . . I'm not gonna spoil it for anybody who thinks I'm good. I know when I'm singing well, but I haven't sung well on record yet. I got a ways to go."[5]

Working in the chapel of Abbey San Encino, by mid-1974 he was already at work on his third album. Jackson had taken nine months to record his last album, *For Everyman*, which—like its predecessor—had consisted of ten songs. It cost in excess of $100,000 to complete, and—in terms of sales—it was only moderately successful. David Geffen instructed Browne that he expected his third album to be delivered much quicker and for significantly less money.

At this point, Jackson's touring band consisted of David Lindley (slide guitar, acoustic guitar, electric fiddle, and electric guitar), Doug Haywood (bass and harmony vocals), Larry Zack (drums and percussion), and Jai Winding (piano and organ). In the summer of 1974, when it came time to record tracks for his third album, *Late for the Sky*, Browne decided to just use his touring band in the studio. That way, when it came time to tour to support the album, everyone would be up-to-speed on the same songs.

Using his touring band in the studio also helped cut down on the time it took to record his new album. According to him, "I suppose I'd rather actually be in a group sometimes. It would be a lot more fun [as part of a band], a lot more kinetic. . . . On my own I tend to just molder around and take my time."[6]

Since he had produced his last album, *For Everyman*, on his own, and it took him nearly a year to deliver it, Browne and Geffen agreed that for his third album Jackson would use a coproducer to expedite and streamline things. They agreed to use Al Schmitt, who had been one of the engineers on the last album.

Schmitt recalled, "Jackson said he wanted me because I wasn't domineering, that I wouldn't take his album away—'He's gonna help me do what I wanna do, help me with some of the shortcuts.' "[7]

The recording process was pretty much nonstop. They worked every day, from early in the afternoon, until late into the next morning. They were truly "musician's" hours, but they were long and consistent sessions. According to Schmitt, "Looking back at that project, the one thing that really stands out—besides his talent, his uniqueness with words, and so forth—is his integrity. He didn't vacillate; he had some strength. There was no shit that was gonna slip by. Not that the rest of us would have let it, but in front you knew that that wasn't going to happen."[8]

Several of Jackson's friends stopped by the studio while he was recording this album, including Linda Ronstadt, Dan Fogelberg, and several members of the Eagles. The feeling surrounding the recording of the *For Everyman* album was that Jackson was creating his album in a self-directed fashion and in that way he wore too many hats. This time around, he was bolstered by the camaraderie of the musicians around him and his friends.

> Several of Jackson's friends stopped by the studio while he was recording this album, including Linda Ronstadt, Dan Fogelberg, and several members of the Eagles.

"It was amazing; he was singing quite a bit better," claimed Al Schmitt. "The difference was he would get things so much quicker. His intonation was better. He had more strength. He could sing longer."[9] That being the case, the *Late for the Sky* album was recorded in six weeks, at a cost of $50,000. Part of the streamlining came in the fact that the album would only feature eight tracks instead of his usual ten. Having two fewer songs freed up space on the record to expand the length of the songs. Two of the tracks were more than six minutes long, and three other songs were more than five minutes long. It was the age of "album artists" garnering airplay on FM radio stations, and this album was to find a comfortable and welcoming home in that format.

Late for the Sky really solidified Jackson's sensitive, detailed, but slightly depressing outlook on life. His decidedly somber subject matter on this album deals with death ("For a Dancer"), impending disaster ("Before the Deluge"), desolation ("Late for the Sky"), and the regretful end of a love affair ("Fountain of Sorrow"). However, that being said, both Jackson's expressive singing style and the voices and music accompanying him are at an exciting all-time high.

The slow and somber "Late for the Sky" opens the album and sets the tone for the other seven songs. Singing slowly and mournfully, Browne tells of a love affair that is not destined to work out. His lover's expectations of him are too great, but in the end he cannot match her vision of him. It is rumored that this song is about his breakup with Joni Mitchell. With a subtle harmony vocal behind him, Browne sounds wonderful on this classic cut.

Jackson recalls of recording "Late for the Sky" with his circle of singing buddies, "It has this great harmony part by Doug Haywood that really makes the song. Doug, Don Henley, J. D. Souther, Dan Fogelberg and I were really the best of friends back in the '70s. Everybody has that group of friends in their life that they're close with at the time when they come of age, and these were mine. I had some of the most hilarious times standing around the mike with them. I'm not a very exacting harmony singer and certainly was less so then, so when we did harmonies they'd have to send me on some errand just so they could get it done. 'Hey, yeah, Jackson, know what? I left something in my car, would you mind going and grabbing it?' I'd come back and the part would be finished."[10]

In spite of its downer title, "Fountain of Sorrow," has a nice lively beat to it, and Jackson finds himself reminiscing instead of lamenting here. Looking at old photographs he discovers in a drawer, he recalls an old lover and what she was like back then. Singing about the moment he snapped that photograph, he is finally able to put this failed relationship in perspective. A beautiful and medium-paced ballad of love lost, "Fountain of Sorrow" was truly his most masterful vocal performance to date.

The slow, pedal guitar–led "Farther On" finds Jackson's narrating protagonist looking for beauty in his songs. He sings of seeing his dreams torn apart and his love affairs all ending dismally. Using romantic allusions to illustrate his moods, he sings of someone storming the gates of his "citadel." Likening his heart to the gates of a medieval city made this song a moody Valentine of classic poetry, set to brilliant country/rock music.

Singing about wandering through life and seeking the perfect love is the subject of "The Late Show." The troubadour again ponders the meaning of his existence. He is in love with a woman he cannot seem to "break through" to, and he is frozen by indecisiveness. Musically, "The Late Show" clearly profits from Don Henley, Dan Fogelberg, and J. D. Souther's soaring harmony vocals. Listening to this song gives the listener a taste of what it would be like if Jackson Browne was suddenly a member of the Eagles. At the end of the song, the narrator is heard getting on his motorcycle and riding away—alone.

The album's raucous rock & roll number is called "The Road and the Sky."

Jackson Browne sings his trademark ballads on the PBS series *Soundstage* in 1977. (Courtesy of Photofest)

John Hall, Graham Nash, James Taylor, Browne, Bonnie Raitt, and Carly Simon at the famed No Nukes Concert in September 1979. (Courtesy of Photofest)

Browne was not only one of the headliners at the No Nukes Concert, he was also one of the organizers of the event. (Courtesy of Photofest)

Band member Waddy Wachtel sings harmony vocal with Browne at Nassau Coliseum on June 9, 1982. (Photo courtesy Michael Brito/Star File)

Jesse Colin Young and Browne sing a harmonious duet at the No Nukes Concert. (Courtesy of Photofest)

Browne is so masterful at writing songs about heartbreak because he has often been unlucky in love. His first wife committed suicide not long after their wedding, and his second marriage crumbled a year after the birth of his second son. (Photo: Chuck Pulin/Star File)

Darryl Hannah and Browne seemed like the perfect couple. In the early 1990s, however, she began seeing John Kennedy Jr. as well. (Photo courtesy Vinnie Zuffante/Star File)

Browne often accompanies himself solo on keyboards, as he does here in Burlington, Vermont, in October 1983. (Photo courtesy Mark Harlan/Star File)

Browne is a gifted singer and songwriter who has a passion for his craft. His socially conscious songs and touching ballads have made him a troubadour for everyman. (Photo: Chuck Pulin/Star File)

On January 2, 1994, Browne reunited with longtime friends and collaborators David Lindley, Graham Nash, and David Crosby for the Disney Channel TV special *Jackson Browne: Going Home.* (Courtesy of Photofest)

New York deejay Scott Muni, Browne, and radio producer Zach Martin at the taping of Muni's radio show in 2002. Browne was a guest on the show to promote his thirteenth album, *Naked Ride Home.* (Photo courtesy David Salidor/dis COMPANY)

On the TV special *Jackson Browne: Going Home*, the troubadour was able to look back on his long and eventful musical career. (Courtesy of Photofest)

A lighter and more fun-loving Jackson sings of not wanting to be serious at all. Not knowing if he is headed for heaven or hell, he sings of hot-wiring a stolen Chevrolet and running around the roads without a care. This was clearly Browne sowing his wild oats and wanting to party down. For this song, Browne plays a ragtime-sounding piano and the slide guitar. Even while being jubilant on a song like this one, Jackson still manages to add allusions of "dark clouds" looming on the horizon.

"For a Dancer" sadly eulogizes the passing of wildly flamboyant Scott Runyon. Jackson sings about Scott dancing in and out of his life, like a carefree clown. He wonders where people go when they die and tries to put the memory of his fallen friend in perspective. A beautiful piano and fiddle-laden ballad, Browne resolves to keep a fire of remembrance going and to dance his sorrow away in honor of the friend who is no longer in his life.

> "For a Dancer" sadly eulogizes the passing of wildly flamboyant Scott Runyon. Jackson sings about Scott dancing in and out of his life, like a carefree clown.

"Walking Slow" is more of a whimsical look at life. Beginning with the sound of someone playing a jug, this jam-session-sounding track finds Browne in much more of an upbeat mood. Jackson sings about walking down the street in his old neighborhood. Describing his life with Phyllis, he sings about how they fight and don't get along. Yet, he doesn't know what he will do if she leaves him alone. In the lyrics of the song, Jackson declares that if he dies, he wants his friends to carry on in his name.

Finally, the album ends with "Before the Deluge," which still stands today as one of Jackson Browne's true masterpieces. Dramatically sweeping in sound, and led by David Lindley's beautiful electric fiddle playing, this is Jackson's ultimate apocalypse-now fantasy.

According to Browne, "In the late '60s, I thought there was going to be a real breakdown in the fabric of society. Those people who were continually given the short end, and being continually oppressed, where going to begin to tear it down. I felt the whole thing was very shaky. In the '60s there were the Watts riots and a lot of demonstrations against the Vietnam War. There was this all-encompassing feeling that there was something really huge that was wrong that people couldn't see. I think that much is, of course, still true. At one point I became a little ashamed of myself for writing the song 'Before the Deluge' in which I project a huge cataclysm. I felt, 'How wrong to idly project such a catastrophic event, to dabble in your imagination with the idea of so many people being wiped out and dying.' But it doesn't keep me from singing the song—I think it was on a lot of people's minds."[11]

While listening to this song, one cannot help but think of Jackson Browne as one of those street prophets carrying a placard that reads: "Repent: The world is about to End!" As dark as Browne's vision is in this song, one cannot help but appreciate how beautiful this song sounds. In the realm of Browne's recurring heartbreak and apocalypse themes, this was a 1970s musical masterpiece.

The cover of *Late for the Sky* was a concept that Browne himself had come up with. It was based on one of the paintings of surrealist Belgian painter René Magritte. By far, Magritte's most instantly recognizable painting is a full-body portrait called *The Son of Man*. In the painting, a man wearing a black suit and bowler stands looking forward out of the canvas while his face is obscured by a disproportionately large green apple hovering in midair.

The painting that Jackson Browne wanted to replicate, with a California twist, was one called *The Dominion of Light*. In it, the sun goes down behind a darkened two-story house surrounded by trees at dusk. Because of the lighting at that time of day, the sky is intensely blue, and clouds are illuminated brightly.

Browne met with photographer Bob Seidemann and asked Bob to replicate his vision. According to Seidemann, he waited for days for exactly the right kind of sundown shot to get the effect that he wanted. The resulting photo depicted a vintage American car from the 1950s parked in front of a two-story house surrounded by lush trees at dusk. Just like in the painting, the cloudy sky behind the house is intensely blue as the sun begins to set over the Pacific.

On the inside of the *Late for the Sky* album, Jackson's personal "dedication" reflected his new life with Phyllis and as a father. After thanking all of his musician friends, he wrote, "For Phyllis and Ethan." With regard to the painting-inspired cover on the album he wrote, "Cover concept by Jackson Browne if it's *all reet* with Magritte."[12]

When Jackson's third album was released, it drew passionate reviews with mixed results. In *Rolling Stone*, Stephen Holden enthusiastically claimed of *Late for the Sky*, "No contemporary male singer/ songwriter has dealt so honestly and deeply with the vulnerability of romantic idealism and the pain of adjustment from youthful narcissism to adult survival."[13]

> When Jackson's third album was released, it drew passionate reviews with mixed results.

In the *Village Voice*, James Wolcott wrote, "Browne isn't a bravura performer—his photographs remind one of a wan Nureyev....Like Dylan before him, he not only expresses the mood of his time but embodies it. *Late for the Sky* is not a romping, rousing album but with its tone of cool despair and undercurrent of hip hopefulness, it reflects the confusions and anxieties of the early '70s. It's an understated work, but the echoes travel for miles."[14]

Late for the Sky was an album that clearly divided the crowd. While similar-sounding act and labelmates the Eagles scored hits by singing about having a "Peaceful Easy Feeling" (1972), drinking a "Tequila Sunrise" (1973), and giving "The Best of My Love" (Number 1 in 1974), Browne was tackling much more morose material. Songs like the sad "Fountain of Sorrow" and the apocalyptic heroics of "Before the Deluge" were too much of a "down" trip for many music fans. To them, Jackson was sounding like the Little Red Hen who ran around all the time saying "the sky is falling!"

When *Late for the Sky* was released, *Crawdaddy* magazine hated it. According to reviewer David Spiwak, "After a while too much of this stuff is depressing.... We've heard this song before and it's time for something else."[15]

Likewise, Robert Martin complained in the *Toronto Globe and Mail*, "If only Jackson Browne had a sense of humor, or could flash a smile or something....I admire Browne's compassion but prefer a little more steel in a songwriter....It is unfortunate because he possesses almost every element required for genius except spunk."[16]

Listening to them back to back, it is easy to see how Jackson's initial trio of albums gave him an indelible reputation for being moody and brooding. That was some people's cup of tea. And for others it was not.

Of all of his friends and supporters, Glenn Frey was Jackson's strongest ally in the business. Speaking of Browne's songwriting skills, Glenn claimed, "There's no wasted words or filler in his tunes. Fuck! That kid's a monster! Jackson's trip is multidimensional. It's there musically and lyrically. It makes it a little harder to gain commercial acceptance, but when you do get it, it's longer lasting. To get right down to it, I'm in awe of him. I've seen audiences go through changes during 'Song for Adam' that were unbelievable."[17]

What happened on the record charts this time around further cemented Jackson's reputation for being an "album artist" as opposed to being a "singles artist." "Walking Slow" (1974) and "Fountain of Sorrow" (1975) were released as singles from this album. However, both songs failed to even make it to the charts.

Regardless, the album was a huge hit. It made it to Number 14 on the *Billboard* charts in the United States, and remained in the Top 40 for eight weeks. Released on September 19, 1974, the Record Industry Association of America (RIAA) Certified *Late for the Sky* "Gold" on December 24, 1974, for sales of over 500,000 copies sold in the United States.

To support the release of the album, in the fall of 1974 Jackson and his band hit the road for an extensive six-month concert tour. Also on the tour was Linda Ronstadt. She concurrently had the song "You're No Good" and the album *Heart Like a Wheel* both hitting Number 1 in the winter of 1974–1975. She was now as successful—if not more successful—as Jackson was at this point, so they alternated who was going to be the opening act and who was going to be the headliner.

As Jackson continued to tour in 1975, his keyboard player, Jai Winding, was replaced by Wayne Cook. The tour bus that Browne and crew used was a reconverted Greyhound. There was also a motor home for the roadies, and an equipment truck. It truly became the Jackson Browne caravan.

> The tour bus that Browne and crew used was a reconverted Greyhound. There was also a motor home for the roadies, and an equipment truck. It truly became the Jackson Browne caravan.

At one point, Phyllis and one-year-old Ethan accompanied Jackson on the road. After Phyllis saw that life on the road wasn't as glamorous as she might have imagined, she flew home, while Ethan stayed with Jackson.

Wayne Cook immediately noted that although Jackson was basically nice and friendly, he had an icy coolness to him and had a big ego about his role as a "rock star." In the middle of the tour, Cook did what he could to get Jackson to loosen up a bit. At one particular concert, as Jackson was taking off his shirt on stage, Cook started playing the Billy Rose song "The Stripper." The crowd laughed, and although he was a bit irritated by his keyboard man's improvisation, he finally saw the humor. According to Cook, after that things on tour were a little more relaxed.

Feeling more comfortable with Cook, one night in Phoenix—during the 1975 tour—Browne cajoled Wayne into a bit of showing off at the keyboards. Since Browne and the band knew that Elton John was in the audience that night, he egged Wayne on. At one point, Wayne performed a 360-degree spin off the piano bench midsong. For a flamboyant conclusion to the show,

Jackson threw himself inside the open grand piano—electric guitar and all. Finally, Jackson was loosening up as a rock & roller!

In the summer of 1975, Jackson, Phyllis, and Ethan went to Paris to visit Phyllis's mother. Browne loved the "City of Light," and he especially loved the fact that no one there recognized him. In the United States, he had become quite a well-known troubadour and rock star, but in Europe no one knew who he was.

Since Phyllis's mother, Nancy Farnsworth, was a songwriter too, he immediately hit it off with her. One day, as he sat at her piano in Paris, she told him of a lyric line she had come up with. He was so inspired by what she said, that he went ahead and finished the song. It was to become the song "Here Come Those Tears Again," which would be included on his next album.

Late in the summer of 1975, Jackson, Ethan, and Phyllis returned to Los Angeles. Not long afterward, Jackson was back on the road doing stray concert dates. Stephen Holden wrote in *The Village Voice* that he had talked to Jackson in September 1975, at the Main Point, a club in the Philadelphia area. According to Holden, "He seemed restless and at loose ends. He is vague about his future plans and said only that in a few weeks he would be going into the studio to produce an album by his friend Warren Zevon."[18]

Jackson's performance at the Main Point was broadcast over a local Philadelphia radio station and was pressed into a two-record set bootleg album. The album is known as a true Jackson Browne collector's item. Since he was set to be the producer of Zevon's debut album on Asylum Records, Jackson was quite familiar with Warren's quirky material. That night he performed three Zevon classics, "Mohammed's Radio," "Hasten down the Wind," and "Werewolves of London." Linda Ronstadt would later cover the first two of those songs, turning "Hasten down the Wind" into the title track of her forthcoming 1976 "Platinum" album of the same name.

Zevon had been kicking around the music business for several years now. In 1969, he had signed with Liberty Records and eventually released the album *Wanted Dead or Alive*. It was not successful at the time. Warren felt that he had one more shot at stardom, and Jackson wanted to do what he could to help him out.

The self-titled *Warren Zevon* album was worth the wait. His songs were filled with irony and dark humor. He wrote of outlaws ("Frank and Jesse James"), prostitutes ("Carmelita"), pimps ("The French Inhaler"), and odes that argued for partying nonstop ("I'll Sleep When I'm Dead"). His songs were serious poetry, and this was an aspect of Zevon's art with which Browne could strongly identify.

From October to the end of November, with December off, and from January to February, Jackson Browne poured himself into his role as Warren Zevon's producer. Obviously, Browne saw much of his own angst mirrored in Zevon's struggles to get his music heard, and in that way he identified with his unknown friend. Jackson wanted to make certain that Zevon had a solo album that would clearly steer him down the right path toward success.

> Reportedly, Phyllis wasn't exactly thrilled with the fact that Jackson was spending all of his waking hours in the recording studio with Zevon. It began to irritate her, and it made her feel abandoned and depressed.

Reportedly, Phyllis wasn't exactly thrilled with the fact that Jackson was spending all of his waking hours in the recording studio with Zevon. It began to irritate her, and it made her feel abandoned and depressed.

At this point, Jackson still had not married Phyllis. He knew that she was feeling unhappy with her life. Wayne Cook recalled her mood from the 1975 concert tour. "She basically was on a bummer a lot," he claimed. "When she was around things would quiet down quite a bit. . . . It was just like somebody [had just] let the air out of a balloon."[19]

Wanting to make everyone happy, Jackson decided that marrying Phyllis would help her feel like she belonged in his life, instead of just being the live-in girlfriend who bore him a child. Surely a wedding would change her mood. In December 1975, Jackson and Phyllis officially tied the knot. She was now Mrs. Clyde Jackson Browne.

In addition, there were also plans underway for Jackson, Phyllis, and Ethan to move to a new residence. The new $750,000 house was located in the Hollywood Hills. It was a big leap from the hippie existence that they were living at Abbey San Encino. In the transition, Jackson turned the mansion over to his brother, Severin.

Jackson had his first "Gold" album under his belt, and he was now stretching out into becoming an accomplished music producer. As 1975 came to an end, it seemed like everyone was happy. But looks could be deceiving.

CHAPTER 6

The Pretender

IN JANUARY AND FEBRUARY 1976, Jackson Browne was busy in the recording studio working on what would become the *Warren Zevon* album. Meanwhile, bored with her life, Phyllis decided to try to revive her modeling career. She went out and got an agent to move forward with her own creative endeavours. Unfortunately, her agent lost his job and never called her to tell her about it. Taking it personally, Phyllis lost interest in the whole venture. After that, she went into another of her deep and brooding depressions.

When Phyllis's old friend Terry Reno spoke to her on the phone, Terry found Phyllis to be in one of her emotional "low" periods. In fact, Phyllis was so depressed that for most of the month of March, she was too upset to take care of her two-year-old son, so she hired a babysitter to care for him while Jackson worked.

On March 24, 1976, Jackson went to the recording studio. It seemed like any other day with Phyllis lately, so he didn't think that anything was out of the ordinary. That night, as the babysitter slept on the sofa, a knock came from the front door of the house. The babysitter opened the door to find that the person knocking was a delivery man with prescription drugs. Phyllis intercepted the pills and went back into the bedroom.

The night passed, and Jackson came home early the following morning. When he walked into their bedroom, he found Phyllis dead of an overdose.

Three days later, Phyllis Major Browne was laid to rest in Santa Barbara. An inti-

The night passed, and Jackson came home early the following morning. When he walked into their bedroom, he found Phyllis dead of an overdose.

mate circle of family and friends were present at the cemetery to bid her good-bye.

In Rich Wiseman's book *Jackson Browne: The Story of a Hold Out*, "an acquaintance of Jackson's" is quoted as having run into Jackson at a store shortly after Phyllis's suicide. Claimed the source, "[Browne was] absolutely rigid, trying to hang on to the world.... It was just obvious that there were pieces of steel stuck to his face. You know, everything was the same: 'Hi, how are you?' But you were looking at a guy whose back teeth didn't open up at all."[1]

Jackson took off the entire month of April to get his head together, in the wake of Phyllis's death. That month his old friend Steve Noonan came to see how he was doing. According to Noonan, Browne was visibly depressed, and Jackson proclaimed to him that he just wanted to bury himself in his work.

At the age of twenty-eight, he was now the widowed single father of a two-year-old son. He was also a recording star who employed his own band. He also had a recording contract, and another full album of music to deliver as soon as possible. Of this period circa 1976, Jackson recalled, "I used to do a lot of coke, so your energy is blown most of the time. And it was in the wake of my wife's death."[2]

In early May, Jackson threw himself into the recording sessions for his fourth album, a project he used to work his way through his depression. In the middle of the month, he performed at an all-star concert in Landover, Maryland. Held at the Capitol Center, the event was a fund-raiser for U.S. presidential candidate Jerry Brown, the California governor. Also on the bill that night were the Eagles, Linda Ronstadt, and Dan Fogelberg.

There were also a couple of other political events that Browne performed at during that period of time. Jackson later explained of this short-lived advent, "That was something that happened, I guess in '76. Historically, it's worth noting that that was the first time they had put all these limitations on campaign contributions. So you could get a lot of money calling every person who bought a ticket a 'contributor.' There was suddenly this loophole—everybody loved that, politicians especially: 'Ha! That's how we'll get the money!' And I did have some experiences with that that I didn't really care for. After about two of those, one for a candidate here in California and one for Jerry Brown, I decided not to do that anymore. I didn't like the prospect of being linked to a particular person's ability to carry out his promises."[3]

Working his way through his grief, Browne continued to forge ahead on his fourth album for Asylum Records. He was joined on this album by several of his close friends. Not only did they show up in

Working his way through his grief, Browne continued to forge ahead on his fourth album for Asylum Records.

the recording studio to contribute to the music, they were also there to support him. The guest artists on this album include Bonnie Raitt, David Crosby, Graham Nash, Lowell George, Albert Lee, Don Henley, John David Souther, Bill Payne, Jeff Porcaro of Toto, and Valerie Carter.

Browne kept working nonstop, partially to keep busy, and partially to finish everything he wanted to accomplish. His one break was a brief camping trip with his son, Ethan. Finally, Jackson completed recording *The Pretender* in September 1976, and only two days later—on October 1—he embarked on a concert tour with the group Orleans. The tour not only took him across the United States, but on his first international tour as well. He performed in Europe, Australia, and Japan. Australia and Japan would become two of Browne's strongest overseas markets.

Not only was this album created at a stressful time in Jackson Browne's life, which colored the songs contained on it, but he also pushed himself to come up with a dramatically fuller sound. One of the differences was to hand the production duties over to Jon Landau, who was Bruce Springsteen's usual producer. Ultimately, this move gave the album more of a snappy rock sound. Also, he began using more drums in his songs. According to him, "It took me until making my fourth album before I realized how cool the drums were!"[4]

When the recording process was over, no one was happier than Jackson. "I remember looking at *The Pretender* when it was finished and going, 'Whew . . . all right . . .' I was glad it was out of the way," he proclaimed. "It reminds me of a story Lowell [George] told me about John Lee Hooker. One of the young guitar players in his band gave him some acid and the two of them sat there for twelve hours and fixated on the rug and didn't say a word. Finally he looked up at this young guy and said, 'Whew. Good. Now that's over, let's go get some whiskey.' That's how I felt about *The Pretender*. You know, 'Let's go play some disco!' "[5]

Jon Landau was fresh from success with Springsteen's incredibly successful *Born to Run*. On *The Pretender*, Jackson is finally more firmly in rock & roll territory with Landau at the helm. This was an obvious ploy to turn Jackson

On *The Pretender,* Jackson is finally more firmly in rock and roll territory with Landau at the helm. This was an obvious ploy to turn Jackson Browne into a more serious rocker, and less an acoustic guitar and vocal troubadour.

Browne into a more serious rocker, and less an acoustic guitar and vocal troubadour. It was a move that clearly widened his musical appeal.

One of the most major changes that came with this album was that top-notch session musicians were brought in to make this a more commercial and complexly layered sound. Russell Kunkel, Leland Sklar, Craig Doerge, and Van Dyke Parks are among the Los Angeles session players who added to the fuller sound of this album. John Hall of the group Orleans added his guitar solo to "Here Come Those Tears Again." And even though David Lindley was only heard on two of the tracks on this album, he was still an active presence in Jackson's music.

This exciting new album opens with "The Fuse," a more optimistic take on the subject matter of "Before the Deluge." Here, Jackson likens the planet Earth to a bomb with a fuse sticking out of it. The protagonist in his song again ponders the meaning of life. He looks for utopia and asks "Oh Lord, are there really people starving still" on Earth? However, he takes more of a "survivor's" stance on his recurring apocalypse visions.

"Your Bright Baby Blues" was a song that he had been singing since 1974. In this slow ballad about a confused lover he wants to reach and touch, Jackson claims that he is finally ready for love. He also sings about his attempts to run away from himself. Midsong, he has a narrative section where he speaks of a friend offering him some hallucinogenic drugs. With that, he goes soaring in his own mind. When he looks down from his high, he sees this person with the bright baby blue eyes. Lowell George and Bill Payne, of the group Little Feat, played the slide guitar and organ, respectively for this song.

On "Linda Paloma," Jackson again takes a journey to Mexico for this South-of-the-Border ballad, which translates to "beautiful dove." Complete with authentic Mexican guitars and mariachi horns behind him, he blends cultures on this effective vacation of a song. This was a refreshing new departure for Browne into "world music."

"Here Come Those Tears Again" was the song that came from Jackson Browne and his mother-in-law, Nancy Farnsworth. An earnest rock love song about devotion, Browne benefits from someone else's vision and presents his least morose love song yet. Bonnie Raitt and Rosemary Butler provide beautiful and strong background vocals to this highly effective song.

Singing to his now-motherless son, Ethan, in "The Only Child," Jackson gives him fatherly advice. Browne warns Ethan to take good care of his memories of his mother and to grow up to be someone who looks out for his "brother." Albert Lee's electric guitar is featured on this track, and Don Henley and John David Souther provide background vocals.

Coming along this same songs-about-family theme, Jackson sings about his own estranged father in "Daddy's Tune." He sings of having regrets over unkind things he said to his father over the years. Jackson complains that Jack Browne was so hard to talk to while he was growing up. He sings of how he became associated with the neighborhood juvenile delinquents when he was a teenager. As the song erupts into a sort of ragtime piano tune, Jackson looks for some kind of resolution with his father.

"Sleep's Dark and Silent Gate" obviously was Browne's way of confronting his grief over Phyllis's death. Taking a gloomy, almost gothic stance on the meaning of life and death, this is a brilliant piece of songwriting. He sings of lying awake in his bed at night, wondering about where all the time has gone and what it all really means.

The final cut, "The Pretender," finds Jackson turning up his nose at the nine-to-five lifestyle of the typical American businessman. He wonders sarcastically what changes the "love-one-another" peace philosophies of the 1960s really made to society, now that they are but an echo of the past. He sings in a third-person stance about "the pretender" who drives to work every day, puts in his eight hours, and goes home to "what?" Perhaps Jackson's most focused song of pessimism about society, this song is tight, snappy, succinct, and snidely critical of "the American dream." The song features the unmistakable smooth and creamy background vocals of his buddies David Crosby and Graham Nash.

It was undeniable that *The Pretender* was his most deeply autobiographical album to date. "It's a description of a period of time in my life," Jackson explained, "and it's something that I really wanted to say. And in saying it, it allows me to forget about it. The fact is that in place of anything really fine and true, people fall back on products

It was undeniable that *The Pretender* was his most deeply autobiographical album to date. "It's a description of a period of time in my life," Jackson explained, "and it's something that I really wanted to say."

and gadgets, the whole game. And they'd rather make love with their dark glasses on. That was like something that actually occurred to me and my wife. And it was just like a funny thing we did that one time. Those kind of things just came back up in songs. It's more about an attitude and a place where people go and a place where I was. Like let me just say, 'When you're talking about "The Pretender," you're talking about a person being like everybody else and being satisfied with what he imagines everybody else is satisfied with.' "[6]

It was Jackson's most introspective material that garnered him the largest amount of plaudits from the critics. In a way, this began to bother him. He later told the *Chicago Tribune*, "Earlier on I got a lot of critical praise—that long, indulgent, long-winded kind. It sort of embarrassed me that I hadn't gotten more attacks, you know, like most of my friends, or that there were really fine artists who weren't being written about at all."[7]

During his *Pretender* concert tour, Jackson Browne played a New York City concert at The Palladium on East Fourteenth Street. In the process, he received one of the worst concert reviews of his career from John Rockwell in the *New York Times*. Entitled "Browne Sings at Palladium; Show Uneven," Rockwell claimed, "It began more or less like Jackson Browne concerts of the past— slow, careful and a bit plodding.... Then it built to a fevered climax in which Mr. Browne seemed almost uninvolved." Apparently, the show ended with an overextended improvisational version of the song "Cocaine." Rockwell claimed that this, like many of Browne's past performances, had dragged along without any thought toward pacing or focus. He also found Jackson's "not particularly distinctive baritone buried in a turgid mix" of the music. The reviewer drove home his discontent by complaining that by the end of the show, the singer "was standing limply in the middle, looking happily confused.... Mr. Browne's new-found relaxation and energy were dissipated by self-indulgence."[8] Oh well, you can't please everyone.

Criticism or not, suddenly Jackson had reached "King Midas" stature, as one by one his albums racked up sales, until all of them surpassed sales of over a half-million copies each. *For Everyman* went "Gold" on October 8, 1976. *The Pretender* was an instant hit for Jackson Browne: it was released on November 10, 1976, and five days later, the RIAA certified it as being "Gold" on November 15. *Jackson Browne*, his debut album, was also certified "Gold" on November 16, 1976. Now, all four of his albums were "Gold," in spite of the fact that only one of his songs—"Doctor My Eyes"—had ever become a major chart hit.

The critical reception for *The Pretender* was again highly mixed. Those who loved him and his somewhat bleak outlook on life and love were deeply touched. And those who weren't, were deeply repelled by his recurring self-indulgence.

In *Rolling Stone*, Dave Marsh wrote of *The Pretender*, "As someone who's always had reservations about admiring [Jackson] . . . I find that Jackson Browne touches me most deeply when he's most specific, least cosmic."[9]

Larry Roher of the *Washington Post* complained of Browne's performance on *The Pretender*, "What's most disappointing is the blandness that pervades Browne's singing on all but a few songs here. For a songwriter who invests his lyrics with so emotional a content, Browne is a terribly deadpan, detached singer."[10]

Whatever negative criticism that *The Pretender* garnered seemed to drip off of him like beads of water dripping off the back of a duck. "The perception was that I wrote an album about my wife's death, which was not true," he argued, "because the album was pretty much written before she died. If you want to listen to 'Sleep's Dark and Silent Gate' or 'The Pretender' or 'Your Bright Baby Blues'—they're not about somebody dying. Even in the bad reviews I got at the time, people accused me of being self-pitying, which was completely untrue. I don't think that the songs were about that. It was not self-pitying at all. I think that it was basically about going forward and still living in the world—just the act of finishing my record. The point is that those things hurt. When people slam you for something that's just not correct, what do you really do about it? What do you do?"[11]

> "The perception was that I wrote an album about my wife's death, which was not true," he argued.

With regard to mining the sounds of Mexico for "Linda Paloma," Jackson waxed theoretical. According to an interview he gave in the *Village Voice*, he claimed, "I've a certain appreciation for Our Lady of Guadalupe and the Virgin Mary and the word *consafos*, which means 'this is predicted by God.' In other words, it means 'believe it and don't fuck with it.' There's a Catholic intensity to certain neighborhoods in Los Angeles, where reverence for the Virgin is personified in the attitude some guy might take with you if you make any inquiries about his little sister. The Aborigines have all kinds of rites that really correspond to Freudian theories and ideas having to do with puberty. And when I think about the Virgin Mary and about the infant Christ child, I think about the reverence you would give to your baby, which is not entirely unsexual. These things are a part of being born into the world, being born a woman."[12]

And then there was his recurring theme of impending apocalypse. According to him during this stage of his life, "When you talk about the end of the world, it has more to do with rebirth. We're depleting the world's natural resources, man. People are starving in American cities, and people are starving in Ethiopia. And wars are carried on for 10 or 15 years. We can't build nuclear power plants on earthquake fissures and get away with it. It's common sense. The deluge is not a huge flood. It's not even wars. It's a series of gigantic mistakes. All it takes is for one of these things to blow up, and you have areas of the globe which will be uninhabitable for the next 280,000 years. I believe it's going to happen. I also believe that there's not much anybody can do to prevent it."[13] Such pronouncements made one want to yell at him, "Hey Jackson: lighten up!"

Jackson was on tour when *The Pretender* hit Number 5 in *Billboard* in the United States. It was his first Top 10 album, and in many ways it marked the fact that he had really tapped into his musical strengths this time around. It was in December 1976 that Jackson's tour went to Europe. One of his favorite concerts from this leg of the tour was playing the city he was born in: Heidelberg, Germany. There were also highly memorable stops in Edinburgh, Scotland, and in London, England. *The Pretender* has the distinction of being the first of his albums to actually make it onto the Great Britain charts, hitting Number 26.

For Jackson, *The Pretender* was the fourth album in a series of deeply introspective works for him. According to Browne at the time, "You can only be lonely so long, you can only feel unhappy for a while. There aren't any of those songs on *The Pretender* and the next album will be easier, happier. . . . It will be quite different. I really feel like I've closed a whole era of my life. I don't feel like talking about these things anymore or writing about [them]."[14]

With his three-year-old son on tour with him, and with a strong and devoted audience of concertgoers clambering to see him perform, Jackson Browne had arrived as a major star in the music business. He had effectively established himself as one of the most serious and deeply personal songwriters around. Now it was time to heal his broken heart and move forward.

CHAPTER 7

Running on Empty

As 1977 BEGAN, IT WAS CLEAR that it was a "make it or break it" period for Jackson Browne. His entire life he had been working up to this point of success and career control. The fact that he was an established star with four consecutive "Gold" albums under his belt drove him to accept as much work as he could take on and complete successfully. This, as well as the quest to put Phyllis's suicide behind him, made twenty-nine-year-old Jackson even more determined to live his life to the fullest. He was about to make several sweeping changes that year, both in his personal life and in his professional life.

During his first global concert tour, Jackson had finally made it as an internationally known rock star, and he was about to lighten up and enjoy it a bit. In February 1977, he was on the Australian leg of his tour to support *The Pretender*. At this emotionally fragile time in his life, who would have guessed that he was about to meet the woman who would make him forget his troubles and move forward?

> During his first global concert tour, Jackson had finally made it as an internationally known rock star, and he was about to lighten up and enjoy it a bit.

It was after a concert in Brisbane, Australia, that he met seventeen-year-old Lynne Sweeney. Although she was a full twelve years younger than he was, there was something about her beauty and innocence that instantly appealed to him. In the past, he had dated Joni Mitchell, Laura Nyro, Nico, Pamela Polland, and Phyllis Major—all of whom were driven women with strong career aspirations and ties to the music business. Young and optimistic, Lynne had absolutely nothing to do with singing, songwriting, or the music business, and this was part of her allure to Browne.

Jackson later explained, "I met her in Australia during the '77 tour. She came to the show. Everybody had a fantastic time that night. After the show, there was a party that the band threw. Halfway through the party, the promoter was having such a good time that he offered to flip me for the bill—and he lost. It was a great night all around. Lynne came to the party, and I started seeing her from then on."[1]

He later explained of that particular and provocative party, "They're just looser in Australia. We had fifty naked people in the pool. There was some sort of sensitivity-training convention at the hotel, so between our tour people and all these sort of freedom junkies, this pool was just steaming, man. I'm surprised we didn't evaporate the whole thing."[2]

Whatever it was that he saw in Lynne that night at the wild poolside party, he was smitten. According to him, "She was [from] Sydney, but I met her in Brisbane. When we played Sydney, she came to visit there. And then over to Perth, and back to Sydney. I think we played Sydney three different times. She was living there [in Brisbane] with a bunch of friends and working in a preschool at the time. Before that, she'd been a model. I think she started modeling when she was quite young."[3]

Following the Australian leg of the tour was Japan. After his concert dates there, Browne revealed that he received a call from filmmaker Francis Ford Coppola, "He invited me to the Philippines when he was shooting *Apocalypse Now*. I was in Japan at the time and I got this message that he really wanted to talk to me. He went through three or four different people to reach me, and it was like I was being called to the Philippines for some important assignment. This was in 1977. . . . Anyway, I had [written the song 'Disco Apocalypse' that he was performing live at the time]. 'Ah,' I thought, 'he wants some music.' But the first thing he said to me was, 'I just wanted to talk to somebody.' And he said, 'Since you were in the neighborhood, I thought I'd invite you to come by.' I was in Japan and it was a goddamn nine-hour plane ride! I must have been visibly disappointed that I wasn't being called on to work, because later he said he was interested in my putting some contemporary lyrics to *La Bohème*. I don't know if it was [a] consolation prize or what. It sounded like a good idea, but I didn't think I could do it."[4]

When twenty-nine-year-old Jackson returned to the United States, he brought Lynne, his new seventeen-year-old girlfriend, along with him. According to Mark Jordan, the piano player who was with Browne for this particular tour,

"He was quite smitten. They seemed to be pretty blissful. It was kind of a relief."[5]

Meanwhile, two singles had been pulled off *The Pretender* album, and both of them were successful on the charts. First was "Here Come Those Tears Again," which made it to Number 23 in the United States in early 1977. It was followed up by "The Pretender," which hit Number 58. Both songs—especially "The Pretender"—became major hits on FM rock radio. On April 12, 1977, the album *The Pretender* was certified "Platinum" in the United States. Finally, Jackson Browne had his first bona fide million-selling LP. This meant that the pressure was on for him to record and release his next album as soon as humanly possible.

Although the heat was on for him to concentrate on his own LP, in April 1977 Jackson went into the Sound Factory Studio in Hollywood to coproduce the second Warren Zevon album. This time around, he was going to share the production responsibilities with Waddy Wachtel. The resulting album was *Excitable Boy.*

Speaking of what was to become the *Running on Empty* album, Jackson proclaimed at the time, "I wanted to make the kind of music that is experienced between people, not the kind that's conceived by one person and sung to a bunch of other people."[6] Out of this idea was born the most successful album of Browne's recording career. As of 2005, it sold in excess of 7 million copies in the United States alone!

Jackson had an American concert tour set for August and September 1977. It was around this time that he began to harbor the idea of recording a brand new album about what it was like to be on a rock & roll concert tour, to be recorded *during* a tour.

> Speaking of what was to become the *Running on Empty* album, Jackson proclaimed at the time, "I wanted to make the kind of music that is experienced between people, not the kind that's conceived by one person and sung to a bunch of other people."

The more he started to think about his next disc, as a new departure and as a concept album, he had one major concern: Was his present touring band strong enough? He decided that it was not. With that, he set about to hire a professional band of studio musicians, who could not only tour with him, but could also produce studio-quality music on and off stage.

With that, he hired a quartet who called themselves the Section and who were signed to Capitol Records. Bass player Leland Sklar, keyboard player Craig Doerge, and drummer Russell Kunkel had all appeared on the *Pretender* album. Together with the fourth member, guitar player Danny Kortchmar, the Section signed on for Browne's new recording venture/concert tour.

In addition to the quartet, Jackson included his longtime music partner David Lindley on the fiddle and lap steel guitar, his longtime harmony vocal friend Doug Haywood, and top-notch background singer Rosemary Butler.

Lindley was happy to be performing live with this particular group of music industry professionals. Speaking of the Section, David claimed that they were all great at consciously creating places for everyone on stage to chime-in with a solo or a new layer of sound, "They leave holes, they're always listening—Craig Doerge especially. Not only does he play straight ahead, but he plays with an eye out here and an eye out there....If you watch Russ Kunkel play drums he's looking, checking out, listening to what other people are playing. That's why you get those magic moments."[7]

Explaining the concept behind *Running on Empty*, Browne said, "These tunes that we've got, were put together around these people, and this experience, that's all."[8]

It was kind of like an audio reality show. "We had a [recording] machine that we carried with us everywhere," Jackson revealed. "And I had a guy who mixed my last album [Greg Ladanyi] right on the road. We'd record rehearsals, in the hotel room and on the bus. Then he'd go back to the studio right after he'd got the tape out of the machine. He'd run straight over and listen, 'cause he was so into it."[9]

Explaining the album concept, Browne claimed, "*Running on Empty* was about trying to demythify rock & roll, the experience. It's mythical stuff anyway. It's slippery stuff, folks. But there's a certain point at which it would do people good to see whose life it is."[10] The really great thing about this album is the fact that it was not only about Jackson's experiences on this one specific tour, but it also took in even the most unheralded members of the tour: the roadies, the soundmen, hell—even the tour photographer got a chance to sing on the LP!

From the very first cut, it was clear that with this album he was on to something new. The very first seconds capture only ambient crowd noise, then the band kicks it into high gear. "Running on Empty" was the perfect metaphor for the physical and emotional exhaustion that Jackson had felt so many times. It was one of only two songs on that album written by Browne alone. In three words, it perfectly defined a mood.

First of all, on the song "Running on Empty," Jackson and his band *really rock*. This was clearly not one of his apocalypse/death albums. The band wails and Browne sings here with a newfound verve and drive. In the opening lyrics, he sings that he has been on the road since 1969, when he was just seventeen years old.

Regarding the song "Running on Empty," Jackson explains, "We recorded it every night for a live album, and this version was, like, the only time it came together. It was just sort of a jam we'd play every night, you know—it was a thing. We wanted it to hold still and develop as a song, so one night my writing partner, Danny Kortchmar, and I stayed up all night, arranged it and taught it to the band that afternoon, after we'd already been playing it for a month. That night it was incredible, and the next night everyone went back to playing it the undisciplined way."[11] The version of the song that they used on the album was recorded in front of a live audience at the Merriweather Post Pavilion in Columbia, Maryland, on August 27, 1977.

The second song on the album finds Jackson plaintively singing of the rigors of "The Road." A song written by Danny O'Keefe, here, Jackson hypnotically spins a tale of highways, dancehalls, motel rooms, coffee mornings, cocaine afternoons, and the long-distance calls that connect touring musicians with their homes and loved ones. With a lonesome violin and acoustic guitars supporting Jackson's "world weary" vocal, this song is one of Browne's finest performances to date. Here everything works in his favor.

"The Road" was recorded in Room 301 at the Cross Keys Inn in Columbia, Maryland, on August 27, 1977, and on stage at the Garden State Arts Center in Holmdale, New Jersey, on September 9, 1977.

The most "tongue-in-cheek" song on the album is "Rosie." In answer to everyone's question about this controversial song: Yes, this *is* a song about masturbation.

"Rosie" is a narrative song written by Jackson Browne and Donald Miller. Donald "Buddah" Miller was the head roadie on this tour. In this story song, the protagonist is a roadie—the show's sound man—who talks about a groupie who was waiting outside the venue awaiting

> The most "tongue-in-cheek" song on the album is "Rosie." In answer to everyone's question about this controversial song: Yes, this *is* a song about masturbation.

the arrival of the trucks. The roadie spots the lonely but friendly looking girl and gives her a pass so she can attend the show. As he fiddles with the controls on the sound board, he gradually runs out of scintillating conversation. The show starts and the groupie turns her attention to the band. When the show ends, the girl ends up being picked up by the band's drummer—and alas, the groupie leaves the sound man alone for the evening.

The chorus is all about the "date" he ends up having sex with again: his own hand. There is an old joke line from the era concerning masturbation. In reply to the question "Do you have a date Saturday night?" one would self-deprecatingly reply "Yeah, the usual one, Rosie Palms and her five sisters."

In the context of the song, Jackson sings that it is "Rosie" who wears his ring, it's "Rosie" who reaches over and physically turns out the light, and it's "Rosie" whom the sound man has sex with that night. This song was just the right amount of sexual silliness that helped make this such a different album for Jackson Browne.

"Rosie" was recorded in a rehearsal room, backstage at the Saratoga Performing Arts Center in Saratoga, New York, on September 1, 1977. The background vocals are "handled" by Doug Haywood and Joel Bernstein, the tour's photographer.

"You Love the Thunder" is the second of two of Browne's solo original compositions on this album. In the lively lyrics of this song, Jackson sings of the mesmerizing force that makes one want to live the life of a musician on tour. Claiming he is addicted to the excitement that rings like thunder and the rain, this is another electric performance from Browne and his troupe. Recorded live on stage at the Garden State Arts Center in Holmdale, New Jersey, on September 6, 1977, this song profits from the unmistakable camaraderie that existed between this particular group of musicians and singers. Everyone sings this song with conviction, fire, and obvious joy.

"Cocaine" was a song credited to Rev. Gary Davis. Here, Jackson and Glenn Frey contribute additional lyrics. A slow, acoustic blues number, Browne sings of his foggy recollections and his allegiance to the white mistress of cocaine. This is in fact such a pro-coke song, that it concludes with the sound of Jackson snorting a line of the white powder.

Years later, after Jackson and many of his friends had already given up habitual use of cocaine, David Lindley said of the tour that yielded the *Running on Empty* album, "On that tour everybody got 'crazy.' *All the time.* When a bunch of people take coke, they get poignant. A lot of people spent a lot of time being 'real poignant' on that tour."[12]

Speaking specifically of the "live" recording of "Cocaine," Jackson later claimed, "At the end of the song, there's a bit where David did his Strother Martin voice and said, 'It takes a clear mind to make it.' I was high, doing coke, and David was trying to tell us, 'Look, making music in front of tape recorders is best done when you've had some sleep and you know what you're doing.' Trying to tell us he was not having a great time. I'm glad that's on there, because, in a way, it's like a little disclaimer. At that time, I think I must have sounded like an ad for coke."[13] Indeed, he did.

This was a song that somewhat labeled Jackson as a "drug guru," in a "Cheech and Chong" sense of the term. In reality, cocaine was a huge part of the tour that produced this album. It was a substance that was used to numb Browne from the tragic suicide of his first wife. It was the height of the sex, drugs, and rock & roll lifestyle he was leading at the time. Eventually, Jackson would see cocaine ruin the lives of many of his friends. But at the time this song was recorded, it all seemed like harmless fun and games.

> This was a song that somewhat labeled Jackson as a "drug guru," in a "Cheech and Chong" sense of the term. In reality, cocaine was a huge part of the tour that produced this album.

Fittingly, "Cocaine" was recorded on tape in private. The performance that made the album was sung (and snorted) in Room 124 of the Holiday Inn in Edwardsville, Indiana, on August 17, 1977.

Guitar player Danny Kortchmar contributed the song "Shaky Town," which was written about the equipment truck and bus drivers on this tour. A slow ballad about following the highway signs from city to city and from gig to gig, it includes a "10-4" reference—in CB radio truck drivers' lingo—which was so popular at that time. "Shaky Town" was recorded in the same hotel room as "Cocaine," on August 18, 1977. Kortchmar also provides harmony vocals.

"Love Needs a Heart" was written by Lowell George, Valerie Carter, and Jackson Browne. It is the album's only true love ballad. Recorded live at Universal Amphitheater in Universal City, California, on September 17, 1977, it is a beautiful performance. The song deals with the need for love—presumably while on the road.

Written by Jackson Browne and Howard Burke, "Nothing but Time" is a lively song about traversing one's way across the country on the highway. Not surprisingly, it was recorded aboard their Continental Silver Eagle bus somewhere in New Jersey. The sounds of traffic in the background on this track are real, and so is the nice jam session feeling. Burke was Jackson's tour manager at the time.

"The Load Out" is a classic 1970s rock recording. It is an ode to the roadies, who day after day and show after show have to unload the stage, the lights, the wiring, and the riggings, only to have to break them all down again and put them back in the truck. Written by Jackson and Bryan Garofalo, it was recorded in concert at the Merriweather Post Pavilion in Columbia, Maryland, on August 27, 1977. Garofalo was the bass player who had toured with Jackson, prior to Jackson having replaced the band for this tour.

> "The Load Out" is a classic 1970s rock recording. It is an ode to the roadies, who day after day and show after show have to unload the stage, the lights, the wiring, and the riggings, only to have to break them all down again and put them back in the truck.

It's just Jackson and his piano as he sings of the roadie's life. For anyone who has ever been a roadie for one of the thousands of rock & roll concerts that have been performed in the last fifty years, this is your song. In this song, Browne proclaims that without the roadies, there would not be a show.

"The Load Out" bleeds right into Jackson's now-famous version of the song "Stay." This song was originally recorded by the group Maurice Williams and the Zodiacs. It was penned by Williams, and became a Number 1 hit for the group in 1960.

Rosemary Butler steps out front for the first featured chorus of the song. Then, in a voice even higher than hers, David Lindley chimes in for his own solo chorus. It prompted Jackson to write in the liner notes: "Featuring a rare vocal appearance by David Lindley."[14] With everyone in the troupe taking a solo spot, this is the perfect way to end the show—by announcing that even Jackson would prefer to "stay" on stage just a little bit longer.

In the space of ten songs, Jackson illuminated just about every aspect of life on the road. He sang of the roadies ("The Load Out"), the truckers ("Shaky Town"), the groupies ("Rosie"), the lust for the music ("You Love the Thunder"), the drugs ("Cocaine"), and the way it wore one out ("Running on

Empty"). It was a full portrait—brilliantly conceived, highly original, and infused with more life than he had shown on any previous recording.

Jackson waxed very philosophically about the rapport he had with his band—the band that helped create *Running on Empty*. According to him at the time, "We all play together a lot, and when these assholes in New York start yelling, 'Incest!', man I want to—I don't know—fuck it. It's a really really good bunch of players who all know each other and help each other. It's like a city in Italy in the 16th century, in which wonderful violins are made by this one and by that one; the students of Stradivarius had their own students. I feel there's a seed of something wonderful there with us; something wonderful's happening."[15]

He knew this was the perfect time capsule for this period of his life: a microscopic look at the inside of a rock tour. "If you look at 'Hotel California,' 'One of These Nights' and those songs, The Eagles sort of got into describing their lives," he claimed. " 'Life in the Fast Lane'—they had a lot to say about it, but I think it's a trap. To that extent, I think I went into the same trap with *Running on Empty*. You describe a life that is not everybody else's life; it's almost like serializing your exploits. I guess it was a hedonistic life: Give kids not only all this bread and all these resources but also this expression—give them a chance to say whatever they want to say. Not everything that we had to say was worth saying."[16]

A couple of song ideas that Jackson had for the *Running on Empty* album didn't make the final cut. The idea of doing a cover of Eric Clapton's "Layla" was considered. Another piece was the proposed "The Wreck of the Marriott," about the fabled "trashing" of a rock & roller's hotel room.

A couple of song ideas that Jackson had for the *Running on Empty* album didn't make the final cut. The idea of doing a cover of Eric Clapton's "Layla" was considered. Another piece was the proposed "The Wreck of the Marriott," about the fabled "trashing" of a rock & roller's hotel room.

When *Running on Empty* was originally released on December 6, 1977, it instantly changed people's perceptions about Jackson Browne. An out-of-the-gate sales success, *Running on Empty* was certified "Gold" by the RIAA on December 28, 1977. It made it to Number 3 in *Billboard* in the United States, and in England it hit Number 28. The first single off the album, the title cut "Running on Empty," hit Number 11 in the

United States. It was so popular that it has gone on to become the signature song of his career. In other words, his "commercial appeal" quotient went up several points because of *Running on Empty*.

The *Running on Empty* album spent two weeks at Number 3 in *Billboard*, but couldn't hit Number 1. In the top position at that time was the soundtrack for *Saturday Night Fever*, which was the disco blockbuster of the year. At Number 2 was Billy Joel's *The Stranger*.

As instantaneous as the sales success of the album was the critical praise for it. Janet Maslin of the *New York Times* claimed that his presentation of songs on record received less of his craft than he put into his clever turn of phrase amid his compositions. However, on *Running on Empty*, Maslin felt that he was free to simply interpret other people's compositions, and in doing so, his singing freed him up to concentrate on his delivery. In her review, she proclaimed, "Although he has been known as a lone wolf who takes things very, very seriously, Mr. Browne is here content to sing, with a great show of camaraderie, about nothing more momentous than the life of a rock & roll band on the road.... Mr. Browne has often had more to say to his audience than he does right now. But he has never been better able to make that audience listen."[17]

Paul Nelson of *Rolling Stone* enthusiastically embraced *Running on Empty* by writing, "As our finest practicing romantic, Jackson Browne has been stuck inside of Mobile with the Memphis blues again for so long that the road probably looks like a realistic way of life to him.... This time Browne has consciously created a documentary, as brightly prosaic as it is darkly poetic, with a keen eye for the mundane as well as the magical."[18]

Both Joni Mitchell's and Jackson Browne's albums had been released by Asylum Records the same week, so there were a lot of parallels drawn between their creative lives during this era. They shared so many similarities—stylistically and creatively—at the beginning of their recording careers. However, now Jackson was becoming more rock and roll oriented, while Joni was veering more and more into the realms of experimental jazz.

In the December 24, 1977, issue of *Billboard*, the publication made Browne's *Running on Empty* and Joni Mitchell's *Don Juan's Reckless Daughter* their two "Spotlight" albums of the week. They reviewed Jackson's disc by pointing out, "The material deals mainly with experiences of the road—brief encounters, loneliness, roadies—all done with Browne's evocative, haunting and penetrating insight. Music is a mix of soft rock ballads and pounding up-tempo tunes."[19]

Carl Arrington of the *New York Post* claimed, "*Running on Empty* captures the thrills, boredom, fun, despair, frustration and exhilaration that happens every day when a band is on tour . . . both authentic and artistically pleasing." Yet, he also pointed out, "Browne has not yet developed the finesse or musical magic of Joni Mitchell, and there are times when his self-expression becomes self-pitying. But he knows how to craft a song and deliver it in a way that moves people."[20]

As stressful and tragic as 1977 had been, 1978 was a great year for Jackson Browne. He had a new love in his life, Lynne Sweeney, he had recorded the biggest album of his career, and he was now viewed as a serious rock & roller, as opposed to a deeply moody and apocalypse-obsessed troubadour. This was Jackson's most joyful rock album, and a time capsule of what it was like to be a highly successful rock star on tour in the 1970s.

> As stressful and tragic as 1977 had been, 1978 was a great year for Jackson Browne. He had a new love in his life, Lynne Sweeney, he had recorded the biggest album of his career, and he was now viewed as a serious rock & roller.

In January 1978, Warren Zevon's album, *Excitable Boy*, was the chart hit that its predecessor had failed to become. This album demonstrated Jackson's skills as a producer. While the *Warren Zevon* album peaked in *Billboard* at Number 189, *Excitable Boy* hit Number 8 on the chart and produced the Top 30 hit "Werewolves of London." Also included on this new Zevon album was a song that Jackson penned with Warren: "Tenderness on the Block."

On March 5, 1978, Warren performed music from *Excitable Boy* in front of a star-studded audience at The Bottom Line in Greenwich Village. That night, Zevon's stylish showcase had Clive Davis tapping his feet, Jackson Browne whistling for more, and a list of luminary contemporaries including Carly Simon, Peter Frampton, and John Belushi. Jackson, especially, looked like he was having a great time that evening.

Jackson took much of 1978 to catch his breath, write new songs, and spend time with Lynne. He also taught a course in songwriting to his son Ethan's elementary school class. While he was on his hiatus, in August 1978, "Stay," the second single pulled from the *Running on Empty* album, peaked at Number 20. In the United Kingdom it hit Number 12.

After a relentless year on the road, Jackson felt like he had been "running on empty." His 1978 sabbatical from his own life in the fast lane was well earned. When he reemerged in 1979, he would have his most high-profile year yet.

CHAPTER 8

The MUSE Concerts

IN TERMS OF BEING A LIFELONG ACTIVIST, Jackson could count several pop music singing peers: David Crosby, Stephen Stills, Graham Nash, Joan Baez, James Taylor, Bruce Springsteen, Glenn Frey, and Don Henley. If there was a cause to be sung about, or a social wrong that needed to be righted, one or more of these stars was usually there. However, throughout Browne's career, the one compatriot with whom he was the closest in the 1970s, was Bonnie Raitt.

She can be heard on his 1973 album *For Everyman* on the song "The Times You've Come," and on his 1976 album *The Pretender* she sang background vocals on the song "Here Come Those Tears Again." He returned the favor in 1975, singing behind Bonnie on four tracks on her *Home Plate* album: "Fool Yourself," "Run Like a Thief," "I'm Blowing Away," and "Your Sweet and Shiny Eyes." During the 1970s, Raitt recorded several of his compositions on her albums, exposing his songwriting skills to her more blues/rock audience. His song "Under the Falling Sky" appears on her 1972 *Give It Up* album. In 1977, she recorded Browne's "My Opening Farewell" on *Sweet Forgiveness*, and two years later on her 1979 album, *The Glow*, she covered "Sleep's Dark and Silent Gate."

In 1979, Bonnie and Jackson continued to collaborate on several projects. Two of these projects were among the most successful benefit concerts of the entire year: a fund-raising concert for Lowell George and the historic MUSE concerts in Madison Square Garden.

In the 1970s, one of Jackson's best friends, favorite collaborators, and singing inspirations had been Lowell George of the West Coast rock group Little Feat. Although Little Feat never scored a big-chart hit, it was—and is—something of a cult-worshiped Los Angeles band. Throughout the 1970s, Little Feat consisted of Bill Payne, Paul Barrere, Fred Tackett, Kenny Gradney, Richie Hayward, Sam Clayton, and Lowell George as the group's leader. They recorded several eclectic and artful albums like *Dixie Chicken* and *Thanks, I'll Eat It Here*. In addition, they had a strong circle of friends and collaborators from the same conglomerate of California rock musicians of which Jackson was an integral part.

Probably the most widely known song written by Lowell George was one that appeared on Linda Ronstadt's Number 1 "Platinum" breakthrough album, *Heart Like a Wheel* (1975). The song was "Willing," and it was about smuggling cocaine and marijuana from Mexico. Many of George's songs had a drug theme to them.

Jackson's own fans were familiar with the members of Little Feat, via several favorite Browne recordings. Payne played the piano on "I Thought I was a Child" on Jackson's *For Everyman* album. Lowell sang harmony vocals and played the slide guitar on "Your Bright Baby Blues" on *The Pretender*, and Payne played the piano on "The Only Child" on that same album. Together with Valerie Carter and Jackson, Lowell cowrote the song "Love Needs a Heart" on the *Running on Empty* album.

In April 1979, Little Feat announced that it was going to break up, and the band members—including Lowell George and Bill Payne—were all going to go their own separate ways. That same month, Warner Brothers Records released Lowell's long-awaited years-in-the-making solo album, *Thanks, I'll Eat It Here*.

Two months later, on June 28, Lowell played to a sold-out house in Washington, D.C., and the next day he died in his Arlington, Virginia, hotel room. At the age of thirty-four, he had suffered a heart attack, brought on by his notorious drug use. His friends, including Jackson Browne, were all devastated by the tragic news.

On August 4, 1979, Jackson was among the friends and comrades of Lowell George to perform at a benefit/tribute concert held at the Great Western Forum in Los Angeles. The successful concert that night drew a reported crowd of 20,000 and raised over $230,000 for Lowell's widow and children. On the bill that night were Jackson, Bonnie Raitt, Linda Ronstadt, Little Feat, Nicolette

Larson, Emmylou Harris, and the Tower of Power Horns. The audience was star-studded as well, as members of Van Halen and California governor Jerry Brown were on hand for the event.

Bonnie sang an emotional rendition of "Here Come Those Tears Again" with Jackson and several members of Little Feat. Bonnie, Little Feat, and each of the soloists performed sets of five or six songs with the same house band, which Bill Payne had assembled for the event. Ronstadt, Larson, and Harris appeared as an all-star trio at one point during the show, and Raitt's solo singing soared on Lowell George's trademark song, "Rock & Roll Doctor." After she was finished singing that particular song, she announced, "People would call out for this one when Lowell was on-stage, and Lowell would tell them, 'Rock & Roll Doctor'? You're looking at him, sucker!'"[1]

Following her set, Bonnie introduced her buddy Jackson Browne. He performed his own composition of "For a Dancer," from the *Late for the Sky* album—about dancing to remember a fallen friend. In his set, he also performed "Here Come Those Tears Again" and "Love Needs a Heart," which he had written with Lowell George and Valerie Carter for his *Running on Empty* album. Browne also sang the song "Peace Divine" with Linda Ronstadt and John David Souther. Ronstadt was reportedly in tears when she performed her sorrow-filled version of Lowell's drug ode, "Willing." Then Jackson, Bonnie, and the entire ensemble rejoined Linda and the band for an all-star finale version of "Dixie Chicken," complete with a celebrity kick line.

Bill Payne said after the concert, "This really wasn't done for money or grandstanding. The reason we were up there is because Lowell George brought us together during his life. He wasn't as well-known as some of the people who were up there that night, but he'd influenced each and every one of us."[2]

That same year, Jackson Browne and several of his closest friends were busy organizing one of the most successful fund-raising and consciousness-raising events of the decade: the MUSE concerts, the *No Nukes* album, and ultimately the *No Nukes* film. MUSE was the abbreviation for the organization Musicians United for Safe Energy.

On July 30, 1979, Jackson, Bonnie Raitt, and the Doobie Brothers were guests on

> That same year, Jackson Browne and several of his closest friends were busy organizing one of the most successful fund-raising and consciousness-raising events of the decade: the MUSE concerts, the *No Nukes* album, and ultimately the *No Nukes* film.

Dinah Shore's top-rated TV talk show. This special ninety-minute version of *Dinah!* was completely devoted to the upcoming series of MUSE concerts in New York City in September and to bring about an awareness of the dangers of nuclear power plants.

Ultimately, Jackson and several of his compatriots—including Crosby, Stills & Nash, Bonnie Raitt, Bruce Springsteen, Chaka Khan, the Doobie Brothers, James Taylor, Carly Simon, Poco, John Hall of the group Orleans, Tom Petty and the Heartbreakers, Gil Scott-Heron, Jesse Colin Young, Ray Parker Jr., and Raydio—lent their time and energy to the cause and to the highly promoted concerts. In the wake of the recent "meltdown" at the Chernobyl nuclear plant in the Ukraine territory of the Soviet Union, it was clear that the entire planet could be contaminated by one single disaster.

According to Graham Nash, "In January of '78, we did some benefits with Jackson Browne to stop the Diablo Canyon plant, which sits near an earthquake fault in San Luis Obispo, California. That's when I wrote the song 'Barrels of Pain,' which is about the low-level nuclear waste lying in barrels off the coast of San Francisco. The whole question of nuclear waste scares the hell out of me. Here in the United States, at the Hanford waste dump, plutonium has already escaped from at least one trench, threatening us with the same kind of explosion. We're committing evolutionary suicide here, and that affects every person on the planet."[3]

On the *Dinah!* show, the program's announcer proclaimed, "Today: the Number One singing group in the nation—The Doobie Brothers, with their hits 'Minute by Minute' and 'What a Fool Believes'. Singer/songwriter of 'Running on Empty' fame—Jackson Browne. Beautiful folk-rock singer Bonnie Raitt joins in a song with the Doobies and Jackson Browne."[4]

Being as they were the biggest hit-makers at the time, the Doobie Brothers were the first of the guest stars to perform on the show that day. After the group sang "Minute by Minute," Dinah Shore sat down with the group, introduced the individual members of the band, and chatted for several minutes. Then Dinah and the Doobies introduced their mutual friend, Bonnie Raitt. According to Shore, the last time Bonnie had been on the show, it was with her father, Broadway legend John Raitt.

Bonnie and Dinah talked for a few minutes, and then Shore said, "You have another friend backstage. Would you introduce him?"

Raitt sincerely replied, "A man who also needs no introduction, one of my

Raitt sincerely replied, "A man who also needs no introduction, one of my best friends, and I think the best songwriter this country has produced so far, Jackson Browne."

best friends, and I think the best songwriter this country has produced so far, Jackson Browne."[5]

The Dinah Shore show was a great open platform for Jackson and his musician friends to express their increasingly more vocal political views. The Vietnam War was over, and the sexual revolution was already a reality. The war was now on to eliminate nuclear weapons and nuclear power. The near-meltdown at Three Mile Island in Pennsylvania had galvanized the battle cry against the promotion of nuclear power, making it one of the most hotly debated issues of the late 1970s and early 1980s. Browne actively began battling against nuclear energy, while promoting the use of solar energy.

If you look at his career path during this period, this particular year became a true turning point for Jackson Browne. The MUSE concerts were the beginning of a highly politically motivated series of songs, concerts, and press statements from him. During the course of the 1980s, he was going to evolve from personally introspective songs like "I Thought I Was a Child," and hippie drug odes like "Cocaine," into more protest-oriented subjects.

On *Dinah!* the Doobies, Jackson, and Bonnie sang their version of John Hall's song "Power," which labels nuclear-produced electrical power as sheer "poison." Introducing "Power," Jackson Browne explained, "This is a song that Bonnie and I have sung together several times at various rallies and events recently, in the last year, year-and-a-half. I first heard it at Seabrook, New Hampshire, when John [Hall] and I were both playing at the occupation of the Seabrook, New Hampshire, nuclear plant...demonstrating against it. And it's become somewhat of an anthem to the antinuclear-power movement, and it's a song that we chose to sing today, because Bonnie, and John Hall, and the Doobies, James Taylor, Graham Nash, and I will be playing at Madison Square Garden this fall—in September—and it's a song that we'll probably be playing together."[6]

The rousing and conviction-filled version of "Power" that followed drew a huge round of applause from the studio audience on *Dinah!* that day.

Bonnie later explained the amazing connection between her and Jackson, and the now legendary antinuclear trailblazer, the late Karen Silkwood. Most people nowadays know who Karen was, due to the 1983 film about her life,

Silkwood, which starred Meryl Streep, Cher, and Kurt Russell. She was killed in
a tragic car accident, which occurred under questionable circumstances in the
early 1970s.

Raitt claimed, "I first became aware of how dangerous the nuclear industry
had become when I read about Karen Silkwood's death back in 1974. Some-
time later the Supporters of Silkwood approached me about doing a benefit to
raise funds for the family case against the Kerr-McGee plutonium company,
which they believed was responsible for her death. Ironically, tickets to a concert Jackson Browne and I were giving a few days later in Oklahoma City were
found in her car when she died. But the kicker for me has been the attempt to
license the Diablo Canyon power plant just a few hours upwind of where I live
in Los Angeles. When it became known that the plant was about two miles
from the Hosgri earthquake fault, I knew there was no other choice but to get
involved. I read all I could and the more I found out, the more frightened and
angry I became. Stopping nuclear power is not just a cause; it's a necessity.
What good is music if you don't have anyplace to play it, or anyone to play it
to?"[7]

Jackson and his friends were beginning to realize that they had a certain
amount of power and influence on the public. By organizing the MUSE concerts, Browne and his hit-making costars
were showing that they, too, had the
power to change minds. But who was to
guarantee that the musicians were using
their power properly, as compared to the
nuclear power–promoting corporations?

> Jackson and his friends were
> beginning to realize that they had
> a certain amount of power and
> influence on the public.

According to Browne, "It's not very much power compared to what *they*
[the corporations] have! But what we have on our side…the threat is real,
being victimized is real, the need for change is real, and these things amount
to something that is true. The need for nuclear power is not true, and their
success lies in the fact that it takes so much money and energy to perpetrate.
Their thing is based on selling something to somebody that they don't need.
That's Madison Avenue. That's Jiffy Pop. That's hair dryers. New and more ex-
pensive ways of using up power for the aggrandizement of oneself. It's been
sold like a drug. Like a mirror that will lie to you!"[8]

Jackson had great expectations for the outcome of the MUSE concerts. At
the time he explained, "If we get a million dollars, a half-million dollars from

tickets or a million from the record...the important thing that will have happened is that we will have plugged people into something."[9]

He also tapped into his longtime interest in the societies of the Native Americans. Just as he had visited Indian reservations as a teenager, the adult Browne visited the Lakota [aka Sioux] tribe in the Black Hills of South Dakota. In the late 1970s, uranium strip mining companies were clearly destroying the land and the environment in their area.

"The American Indians are the original ecologists," Browne explained in 1979. "The way they lived for centuries was in total harmony with their environment. I think the concept of an ecological balance is relatively new to our own society. It has a lot to do with respect. Respect for life. Respect for Creation. If you respect your own life, you can respect the life of another. It's easier to ignore the threats posed by the nuclear power industry if there's nobody you feel responsible for. I suppose the person who made it possible for me to focus on this issue was my son. I want my son to be able to have his own children without being afraid that the increased levels of radiation in the environment could cause them to be deformed."[10]

> "The American Indians are the original ecologists," Browne explained in 1979. "The way they lived for centuries was in total harmony with their environment. I think the concept of an ecological balance is relatively new to our own society. It has a lot to do with respect."

The MUSE Concerts for a Non-nuclear Future were held September 19–23, 1979, at Madison Square Garden. On September 23, there was also a huge rally on one of the landfill plots in lower Manhattan, where Battery Park City now sits. The opening night of the MUSE concerts was unforgettable.

John Hall began the show at 7:30 P.M. with a twenty-minute set. Bonnie Raitt came out and did a number with him ("Good Enough"). She performed her set, and at the end of it she was joined by Jackson Browne. My watch showed a quarter past midnight when the Doobie Brothers came out and did "Take Me in Your Arms," which began a full set. Then the whole cast, including Jackson, came out on stage and John Hall did the final announcements. With Doobie Brothers producer Ted Templeman in the background, everyone began singing "Taking It to the Streets" and then "Power." At 12:55 A.M., the show ended.[11]

On the resulting documentary concert movie and soundtrack album, *No*

Nukes: From the MUSE Concerts for a Non-nuclear Future, Jackson can be heard with the Doobie Brothers, Carly Simon, John Hall, Bonnie Raitt, Graham Nash, Nicolette Larson, Rosemary Butler, and (unbilled) Phoebe Snow on "Power" and "Taking It To the Streets." In addition, Jackson performed his own song "Before the Deluge," and he did a duet version of his hit, "Stay," with his rock & roll hero, Bruce Springsteen and the E Street Band. Rosemary Butler sang the falsetto parts. In addition, Jackson, along with Graham Nash, Rosemary Butler, Doug Haywood, and Suzi Young, sang the background vocals to Jesse Colin Young's anthemlike version of the classic Youngbloods' rock song of peace: "Get Together."

One of Jackson's most impressive performances did not make it onto the soundtrack album, but it would remain one of the true highlights of the resulting film. That song was his rousing version of "Running on Empty."

Doing the duet version of "Stay" with Bruce was one of Browne's favorite aspects of the MUSE concerts. In Jackson's mind, Bruce Springsteen was the ultimate rock hero. According to him, "He's my favorite. [Bruce] definitely had an impact on me—not that I could come close to rocking out like he rocks out. I mean, Bruce is a real rocker. I think I'd be flattering myself if I said I was a real rocker!"[12]

The original three-disc album was released only months after the concert, in December 1979. Amid the five-night series of concerts, the varied lineup included Tom Petty and the Heartbreakers, Gil Scott-Heron, Chaka Khan, Poco, Raydio, Sweet Honey in the Rock, and Crosby, Stills & Nash.

At a press conference held the week of the concerts, Bonnie verbally attacked one reporter who accused the musicians of being "too powerful and too pushy."

"Artists traditionally have been in a position to get public attention," Bonnie proclaimed. "Now if the media had reported accurately about the dangers of nuclear power...if they hadn't consistently mis-estimated crowd sizes at anti-nuclear demonstrations....Our responsibility is to focus media attention if just the movement people had been here today [and not the bands], you probably wouldn't have even covered this!"[13]

In *Rolling Stone* magazine, writer Daisann McLane claimed that it was Browne who really invested the most time and energy into the *No Nukes* cause. According to her, "Jackson Browne, more than any other person, put his reputation, friendships and artistic integrity on the line. He brought in many of the major performers through his own preeminence, dedication and sincerity, which has been demonstrated by doing other, smaller benefits."[14]

Jackson had truly taken the cause to heart. "We're going to have to think about what we need and what we want. About what's important," he claimed at the time. "We hear that we must make sacrifices in order to become an energy self-sufficient nation. And that's true. Sacrifice is a very healthy thing, a way of coming in touch with what's important. But when we hear these multi-national corporations that control the energy telling us that we have to become self-sufficient, they're not talking about people. They're talking about their own interests. What they're talking about is protecting their profits. If they really wanted energy self-sufficiency for the people, they'd be developing solar technology. They'd be promoting conservation, not selling us more and more extravagant uses of energy."[15]

According to a press release sent out by Elektra-Asylum Records, "The M.U.S.E. concerts attracted nearly 100,000 paying fans to Madison Square Garden in what may be the biggest series of benefits ever held in this country. The shows, all of them more than four hours long, were recorded by the 24-track remote unit of New York's Record Plant with a rotating corps of engineers. The [recording] yielded about 20 hours of music, and that was only the beginning. The M.U.S.E. artists then had to evaluate their tracks and decide, with some consultation, which songs and performances should be included on the record. Once the choices were made, those tracks had to be mixed and sequenced to give *No Nukes* a smooth flow and coherence. The main burden for assembling the record however fell most heavily on M.U.S.E. board members Jackson Browne, Graham Nash, John Hall, and Bonnie Raitt."[16]

To fit in all of the major acts, the *No Nukes* album was to fill three two-sided vinyl albums. Someone had to function as the producer, and that task fell on Browne, Nash, Hall, and Raitt. There was a big rush put on the project to make sure that the album was released by Christmas of that year. The man who ended up putting in the most hours on the project was Browne.

Jackson realized that the cause was worth the effort. He knew he had an audience and that he had a strong viewpoint he wanted to express. To him, the corporations who were promoting nuclear power were truly the enemy of the public and of the environment.

"I guess I think of the corporate mentality as the enemy," he claimed. "These people have to be called 'the enemy,' because whether or not they are consciously trying to kill us—or whether they are just being negligent—they threaten our very existence, and they threaten the life of this planet. They're just so plugged into their own ambitions that all they see is the next rung on the ladder, and they don't care who they're standing on. For most people, this problem gives rise to a tremendous feeling of hopelessness. Do you lay down and let these corporations roll over you? Are you going to play dead? Can you leave your life in the hands of these people? It seems to me that we really have no choice but to fight. Each of us must do what we can. We have to educate ourselves and we have to educate each other, and I think we have to take control—while we still have the chance to. And if we don't, maybe we don't deserve to be here. And we can just go ahead and let the mutant sponges inherit the earth. But myself, I like people. I'd like to see a few of them around in a few years from now. In a society that's founded on the idea of getting away with all you can get away with, it's really encouraging to see people working for the good of the whole. I respect that power in each one of us that decides what the quality of existence will be."[17]

To publicize the release of the *No Nukes* album, the whole antinuclear cause received a huge boost in the arm when *Rolling Stone* magazine put several of the MUSE concert stars on the cover of its November 15, 1979, issue. The seven rockers on the cover were Browne, Bruce Springsteen, Bonnie Raitt, Carly Simon, James Taylor, Graham Nash, and John Hall.

In January 1980, the *No Nukes* album reached Number 19 on the *Billboard* magazine album chart. Later that year, the *No Nukes* film documentary was released, and it became something of a cult hit of its own. In spite of its appealing lineup of singing stars, the film and album did not become quite the blockbuster duo of products that the MUSE organizers had hoped they would become. However, the *No Nukes* album was certified "Gold" in 1980 for sales in excess of 500,000 copies, and it became a "must have" item all over again when Elektra/Asylum Records released it as an impressively packaged two-CD set in 1997.

Jackson Browne later defended the whole project by stating, "M.U.S.E. was kind of an experiment. One of the things that really didn't work was that when you shed a lot of media attention on something for a brief period of time, when it goes away people think that the problem has gone away. Also, it was measured in terms of whether it reached its stated goals. Because we didn't make $3 million—we only made a million and a half, and some of that was spent on a movie—it's kind of portrayed as being 'unsuccessful.' What happened before *No Nukes* was Bangladesh. Before that you had Woodstock. And Woodstock was a political event, if you realize that we were at war in Vietnam and this was half a million people coming together to express an ideal of peace."[18]

More than any other project, the MUSE concerts and the *No Nukes* album and film firmly established Jackson as both a political activist and a socially conscious balladeer. It not only solidified his image in the public's eye as a conviction-filled voice to listen to, but it also made him someone to look toward when it came to political issues. If there was a cause that needed to be illuminated, Jackson Browne was there.

CHAPTER 9

Hold Out

THE YEAR 1980 FOUND JACKSON BROWNE working on his latest album. Although the MUSE concerts and producing the *No Nukes* album had kept him busy, he had managed to fit in several months of downtime from his career right after the release of his best-selling *Running on Empty* album.

It was hard to believe that by 1980 it had been four years since he had produced a new studio album. And it had been over two years since the release of his unique live concept album. Jackson was able to take a break from the grind of cranking out a new solo album every year.

In 1980, speaking of the time that he did take off, he revealed, "About a year and a half ago [1978–1979], there was a period of about a year when I wasn't really doing much of anything except hanging out with Ethan. That time was great and I taught an elective course in songwriting at his grammar school. It was fun... I thought it was tremendous. Three kids wrote a song called 'You're Still Good.' The refrain was 'You're still good if you can rock & roll.' Kids have a very exacting way of speaking, you know. Like if I asked Ethan, 'Did you have a good time at so-and-so's house today? Was it good?' And, he'd say, 'Well it was a little bit good.' Now 'a little bit good' is pretty exacting, even if it's not a real graceful way of speaking. And 'You're still good if you can rock & roll.' 'You're Still Good' had a story about this guy who apparently was a real mess at everything else, but he could still make it because he could rock & roll. Except halfway through the song, he got murdered on a train. Someone stabbed him with a knife. I didn't understand that part. But I found that when I'd make suggestions to these kids about changing something, they'd talk it over and come back and say, 'We decided to leave it the way it was.' ... One girl had this amazing little whiskey voice. She must have had a cold or something, because you could hear every little rasp in her voice. Her song was really lovely. It was just the kind of song you'd want an eight-year-old kid to sing."[1]

Browne also revealed, "I started to study acting about a year and a half ago with a teacher named Jeff Corey. He's a wonderful teacher. Then I had to stop to make my album. I'm probably like everybody else when they see an incredible movie with an incredible actor. You see Jack Nicholson or Robert De Niro and you think, 'God, could I do that?' I guess I wondered if I could act. Anyway, a friend of mine introduced me to a friend of his who's a screenwriter. My friend told me, 'This guy writes screenplays the way you write songs, so you ought to meet him.' I did, and we got an idea for a movie and started writing the story. We got a deal and everything. He's writing the screenplay now: Jeff Fiskin. He's very good."[2] Browne ended up collaborating with Fiskin on the script.

Explaining the proposed film's concept, Browne said, "It's about this artist—I suppose you'd call him a conceptual artist—but it's really about a relationship. Having written the story and a song for the film, I think that the character is really close to my own, but I don't know. See, I might not be in the movie. I didn't really write it to be in it. I told the producers and Jeff that I'd like a chance to be in it if it makes sense at the time. And they said they'd be looking for that to happen if I could act, if I liked the script and so forth. But we don't have a script yet. . . . It's called *A Change of Plans*, or *Change of Plan*."[3]

This was not to say that Browne wasn't in the press. In fact, several rumors about what he was up to had circulated. Jackson said, "*The Los Angeles Times* printed a couple of stories that said I was making a movie. They claimed I was studying acting seven days a week or something, and that was never true. At one point, I read in the *Times* that I was making a movie about my life. Supposedly, I'd written this film about a person whose wife dies, and how he's got to raise his young son by himself. I couldn't believe it! It's all untrue. This is bad information or stupid guesswork, that just gets repeated again and again until it becomes common belief. And there's very little that I can do to stop it. Then I was talking to Paul Simon a few months later about his movie [*One Trick Pony*]. I asked him what it was about. And he told me that it was about this guy who's on the road who has a young son. I guess they

> Whatever the rumors were, Jackson soon abandoned his cinematic and acting dreams and returned his focus to his recording career.

just got me confused with another rock & roll singer who was making a film."[4] Whatever the rumors were, Jackson soon abandoned his cinematic and acting dreams and returned his focus to his recording career.

By early 1980, Jackson was busy working on his next album, which would ultimately be entitled *Hold Out*. Released on June 27, 1980, *Hold Out* became Jackson Browne's first and only Number 1 album. Expecting a continuation of its predecessor—the incredibly successful *Running on Empty*—people instantly bought it and were confounded and disappointed in what they heard. And for anyone who loved the deeply personal and touching acoustic guitar-accompanied Jackson Browne of the early 1970s, they, too, were met with something distinctly different.

The song "Disco Apocalypse," which opened the *Hold Out* album, was one of Jackson Browne's all-time worst miscalculations. It had the synthesizer sound of a disco song from the era, it had an uptempo rock/dance beat to it, and it completely confounded fans. Lyrically, it was a song about the disco craze of the 1970s.

The first problem was that 1980 was the year that the bottom fell out of the whole disco market. "Punk" and new wave music were the new crazes. So, if this was going to be taken seriously as a dance song, it was released a year or two too late to find success with that market.

If it was to be taken seriously as a rocker's way of poking fun at disco, it also totally missed the mark. The song "Disco Apocalypse" actually dated back to the 1970s. In fact, Jackson used to sing it in his hotel room during *The Pretender* tour. He later explained, "That was 1976. 'Disco Apocalypse' was a phrase I started saying, an exclamation. It was like saying 'Ooh Fellini' or something. What happens is that you get this little phrase or thought and you have an idea of what it could mean. But it doesn't mean that yet. Not until you've created a song around it."[5]

Interestingly enough, as a folk-based rocker, Jackson was not someone who was antidisco. According to him, "I remember listening to this song by Harold Melvin & The Blue Notes, 'Wake Up Everybody.' God, it was embarrassingly hopeful. But for some reason, it just stuck with me. And stuff like 'Disco Inferno' [by the

Interestingly enough, as a folk-based rocker, Jackson was not someone who was antidisco. According to him, "I remember listening to this song by Harold Melvin & The Blue Notes, 'Wake Up Everybody.' God, it was embarrassingly hopeful."

Trammps]—that's some of the best music ever made, I figure. It's records, you know. When a lot of people think of disco, they probably think of the same foot pattern and the same hi-hat patter going on, through the whole tune. That and a lot of innocuous words. But good music is good music. And disco was a force, you know. It went on for quite a while and everybody had their disco song. Various friends of mine were real worried about 'Disco Apocalypse' before it was finished and I had all the words. It's actually a little dated now. If I could have finished it two years ago and put it out as a single . . . I don't know what people are going to think of it. I know they're sort of allergic to the word 'disco.' "6

On the first night of the MUSE concerts, Jackson decided to try the song out in front of that crowd. When he announced that he was about to sing "Disco Apocalypse," the crowd actually booed him at the mention of the word "disco." He should have taken this as a sign. The next night he sang the song without telling the audience the title of the song, and they applauded when he was done.

This was to remain one of Jackson's most out-of-step and most misunderstood songs. Rod Stewart went successfully from rocker to disco on "Da Ya Think I'm Sexy." And the Bee Gees did it with "Stayin' Alive." But if Jackson wanted to take a rock & roll stance to make fun of disco, he needed to actually say something more poignant than this. He proved that he could not dance in between rock and disco. He never successfully captured either genre on this cut.

The slow and plodding ballad "Hold Out" is about trying to decide between two forces. Should he choose true love, or eschew it for career glory? Jackson explained at the time, " 'Hold Out' is from the same period of time. I started writing that song at the same time I started writing 'Disco Apocalypse.' That was when I was finishing *The Pretender*. See, I always thought that *Running on Empty* was going to be a momentary diversion while I bought myself more time for the next studio album. *Running on Empty* was an idea and it was a digression. It wasn't written as an album the way *The Pretender* and *Hold Out* were. Another reason I like 'Disco Apocalypse' is because Rosemary Butler gets to sing a solo part. It's sort of like what we were doing, when last heard from, in 'Stay' at the end of *Running on Empty*."7

The song "That Girl Could Sing" is clearly about Jackson's love affair with Joni Mitchell nearly a decade earlier. According to Browne, "Well, when you leave a relationship, you're out on the street, you know. And 'That Girl Could Sing' was a song about a real person I knew. Here I was, someone who didn't believe in love but in my own personal search—and I found myself drawn to somebody who was free. So what did I do? I immediately became the person I didn't want to be. I wanted to *possess* that woman. It was a complete turn-around from what I'd said the week before. Then at the point at which I made my peace with that—saying to myself, 'I guess the sanest thing she could have done was to leave, to disappear without explaining'—I found myself out on the street again."[8]

"Boulevard," the fourth cut on the album, found Jackson describing the glitzy and grimy street scene on Hollywood Boulevard. The album's most straight-ahead rock song, Jackson sings of the hookers on that famed street of broken dreams.

According to Jackson, there was a calculated sequencing of the songs on the *Hold Out* album. "One connection between 'Boulevard' and 'Of Missing Persons' is that in both songs I'm talking to young girls. In 'Boulevard,' the girl could be a runaway, someone who's just passing through, hopefully. But everybody's saying, 'Nobody knows you. Nobody gives a shit. Your folks are home playing *Beat the Clock*'—a TV game show from the '50s."[9]

Explaining the song "Of Missing Persons," Jackson said at the time, "Its [dedicated] to Lowell and Elizabeth's little girl, Inara. But the song is about Lowell. It was written the night after we put on the tribute concert in Los Angeles.... He was supposed to be playing the Roxy on July the Fourth. July the Fourth is Inara's birthday. And every year they'd give her a huge birthday party, a huge barbecue. It was sort of a gathering of the clan and various far-reaching members of the community who liked to be together. So 'Of Missing Persons' is about this day and about a birthday that turns into a wake."[10]

Describing its sequence on the album, he claimed, " 'Of Missing Persons' sort of brings you in from the 'Boulevard,' where nothing matters, to where you really hope that someone can see the values. In this song, I'm talking to an even younger little girl. And I'm talking about her parents, particularly her father, who was—as they say—'a wild and crazy guy.' He was 'a leaper' and 'a bounder.' "[11]

Jackson missed Lowell George. Just like he had resolved death with a eulogizing song on "For a Dancer" and "Song for Adam" the slow ballad "Of Missing Persons" helped ease the pain of his friend's passing. "Lowell was one of the

Jackson missed Lowell George. Just like he had resolved death with a eulogizing song on "For a Dancer" and "Song for Adam" the slow ballad "Of Missing Persons" helped ease the pain of his friend's passing.

most amazing persons I will ever know and one of the best friends I'll ever have. But he was a father too. He was a parent too," Browne reminisced.[12]

Without a doubt, the most touching and musically successful song on this album was the midtempo love ballad "Call It a Loan." Written by David Lindley and Jackson, it was clearly about the woman in Browne's life: Lynne. He was realizing during this period of time that he didn't want to lose the love of his new live-in girlfriend. " 'Call It a Loan' is a real turning point as far as the personal relationship on the album goes," he claimed. "Quite unexpectedly, you feel the strange and foreign sensations of love. And you think: 'Shit, what if I don't want this to end.' "[13]

The album ends with its seventh song, the eight-minute epic "Hold on Hold Out." This was one of the happiest periods in Jackson Browne's life, and this song clearly epitomizes this. Written with Craig Doerge, Jackson explained at the time, "Then the album evolves positively into 'Hold on Hold Out.' . . . I was speaking not only of myself but to that idealistic person who exists in me, in Lynne and in a lot of other people. I was talking to anyone who believes that the planet is going to survive and that the race will quite likely go on for several thousand years and fulfill a destiny. And the spoken section at the end of the song sort of neatly ties up the album, I think.[14]

One of the most revolutionary inclusions in this song was the fact that he actually used the words "I love you," addressed to the subject of the song. Clearly, this person was his girlfriend, to whom Jackson dedicated this album with the words in the liner notes: "This is for Lynne."[15] At the end of the song, Jackson goes into a spoken word segment, where he talks about his heart having finally found love in his life.

Speaking of the dedication, Jackson admitted, "Yeah. It says, 'This is for Lynne.' She's the girl in the songs. She's in at least three of them on the new album, and I forget how many on *Running on Empty*. She's the 'Hold Out' yeah, but I'm a hold out too."[16]

In 1980, Jackson really proved that his songwriting style had lightened up considerably.

In 1980, Jackson really proved that his songwriting style had lightened up considerably. According to him, "When I first started writing songs, I was aware of a couple of things: I never said 'baby' in a song and I never said 'I love you.' Those words were in almost every song—particularly Beatles songs—in the '60s, but I was aware that they weren't in mine. But, ah, they're in there now. They seem like natural punctuations of my thoughts. I'll tell you, the whole album kind of surprised me. I think I knew at one time what each little piece was supposed to say, but when I finally saw it coming up in the so-lution—developing, as it were—I suddenly realized what it was about and I was ecstatic. But I also had to make some changes in a way I was living. I saw what had been going on in my life for the last year and a half. I saw where it was going and I liked it. I realized that my life had changed. I was just the last person to know. I mean, it wasn't that I had to change my life, and it was that my life *had* changed."[17]

In Jackson's mind, was the *Hold Out* album a thematic album about finding love? He argued, "I hate the term 'concept album.' *Running on Empty* and *Desperado* were 'concept' albums, I suppose, as opposed to *Hold Out* or *Hotel California*, on which a real direction—a real train of thought—was taken and followed through all the way. This will probably sound immodest as hell, but that's the thing I admire most about my work, and when I see somebody else do it, I get real excited. I believe this kind of approach gives rise to a lot more music, a lot more content than thinking in terms of, 'Hey, we got a couple of up-tempo numbers, now we need a ballad, or vice versa.' Those kind of physi-cal considerations I don't think about a great deal. I have a particular penchant for writing in sequence, recording in sequence—we even tried to mix this LP in sequence. I don't mean that the songs were written in the order in which they appear. But as they were written, they were places in sequence."[18]

His life had evolved, and his singing style changed. On *Hold Out*, he had emerged as a stronger and more self-assured person. "I think it's changed be-cause of the writing, to tell you the truth," he explained. "See, singing is writing, play-ing is writing—that's something I learned from Lowell George. How you sing and play determines how you write, and I think that with my love of Little Feat's music and looking at Lowell and considering him a maestro, I began to sing more when I wrote. As I'd write a song, I'd really *sing* instead of just walking through it and singing it later. So a lot of the way *Hold Out* is sung is written into the songs."[19]

> His life had evolved, and his singing style changed. On *Hold Out*, he had emerged as a stronger and more self-assured person.

In *The Aquarian*, Lydia Carole DeFretos wrote, "*Hold Out* could also be viewed as Browne's progression into the '80s. From the synthesizer propelled sounds of the opener, 'Disco Apocalypse' straight through the soaring guitar on the single, 'Boulevard,' this contained more rock than ever before.... Perhaps the key to what made *Hold Out* work so well, was that it was conceived, performed and recorded with a clear-cut sound and style."[20]

On the other hand, William Ruhlmann, in the *All Music Guide to Rock*, looks back at this album to claim, "If Jackson Browne had convincingly lowered the bar set by his first three albums on his fourth [*The Pretender*] and fifth [*Running on Empty*] ones, his sixth, *Hold Out*, found him once again seeking some measure of satisfaction, albeit in reduced circumstances.... 'Disco Apocalypse' was merely foolish instead of whatever it may have been intended to be (satire? drama?).... *Hold Out* represented an earnest attempt that nevertheless fell short."[21]

Meanwhile, on July 18, 1980, the *No Nukes* film opened in New York City. Marketed as more of a specialized art film than a mainstream release, it had its debut at Cinema I in midtown Manhattan. Speaking at the time about the editing process of the film, Browne revealed, "At various points I was able to sit in and watch people cutting it...develop[ing] it as a movie. And the thing I was most pleased with seeing in the final stages, which I'm sure is still there [was the camaraderie]. I'm sure there's a lot wrong with the movie. Not only are there musicians left out...there are some people in the movement who aren't represented. In some respects this is a rock & roll movie that was designed to: A) try to generate some income that could be put in the right hands; and B) educate, inspire, or rally people. But we don't want to forget that it's just a movie."[22]

Reviewing the film in *Rolling Stone*, Janet Maslin claimed, "The MUSE/*No Nukes* Concerts of 1979 were a high-water mark of inspiration and optimism... a stunning testimony to the depth of the shared beliefs of the generation which came of age in the '60s."[23] In his *1998 Movie and Video Guide*, Leonard Maltin gives *No Nukes* three out of four stars, claiming, "Super Springsteen joins several appealing, if long in the tooth, fellow rock stars to protest nuclear power. Pleasant if not magnetic concert film documentary."[24]

The day after the film opened, July 19, 1980, Jackson headlined Nassau Coliseum in Queens, New York. Reviewing the concert, Robert Palmer of the *New York Times* found that Browne was now at the height of his game as a performer. Being a part of the MUSE concerts in Madison Square Garden had clearly added a newfound confidence in Jackson's performing style. Palmer pointed out in his review, "In the past, Mr. Browne's concerts have tended to be song recitals that concentrated on his confessional ballads and failed to build much momentum.... But Mr. Browne has now demonstrated that he has licked this problem.... Mr. Browne was evidently enjoying himself; he was moving more, and more freely, than he used to, and wringing one energetic performance after another out of his band."[25] Jackson's touring band at this point included Bill Payne (piano), David Lindley (fiddle and guitar), Bob Glaub (bass), Doug Hayward (vocals), and Rosemary Butler (vocals).

Palmer also pointed out, "How many performers would show huge colored photographs of their fiancee while singing about her?"[26] Yes, Jackson was truly in love this time.

Jackson Browne's *Hold Out* album remains one that his fans either love or hate. There seems to be no middle ground. *Hold Out* was certified both "Gold" and "Platinum" on September 15, 1980. The Number 1 *Hold Out* album was also to produce two modest hits for Jackson that year. "Boulevard" made it to Number 19 in the United States. And "That Girl Could Sing" peaked at Number 22 later that year.

On January 17, 1981, Jackson Browne married Lynne Sweeney. He was thirty-two at the time, and she had just turned twenty-one. He seemed to be very much in love with her. Speaking of her at the time, he claimed, "She was modeling when she was about 13 or 14. And she pretty much chucked it. She wasn't very interested in it when I met her. It wasn't until after she came with me to the United States and was here for a while that she got back into it. It was a job, something to do to make money and take her places. It's taken her to Europe and Japan and back to Australia and to New York and Germany. For huge periods of time—what seemed to be huge periods of time, anyway— she's been away. She's going to school now."[27]

> On January 17, 1981, Jackson Browne married Lynne Sweeney. He was thirty-two at the time, and she had just turned twenty-one. He seemed to be very much in love with her.

She was attending Antioch College, and according to Jackson at the time, "She's studying human development and child psychology among other things. We've got a family, you know. I'd like to study those subjects myself, but I think I might be able to learn a lot about them because Lynne's studying them. And because we're *doing* it. We're developing humans here, here in our laboratory," he laughed.[28]

In 1981, Jackson Browne produced the debut album by David Lindley, entitled *El Rayo X*. After all the years that Lindley supported Browne, Jackson took delight in helping his musical buddy to at long last define his own sound. Signed to Asylum Records, Lindley made it a showcase for all of his instrumental talents.

In May 1981, Browne was one of twenty friends of David Crosby's who confronted him at his Mill Valley, California, house and staged a drug intervention. At this point, Crosby had let his chronic drug use rule his life, and it threatened to ruin his career. Jackson, Paul Kantner and Grace Slick of the Jefferson Airplane, Graham and wife Susan Nash, several other close friends and lovers, plus a physician and a professional psychiatric social worker surprised and confronted him—and let him know their feelings about his substance abuse and his obvious self-destruction.

> In May 1981, Browne was one of twenty friends of David Crosby's who confronted him at his Mill Valley, California, house and staged a drug intervention.

In the middle of the intervention, Crosby excused himself, went into his bathroom, and attempted to freebase some more cocaine, to get him through this surprise confrontation. Graham Nash followed him into the bathroom and started a huge argument with Crosby.

As Jackson recalls, "After [Crosby] finally said, 'Okay, great. I'm gonna go [to the hospital detox program], I'm gonna go,' he excused himself and went into the room to hit the pipe and Graham was outraged. Then me and [Carl] Gottlieb kind of second-staged it, right? . . . After the intervention, it was clear that we did everything we could."[29] Although his friends did successfully get him into the detox program at Scripps Hospital in La Jolla, California, he almost instantly checked himself out. It was to be a long while, following an eventual arrest and jail time in Texas, before Crosby was to rid himself of his drug demons. Throughout all of this drama, however, Browne remained a faithful and supportive friend to Crosby.

In June 1981, Jackson Browne played at a benefit called "Survival Sunday," which was sponsored by the Southern California Alliance for Survival. Now that he had such strong political convictions, he was openly speaking out, and he wasted no opportunity to make his opinions known. When he took the stage that day at the Hollywood Bowl, he announced to his audience between songs, "I want to sing a song for the Nuclear Regulatory Commission. I was up at San Luis Obispo and they had these hearings. And for all the information that was presented to them, all the people talking about safety, the only thing that was really obvious was that these gray-flannel-suit heads *were not listening*. They had already made up their minds before the information was presented. I think if you let them put a nuclear power plant on top of an earthquake fault right next to where you live, they'll put one anywhere. On the other hand if you shut it down they'll stop putting them anywhere. This song goes out for them and it's for the people of San Luis Obispo who need our support when they blockade that plant."[30]

With that, Jackson proceeded to rock into a doctored-up rendition of Chuck Berry's "Whole Lotta Shakin' Goin' On," which claimed, "We don't need Diablo, we got the power of the sun."[31]

Browne sang five songs, including a duet with Gary U. S. Bonds on his song "The Pretender." He also had Bruce Springsteen on hand to sing an acoustic duet version of Bruce's "The Promised Land."

In August of that year, the federal government okayed testing at the San Luis Obispo power plant. An antinuclear group calling themselves the Abalone Alliance arranged a press conference to make their stance known. To make the event more newsworthy, they had actor Robert Blake and Jackson Browne as their celebrity speakers.

There were plans underway to form a human blockade at the site, to prohibit the workers from Pacific Gas and Electric from entering the plant. Did Blake and Browne feel that they needed to be part of the human blockade—which would undoubtedly be arrested by the police—as an act of protest? According to Blake that day, "I don't think jail is the strongest card I play." And Jackson proclaimed, "I don't think my body is worth any more than anybody else's."[32]

In September, the protesting human blockade went ahead as promised. On the first day of the protests, 450 people were arrested. On the third day, the number of arrested was at 900. Finally, on the fourth day, Jackson Browne joined the fray, and he was among a group of thirty-six

> Jackson Browne joined the fray, and he was among a group of thirty-six people arrested at the front gates of the plant. On that evening's news, it was Jackson's face that was smeared all over the newspapers.

people arrested at the front gates of the plant. On that evening's news, it was Jackson's face that was smeared all over the newspapers.

If the MUSE concerts in 1979 were the start of Jackson's openly political era, getting arrested that day at the San Luis Obispo power plant in 1981 served as further proof that if he was, as the saying goes, "in for a penny," he was also "in for a pound."

According to Jackson, no one was more surprised than he was that everyone in his age group didn't embrace his beliefs. "You'd be talking to a journalist from *The Village Voice* about the M.U.S.E. concerts, 1979, somebody you'd hope would be a progressive or liberal type. But what you'd hear would be, 'This is really good of you; you don't have to do this.' And you'd have to say, 'Hello. This is about the health and safety of people everywhere, and it is something I have to do, and you should feel that way also.' People always want to set you off in the celebrity ghetto," he claimed.[33]

In January 1982, Jackson's wife, Lynne, gave birth to his second son, Ryan. Whether it was the birth of his second son, the death of Lowell George, observing the mess that drugs were making of David Crosby's life, or a culmination of a lot of things, in 1982 Jackson stopped doing cocaine. According to him, at the time he was most impressed by comedian Richard Pryor, who kicked drugs the hard way. In a well-publicized tragedy, Pryor had been free-basing cocaine, when a sudden blast of flame set fire to the highly flammable polyester clothing he was wearing. What happened to Pryor became one of the most famous and blatant cautionary tales of just how dangerous drugs really were. Fortunately, that particular accident cured Pryor's lust for free-basing coke.

Browne said about Pryor, "He showed that you could stop being a drug-crazed or alcohol-crazed person. I admire Warren Zevon for that too, because it's not easy to change when people love you so much the way you are. But some people spend so much of their careers so loaded that they think that's where the talent comes from."[34]

Is that how Jackson saw himself and his cocaine use? He explained in 1983, "Yeah, you know it's really easy to shut everything else out. I never got seriously addicted to . . . well, I don't know if I did, because I don't know what constitutes a serious addiction. I took a lot of different drugs, tried everything and figured, 'Well, I don't have an addictive personality, so I can have as much of this stuff as I want.' "[35]

According to him, "Over a period of years, you might spend most of your

time that way [stoned]. Gradually, I woke
up and realized, 'Gee, if I wasn't so fucked
up, I would have done those things differently.' Now I've stopped. It's better to
be awake you know?"[36]

He also reported that now that his cocaine days were through, so were his days
of performing the song "Cocaine" in concert. According to Browne, "A couple of
years ago, we [the band] said: 'What is this, a song or a cheer?' And we stopped
doing it. And when I listen back, David [Lindley] was right: it does take a clear
mind to make it."[37]

Craig Doerge, his keyboard player at the time, claimed, "I don't think musicians were aware of their power throughout the '70s. I think all of us in show
business have a greater responsibility than we realized at the time. We weren't
aware of how much show business influences teenagers and the rest of the
world, so when Jackson Browne was singing that song 'Cocaine' on his
[Running on Empty] album, it was an influence, even though Jackson would be
the last person to suggest that a kid should do any kind of drugs at all; he's
very much against them now."[38]

During this same era, there were also some political rallies Jackson became
involved in that did not unfold smoothly. On June 6, 1982, a crowd of over
85,000 people gathered at the Rose Bowl. The event was an antiwar benefit,
and it was promoted as "Peace Sunday." Among the people on the bill were
Stevie Wonder, Linda Ronstadt, Dan Fogelberg, Stevie Nicks, and Crosby, Stills
& Nash. Also, Bob Dylan was on hand as a last-minute addition and as a special guest performer. Apparently, both Joan Baez and Bruce Springsteen were
there as well. Although they were not officially on the bill, Jackson was determined to get them on the stage that day.

Jackson later recounted the story, "This one huge peace rally in 1982—
'Peace Sunday.' The group that held the permit for the park said, 'If you don't
use our slogans and let us define the name of the event and what will be
draped across the front [of the stage], then we won't give you the permit and
there won't be any rally. It was a matter of some fairly radical people having a
problem with being seen in agreement with some fairly moderate people. No
one could agree and the permit did lapse. In the end the city officials got to-

> According to him, "Over a period of years, you might spend most of your time that way [stoned]. Gradually, I woke up and realized, 'Gee, if I wasn't so fucked up, I would have done those things differently.' Now I've stopped. It's better to be awake you know?"

gether and said, 'Please can we give you a permit for the park, instead of your doing this thing in the street?' But even then there were problems. They didn't want Joan Baez to sing, and they didn't want Bruce Springsteen to sing. Evidently, it was just about somebody having their control circumvented. I didn't know a thing about it, but I brought them on and everybody got to hear Joan Baez and Bruce Springsteen. But you get the feeling sometimes that the movement is full of people that are just malcontents."[39]

Jackson was busy throughout 1982 touring the globe. He was one of the headliners for the Concert for Nuclear Disarmament, which was held at Nassau Coliseum on Long Island on Wednesday, June 9. Also on the bill were Linda Ronstadt and James Taylor. In the *Village Voice*, Don Shewey wrote, "Jackson Browne showed off his freshly polished arena persona—much less intimate than the troubadour from his club days with now-gone David Lindley, but 'For Everyman' was moving as ever."[40] The concert was reportedly held to offset the costs of the upcoming rally and megaconcert later that week in Manhattan.

On Saturday, June 12, he was a major part of a huge rally propounding nuclear disarmament, which was held in Central Park in the middle of New York City. Also on the bill that day were Linda Ronstadt, Gary U. S. Bonds, Bruce Springsteen, and James Taylor. The event garnered a ton of publicity and drew a crowd of 750,000.

During the European leg of his touring, Jackson performed at the Lisdoonarva Music Festival in Ireland and at the Glastonbury Fayre in England. He was also one of the stars to perform at the Sixteenth Annual Montreux Jazz Festival in Montreux, Switzerland.

Back in the United States, Browne was one of the headliners at the U.S. Festival series of concerts, held in San Bernardino, California. Also starring at the U.S. Festival were Fleetwood Mac, the Grateful Dead, and the Cars.

Jackson finally broke his own rule against using the word "baby" in his songwriting by composing the biggest hit of his career: "Somebody's Baby." Written for the soundtrack to the film *Fast Times at Ridgemont High,* the lively, catchy, and pleasant song was instantly appealing.

In October 1982, "Somebody's Baby" hit Number 7 in the United States. It was

> Jackson finally broke his own rule against using the word "baby" in his songwriting by composing the biggest hit of his career: "Somebody's Baby."

truly the catchiest and most accessible song he had ever recorded. Oddly enough, at his own insistence, it was not to be included on any of his albums until his *Greatest Hits* package in the late 1990s.

Throughout the 1980s, Jackson Browne seemed to be stylistically all over the map. He was singing songs about disco, without being "disco." He courted the synthesizer rock of the era, but never really crystalized a true sound all his own during that decade. With "Somebody's Baby," it seemed that he had really embraced the idea of being a hugely successful pop star. In many people's minds, this was the best song of his entire career. To others, seemingly himself as well, it made him feel he had somehow sold out, by putting commercial concerns ahead of integrity. He said at the time, "It was hard to write a song about so little."[41]

Only Browne could create the most popular and enduring song of his entire career and express embarrassment about it. In the minds of the general record-buying public, "Somebody's Baby" was the breakthrough song of his career. However, instead of continuing to mine more hits like this one, Jackson Browne had other ideas as to where his career was heading in the 1980s.

CHAPTER 10

Lawyers in Love

LYNNE HAD MET AND MOVED IN with Jackson Browne in 1977. They lived together for four years before they finally tied the knot in January 1981. In January 1982, she gave birth to their son, Ryan. However, before Ryan's first birthday, their marriage was hitting the rocks. It wasn't long before she packed her bags and headed back to Australia. In 1983, as he was working on his seventh album, his marriage to Lynne was in the hands of the divorce lawyers.

That year Jackson said to the press, "Well, it's probably no big secret. Lynne and I are not . . . we're not going to stay married. We're not going to be married anymore. You know why I feel so awkward? Because I don't know what to say about this. That's the honest truth. Lynne and I are getting a divorce. We still love each other; we'll still be friends—that's not going to change. And if I told you all of this, you'd ask, 'Well, then why are you breaking up?' And I just don't know what to say."[1]

While he had been recording the *Lawyers in Love* album, his band members knew that he was having trouble on the home front. His arranger and longtime friend Danny Kortchmar pointed out that Jackson wasn't one to wear his problems on his sleeve. "He never came in all moody or burned out because the marriage wasn't working," Danny explained. "When he gets into the studio to work, he's a fanatic—whatever is happening in his personal life has no effect on his work habits."[2]

Danny also noted that when Browne focused on his work, his personal

problems somehow seemed irrelevant. "It causes complete chaos. It's very difficult for everyone around him, because he becomes more committed to work
than almost anything else."[3]

On August 1, 1983, Elektra/Asylum Records released Jackson's seventh album,
the much misunderstood *Lawyers in Love.* It was coproduced by Jackson and
Greg Ladanyi. Regarding *Lawyers in Love,* Jackson admitted that the title of the
album itself was "pretty sarcastic and maybe a little haughty."[4] Indeed it was.

The cover of the album also helped further muddy the waters of understanding. In the illustration, there is a yellow full moon–filled sky, and in the
foreground a young man in a suit looks cautiously at his surroundings—as
well he should. Popped out of the sun roof of his BMW, he has an oar in his
hands, and his car is afloat in what appears to be the middle of the East River
in a partially water-submerged New York City. Is this the apocalypse that
Jackson had been singing all these years? Is this his way of saying that lawyers
now run the world? Is he bitching about the lawyers handling his divorce?
What the hell did all this really mean?

In the opening track on the album, "Lawyers in Love," Jackson sings of the
human race in their designer jeans, spaceships coming to America, eating off
of TV trays, and watching TV's *Happy Days.* Then he sings of "the Russians"
escaping from Washington and how the moon will be colonized soon as a vacation spot for lawyers who are in love. And we thought he gave up drugs at
this point?

Regarding "Lawyers in Love," Browne explained, "It was meant to be funny.
It was a satire. But I think when it came out it baffled people. People think if
you've written about suicide you can't possibly have a sense of humor. Some
people thought there must be some secret meaning. A couple years later a few
brave souls ventured a guess that it was about the ascension of yuppies. The
fact that it was so misunderstood indicated to me that the problem I was addressing was more pervasive than I thought."[5] This song left a lot of people
cold. And, no one seemed to understand Jackson's sense of humor.

"On the Day" deals with being open to letting love find you. To the sound
of this medium-paced rocker, Brown sings of praying that when love finds
"you," your love is strong enough to hold the one whom you wish to attract.
Obviously, he was licking the wounds of his shattered heart on this one. He
searches for an answer as to why his lover has left his life.

"Cut It Away" was clearly meant as a song to mend Jackson's freshly broken heart. His dream marriage to Lynne turned into a disaster. Here, he sings of cutting away the pain so he can get over the heartbreak. Addressing his lover and telling her that she should have left long ago made this a bitter tune indeed.

Speaking of his trio of Lynne-inspired songs from this period, Browne argued, "I think it's really unfair that people think that those are songs I wrote about my wife. 'Hold Out' and 'Hold on Hold Out' were really songs to myself, about myself—about a part of me that is willing to try to love, to try to give, receive, let somebody in. In one song, I said, 'I can't.' And then in the other, I said, 'Maybe I can.' By getting married, it made it seem that when I said, 'I love you,' I was saying, 'Okay, now we can all live together happily ever after.' But that's not what 'Hold on Hold Out' is about. And in 'Cut It Away,' I don't really refer to those songs."[6]

He opened the door to his heart, and he got his fingers slammed in it. "Cut It Away" was partially a cry for help, and partially his way of healing.

Jackson's composition "Downtown" was one of the purest rock songs on the *Lawyers in Love* album. Here, he sings of rocking out when he is downtown cruising around. Downtown is where he can play his music as loud as he wants and where he is free of the judgment of others. Obviously, he is focusing on forgetting his broken heart on this one.

According to him, "The intimate, confessional and introspective song really had its time. The middle of the '70s, the first half. But then you got a lot of really bad examples of it.... So it always interests me to hear from people who liked *Late for the Sky* best, because those songs—at least six out of the eight—were really the culmination of a period that I just don't feel anymore. It was my literary period: long-form, rambling songs in iambic pentameter with that run-on philosophical attitude. I was wistful, searching bleary-eyed for God in the crowds. I'm writing a song in that style now, because I'm writing a screenplay. I need the main character's old songs as well as his new ones. And it's like trying on my old clothes—they're from a time in my life that I don't feel anymore. I think that attitude is somehow reflected in the new song 'Downtown,' but it's much more spare and realistic."[7]

"Downtown," with its bleeping synthesizer sounds, has a true 1980s pop beat to it. It was a song that Browne could truly lighten up with, and for one cut really rock out without any hidden meanings or deep life lessons attached. It is Craig Doerge's synthesizer work that drives much of this song and gives the music a distinctive bounciness to it.

At this point in time, it had now been two and a half years since David Lindley left the Jackson Browne camp to concentrate on his own career. Since that time, Jackson had put together a band that he had such a strong rapport with, he began to actually enlist their ideas for his songwriting.

According to Browne in 1983, "I started to take unfinished songs to the band and respond as a writer to their suggestions. Your instrument is actually the medium with which you're going to perform the songs. The band is now my instrument."[8]

Out of this mold came "Tender Is the Night," which he cowrote with Russell Kunkel and Danny Kortchmar, and "Knock on Any Door," which he cowrote with Danny Kortchmar and Craig Doerge. "Tender Is the Night" was the strongest bit of lyric poetry from this album, and it still holds up today as a masterful and commercial pop song about looking for someone to love. It is the *Lawyers in Love* album's one true gem.

> According to Browne in 1983, "I started to take unfinished songs to the band and respond as a writer to their suggestions. Your instrument is actually the medium with which you're going to perform the songs. The band is now my instrument."

"Knock on Any Door" asks the musical question: How can you survive a broken heart? Although not as distinctive as "Tender Is the Night," "Knock on Any Door" is a pleasant rocker that Browne poured his heartbroken thoughts into. In the lyrics of the song, Jackson sings of knocking on doors and peering into windows, looking for love. He sings of heartache and disappointment. Musically, it sounds very much like the kind of song that Hall and Oates were recording at that time.

In "Say It Isn't True," Jackson is again addressing what he feels in his heart in the face of apocalypse. Here, he sings about laying in bed thinking about how miraculous life is in general, and how nuclear war could make it all instantaneously come to an end. To a slow beat that sounds like the beating of a heart, Jackson wonders how life can go onward so brilliantly, yet all end if someone pushes the button to start a nuclear war. Using a multitrack technique, on one track he sings the plaintiff chorus "Say It Isn't True," while on another track his speaking voice ponders the needlessness of war. Defending the honesty of "Say It Isn't True," Jackson proclaimed, "It's absolutely a prayer. It's me not caring if anybody thinks I'm corny."[9]

On the album's eighth and last song, "For a Rocker," Jackson again sings of the passing of one of his rock buddies—presumably Lowell George. This time around, however, instead of composing a maudlin death dirge, Browne himself described the message behind the song as "Fuck it, let's dance!"[10] In the song, he claims that he is going to say his final good-bye's to a rocking friend, so let's open up the wine and send him off in style.

In the liner notes of *Lawyers in Love*, Jackson dedicated the album with the words "For Ryan and Ethan." He then wrote "Thanks to Lynne Sweeney."[11] Was this his way of saying "Thanks for breaking my heart" or "Thanks for turning the sharklike divorce lawyers loose on me"?

In *Time* magazine, Jay Cocks proclaimed, "*Lawyers in Love* is, in fact, a particularly neat juggling act from rock's foremost romantic prestidigitator. Part departure and part consolidation, it is the sturdy cornerstone of one of the year's strongest albums."[12]

On the other hand, Lydia Carole DeFretos of *The Aquarian* wrote, "Even devoted Browne followers were concerned when *Lawyers in Love* was unveiled in 1983. Was this the same poet who had so eloquently warned us of the dangers of our own destruction on the Earth? Now his major concerns were things as trivial as 'designer jeans' and a 'shirt so unbelievably bright.' What had happened to the man who led the crusade against nuclear power, and even had himself arrested at a demonstration to make his point?...Many of us still kept the faith, hoping that the inferior quality of *Lawyers* was just a mistake or a phase he was going through."[13]

In the *Village Voice*, Michael Hill stated, "With *Lawyers in Love*, his first album in three years, a new J.B.—older, wiser, remarried, the father of two, and a polished pop star—has assumed the rocker's role in earnest. And while he's up to date enough for MTV, he's too sincere to have much fun with the part."[14]

And William Ruhlmann, in the *All Music Guide to Rock*, says of *Lawyers in Love*, "The craft, and the familiar tightness of Browne's veteran studio/live band, couldn't hide the essential retread nature of much of this material."[15]

One of the biggest disappointments about this album was the fact that "Somebody's Baby" was not included on this album. Reportedly, it was omitted at his

> One of the biggest disappointments about this album was the fact that "Somebody's Baby" was not included on this album. Reportedly, it was omitted at his own insistence. It was another one of Jackson's decisions that surely confounded the record company executives at Asylum.

own insistence. It was another one of Jackson's decisions that surely confounded the record company executives at Asylum.

At a concert in an outdoor suburban amphitheater in Detroit called Pine Knob, Steve Pond of *Rolling Stone* caught Jackson's act and found him performing in a pair of aqua-colored shoes that matched his aqua-colored leather jacket. He opened his show with his latest—and biggest selling—hit of his career: "Somebody's Baby."

In "Jackson Browne Adapts," Pond posed the pointed and potent question, "What's going on here? After ten years of intimate communion with his adoring audience, has Jackson Browne really been reduced to this: a pair of tacky blue-green shoes, a batch of throwaway rock ditties? Talk about 'running on empty!' "[16]

In his own defense, Browne explained at the time, "For the past six years I've been meeting people who tell me they prefer *Late for the Sky* to anything I've done since."[17] Was it time for something new? A new direction? A new message?

It was a new era for Jackson Browne's career. He had given up cocaine. He had gone liquor-free. And his marriage to Lynne was over. Obviously, he was floundering a bit.

Browne argued, "I began writing about myself, but after a certain point, celebrity catches up with you, and it looks like you're opening your life up like a book. That's not so great. Not great at all. So this time, there was a conscious effort not to serialize my life and times. It's not interesting to me, and if it's interesting to other people, maybe that's not so healthy, I've often thought, 'What can these people be interested in? It's . . . it's *unhygienic*!' "[18]

With Browne's marriage on the rocks, his longtime band members pondered Jackson's difficult position. According to Danny Kortchmar, who frequently played with James Taylor, "In the '70s you were supposed to be sensitive, poetic, introverted. But it gets boring walking around in '60s peole[sic] dress, when sometimes you feel like putting on sleeveless T-shirts and slicking back your hair. I think Jackson was feeling burdened by the image of 'Jackson Browne' as a tragic figure, a thoughtful, brooding guy who reads poetry and plays concerts for weepy college girls. I was saying, 'I'm a rocker,' and a lot of the guys in our circle were embarrassed to admit that they'd want to do that. It might offend your friends—what if James Taylor heard you say that? But it intrigued Jackson. He liked the idea of standing up and saying, 'I'm a rocker.' "[19]

His buddies were walking on emotional eggshells around him. Bass player Bob Glaub claimed at the time, "He hasn't changed drastically since I met him. He's just been through a lot more shit since then: two marriages, two kids, how many albums? A lot of shit."[20]

"Buckets," conceded David Lindley. "A lot of people would fold—I would have. But he handled it. Came out scorched, but intact."[21]

For the tour to accompany the *Lawyers in Love* album, Jackson's nine-year-old son, Ethan, came along with him. According to Browne at the time, "He sees what the work is like. And he also sees a lot of sycophants and hangers-on, who want to make friends with him to get closer to me. But he's pretty wise about that stuff. This isn't a great place for kids, but he really wanted to be with me on tour. Anyway, I won't be seeing him for a while because he's going to spend some time in Australia."[22]

As quirky as it was, *Lawyers in Love* made it up to Number 7 on the *Billboard* charts in the United States. And in England it hit Number 37. The album also spawned three hit singles in the United States. The title track went to Number 13, "Tender Is the Night" peaked at Number 25 in November of that year, and "For a Rocker" made it to Number 45 in February 1984.

When the single version of "Tender Is the Night" was released, it gave Jackson a presence on the TV sensation that was sweeping the United States: MTV. This was a new venture, and record labels were happily supplying MTV with videos as marketing tools to sell albums. The "Tender Is the Night" video also gave the public a glimpse at the troubadour and his new girlfriend, Daryl Hannah.

Lawyers in Love was nowhere near the hit that *Hold Out* had been. And neither album could even touch the sales success of *Running on Empty*. On November 8, 1983, *Lawyers in Love* was certified "Gold" for sales of over 500,000 copies. As a former multi-"Platinum" selling artist only five years ago, in a matter of two albums, Jackson overdiversified his music to the point where he was losing his audience.

> *Lawyers in Love* was nowhere near the hit that *Hold Out* had been. And neither album could even touch the sales success of *Running on Empty*.

In 1985, Jackson Browne was one of forty-nine artists to contribute his vocals to the charity/protest song "Sun City." Meant to protest the apartheid in South Africa, the song was produced by Little Steven Van Zandt and remix master Arthur Baker. This was an era in which a lot of pop and rock stars made their political voices heard on huge all-star hit singles with the most successful one of all being "We Are the World." There was also Ferry Aid, Farm Aid, Live Aid, and the list goes on and on.

"Sun City," which made it to Number 38 in the United States and Number 21 in the United Kingdom, was one of the most popular records of this mega-superstar wave of the era. Not only is Jackson Browne one of the star singers to appear on the record, so were several of his idols and compatriots. In addition to Browne, "Sun City" also featured Hall and Oates, David Ruffin and Eddie Kendricks of the Temptations, Bonnie Raitt, Ringo Starr, Pat Benatar, Bruce Springsteen, Darlene Love, Clarence Clemons, Nona Hendryx, Jimmy Cliff, Run-DMC, Joey Ramone, Bono, George Clinton, Peter Gabriel, Ruben Blades, Bob Geldof, Gil Scott-Heron, and a host of other notables. Even jazz greats Miles Davis, Herbie Hancock, and Ron Carter got into the act. Most importantly, "Sun City" also found Jackson sharing space on the song with two significant legends from his past: Lou Reed and Bob Dylan.

Naturally, Jackson Browne embraced the whole spirit of using all-star albums to further political causes. He pondered at the time, "People are fond of pointing out that there was a lot of activism in the '60s and then the '70s were sort of dormant. Now in the '80s there seems to be a lot of concern again. Maybe things work in cycles. But I would say that there is a progression. Within a year or two of an event that centered on extreme hunger and starvation in Africa, you were also having events with many of the same artists discussing human rights. It's possible to really begin connecting these issues. The issues of hunger and peace are related—specifically by the arms race and by the fact that our world's resources are going into technologies that can't be used, while people go hungry."[23]

> Naturally, Jackson Browne embraced the whole spirit of using all-star albums to further political causes.

Jackson again found himself at a crossroads. His music now seemed to be all over the map with *Lawyers in Love* being one of his most confusing albums. No longer was he writing deeply personal ballads. He was still drawing his songwriting inspirations from the world around him, but he was feeling that he needed new inspiration and a new cause to fire his enthusiasm. This time around it was not at his doorstep. He was going to have to travel out of the country to discover what it was. But he was indeed about to find it.

CHAPTER 11

Lives in the Balance

THERE ARE SEVERAL DISTINCT PHASES to Jackson Browne's career. First, there was his deeply personal and diarylike song phase, as personified by his first three albums. Then there was his smooth and sincere *Late for the Sky*, which many fans considered his true masterpiece. Then there was his superstar rocker phase that he sold millions of copies of, *Running on Empty*. Next came his experimental early 1980s pop/rocker phase for two albums. Now, in 1986, with his *Lives in the Balance* album, he began his next phase: his not-so-popular on-the-political-soapbox era.

In the process, he was going to lose or alienate the vast majority of his audience. While countless recording acts all but turn cartwheels in an attempt to attract and hold their core audience, it seemed like Browne was about to do everything he could to sacrifice his commercial appeal for his newfound social consciousness.

> While countless recording acts all but turn cartwheels in attempt to attract and hold their core audience, it seemed like Browne was about to do everything he could to sacrifice his commercial appeal for his newfound social consciousness.

Jackson's life was going through several changes around this period of time. One of the most notable developments was that he was now dating actress Daryl Hannah. They had originally met in the early 1980s when he was performing in concert in Chicago. He had brought her up on stage during his act, and they began a bicoastal and often stormy relationship. Although the pair was to frequently battle with each other, over a period of ten years they went through an on-again/off-again relationship. This was to grow and develop into Browne's longest lasting love relationship, and one of the most controversial.

During this era, the one truly upbeat project that Jackson was involved in was a duet he recorded with saxophone player Clarence Clemons. Along with Little Steven Van Zandt, Clemons was a member of Bruce Springsteen's famed E Street Band. Jackson became friendly with the saxman—via *No Nukes* and "Sun City."

When he recorded his *Hero* album, Clarence invited Jackson to sing a duet with him on a song called "You're a Friend of Mine." When he went into the studio, Daryl accompanied him and provided additional vocals on the track. In January 1986, "You're a Friend of Mine" peaked on the *Billboard* Hot 100 chart at Number 18 in the United States.

Browne had been working on his own album for a while, and it was the product of his latest quest for truth and inspiration. Since Jackson had such a varied style, his fans were uncertain as to what to expect from him this time around. What they got was a political science lecture set to music.

Released on February 19, 1986, the *Lives in the Balance* album was something of a curiosity, and in many people's opinion a huge mistake. Just don't try to convince Jackson of that.

There are two sides to every story. In Jackson Browne's defense, he was invited down to Central America to take a look at what U.S. foreign policy was doing to the innocent people of Nicaragua. He found that the U.S. Central Intelligence Agency (CIA) had been supplying guns to a certain faction down there, and as a result the innocent and poor citizens of that country were emerging as the victims of such policies. Jackson was so moved by what he saw firsthand that he decided he would use his celebrity status, and his next album, as a platform to put a spotlight on the problems U.S. foreign intervention—and specifically the Reagan-led White House—had ultimately caused.

For the rest of the 1980s, Jackson was to use his albums, his time, his energy, and his concerts to make political statements. Along the way, he blasted Presidents Ronald Reagan and George H. W. Bush, the CIA, and any other powers or factions he felt needed exposing.

Browne had only the purest of intentions in doing this. His entire career had come out of a political, folk music–based kind of humanistic perspective. While his idols Woody Guthrie and Bob Dylan had stood up for social equality and justice in the early 1960s, and his contemporaries—like Crosby, Stills & Nash—had protested the Vietnam War in the late 1960s, Browne had cast his net at finding his own personal causes. In Central America, he found it.

The other side of the coin was the fact that Jackson Browne was now courting career suicide. He was a recording artist who had garnered millions of record-buying fans who identified with his deeply personal and introspective songs in the early 1970s. He was also a concert performer who had a long history of chatting with his audiences between songs, often telling charming things about himself and his opinions.

> The other side of the coin was the fact that Jackson Browne was now courting career suicide.

Then, in 1986, with the *Lives in the Balance* album, he traded songs about personal relationships and the pursuit of love for political songs that were heavy-handed and moralistically message laden. And, in concert, instead of talking about his life in between songs, he used the spotlight to make statements about his political beliefs.

Part of his newly developed activism was an outgrowth of his association with Little Steven Van Zandt, the organizer and producer of the "Sun City" recording. Being a part of that recording made him realize that one song could make a difference in bending public opinion.

According to Jackson, "I think most people write a political song because of an issue or because the subject has touched them in some way. If they become known as political songwriters, it's really a way of categorizing them. Steven Van Zandt—you could call him a political songwriter. Actually, until his album *Voice of America*, I never would have thought of putting out an album of all political songs. Because people have a vague feeling that politics is all about bullshit and deception. I always felt a little bit like apologizing for anything that dealt with political subjects. You know: 'I'm sorry I have to mention this, but not everything is as it should be.' Somebody like Steven is all the more brilliant because a person who makes rock & roll the way he does, and wears leopard pants and snakeskin boots and skull earrings and wears his Telecaster [guitar] somewhere between his ass and his knees—for him to be singing the word 'justice,' is very powerful."[1]

He also claimed that he didn't intend on making every song on his *Lives in the Balance* album about the problems in Central America. It was just that those songs seemed to eclipse everything else he had planned to record. "I had already started [writing] 'For America' and 'Lives in the Balance' before I went to Central America," he said. "When I went down there, I met some Nicaraguans. Everywhere you go, if you're a musician, you're handed a guitar, you're asked to sing. I think of those purest of motivations I had when I was 14 or 15, the idea of playing the guitar and singing about something and moving people, expressing something inside me. Those are, I imagine, the reasons people become singers there, too. I realized that their songs were about everything from love to the reconstruction of their society. I thought it would be too hard to talk about those things in a song. And it isn't easy. There are all these songs that we don't think of as political that comment on things that are political. Like I would never have known that the [Tears for Fears] song 'Shout' was about cruise missiles, but I would imagine that Tears for Fears fans knew. If the band did any interviews, they would have occasion to know. Look at Ry Cooder's song 'Borderline.' It's a beautiful, human song about people who come here expecting something, and Cooder's currently not known as a political songwriter. But there's his song, and it has political implications."[2]

He had been searching for a new focal point for his music for a while. He was tired of singing about his own lovelife and sad eulogies to friends who had died. He needed a new spark. It was during his trip to Central America that a light went off in his head.

"I want people to think about themselves, about their own lives and situations, when they hear these songs, not about me breaking up with my wife or something," Browne said.[3]

> "I want people to think about themselves, about their own lives and situations, when they hear these songs, not about me breaking up with my wife or something," Browne said.

Surveying his position at the time, he claimed, "It's like I have to do something, right? And if it's say, going to Central America, I felt like I had to try to put into perspective something that was really unclear. There's nothing about the other struggles in pop music that appeals to me. I don't dress very well, and I'm not very young anymore. I don't play guitar a lot. Really, I'm a songwriter, and these are subjects that came out."[4]

In his own defense, from the perspective of 2002, Browne proclaims of the whole *Lives in the Balance* experience, "I don't want to be a 'bad example' or a 'cautionary tale.'" Yet he admits, "All right. I remember coming back from Nicaragua, having seen people show the highest kind of idealism and sacrifice to a situation that was getting worse and worse. I thought it was more important than any considerations of one's own personal success."[5]

According to Eric Alterman in the highly political publication *The Nation*, "Browne is often singled out as an artist whose audience abandoned him once he became explicitly political in the mid-1980s and started writing about the murderous effects of U.S. foreign policy in Central America and elsewhere."[6] Well, that was exactly what was about to happen.

Released on February 19, 1986, and produced by Jackson, the *Lives in the Balance* album opens with the upbeat rocker "For America." In its lyrics, Browne questions the America to which he pledged allegiance as a child. While the guitars wail, he questioningly sings about the mothers and fathers who lost sons in the futile Vietnam War, and he wonders if they realize that their freedoms are not always guaranteed. He complains of the apathetic blank stares from a generation of people coming of age. He admits in the song that he was out singing about the United States while others died and bled for it. Now he wonders when everyone is going to wake up and realize that the government is actively lying to the public.

Musically, the song "Soldier of Plenty" is beautiful and rhythmic and evokes the sounds of the rainforests of Central America. Here, Jackson condemns the U.S. government supplying guns to certain factions in Nicaragua as a solution to problems. Browne indicts the government for supplying guns instead of sending food to the poor.

Jackson explained, " 'Soldier of Plenty'—I remember writing the first verse and going to sleep and the next morning looking at this thing: 'God is great, God is good / he guards your neighborhood.' I thought: 'What are you talking about? Can you really be singing a song about this?' I didn't know what the song was about until it was written. So, when you ask, 'What do you think you're going to accomplish with one of these songs?,' the answer is: 'I don't really know.' But I know that in going to Central America, I was really moved to want to do something. I thought it would be worth anything to get a point across, perhaps to let people know that the issue is not whether or not one of the poorest countries in the world is a threat to our society, but whether or not they have the right to the same opportunities we have."[7]

After stating his case politically with "For America" and "Soldier of Plenty," for some odd reason Jackson next swings into a pair of nonpolitically motivated songs. While "In the Shape of the Heart" and "Candy" are two of the

In the 1980s, Jackson Browne shifted his focus from introspective songs to more politically based material. His albums *Lives in the Balance* and *World in Motion* found him questioning the policies of the American government. (Photo courtesy Mark Harlan/Star File)

Daryl Hannah and Browne on the "red carpet" at the Academy Awards. For over a decade, they were a hot superstar couple. (Photo courtesy Vinnie Zuffante/Star File)

Bruce Springsteen has long been Jackson's rock idol. They became friendly when they were both on the bill at the M.U.S.E. Concerts in 1979, and they have performed together several times since. (Photo courtesy David Seelig/Star File)

Browne with Bonnie Raitt, David Crosby, and Richard Belzer at a benefit for the charity MusiCares. Both Raitt and Crosby have been longtime friends of Browne's. Raitt has recorded several of his songs on her albums, including "Sleep's Dark and Silent Gate" and "My Opening Farewell." (Photo courtesy Brett Lee/Star File)

2004 was a very high profile year for Browne. He was inducted into the Rock and Roll Hall of Fame, *Running on Empty* was re-released with bonus tracks, and the two-disc retrospective *The Very Best of Jackson Browne* hit the stores. (Photo courtesy Vinnie Zuffante/Star File)

On March 15, 2004, Jackson Browne was inducted into the Rock and Roll Hall of Fame. According to him, the gala, which was held at the Waldorf Astoria Hotel in New York City, was one of the single most exciting evenings of his long career. (Photo: Phillippe Noisette/Star File)

One of the most anticipated events at the annual Rock and Roll Hall of Fame presentation is the All-Star Jam. The 2004 rocking legends included (*left to right*) Kid Rock, Browne, Dusty Hill of ZZ Top, Tom Petty, and Keith Richards of The Rolling Stones. (Photo: Bob Gruen/Star File)

Jackson and his son Ethan on the red carpet at the premiere of the film *Raising Helen* at the famed 1926 landmark El Capitan Theatre in Hollywood, May 26, 2004. (Photo: Jeffrey Mayer/Star File)

Dave Matthews and Jackson have a discussion at a humanitarian fundraiser to "Support the Bushmen of Botswana." The event was held in Beverly Hills, California, on August 28, 2004. (Photo: Jeffrey Mayer/Star File)

album's strongest cuts, they completely undermine the intense mood the two political numbers created.

Listening to "In the Shape of a Heart" by itself reveals it to be one of Jackson's most successful personal relationship songs. He sings about his lover being gone, and his regrets that they had quarreled. He also sings about there being a hole in the wall, about the size and shape of a fist. Is it about Jackson and Daryl quarreling? Is it about Lynne's having left him?

It is followed up by the medium-tempo song about a girl named Candy, who is waiting for true love. Written by Greg Copeland and Wally Stocker, the bouncy "Candy" features background vocals by Bonnie Raitt and Doug Haywood.

Listening to "In the Shape of a Heart" by itself reveals it to be one of Jackson's most successful personal relationship songs. He sings about his lover being gone, and his regrets that they had quarreled. He also sings about there being a hole in the wall, about the size and shape of a fist.

Then, it is back to social awareness songs with "Lawless Avenues." Written by Jorge Calderón and Browne, this narrative song is about living in a city with a dangerous barrio area. Singing about gang violence and the hopelessness of living in a dead-end part of town, Browne is backed up by Calderón both on the bass and in his Spanish-language background vocals.

The song "Lives in the Balance" pulls out all of the finger-pointing political stops. Jackson warns the U.S. government that it is playing with innocent people's lives when it meddles with foreign affairs. Browne claims that America is running close to entering another Vietnam-style war. He blames corporations for selling presidential candidates to the public like they are selling jeans.

This song was to be Jackson's political awareness anthem. He enthusiastically claimed, "There's only so much information you can get out in a song, but a song is an emotional thing. And if it leads people to get information, then it's a powerful tool."[8]

"Till I Go Down" takes a reggae beat and is melded by conviction-filled antiwar lyrics. Vowing that he will never turn his back on the government, Browne claims that he is going to remain vigilant to his cause. He takes a stance against President Ronald Reagan, who, according to Jackson, only worships the dollar bill.

Perhaps the harshest views that Jackson expressed on the *Lives in the Balance* album came in the song "Black and White." Here, Jackson rails against complacency in the face of time running out on the world. He likens sitting down wondering what life is really all about to hastening disaster. This is the album's big "voice of doom" song. Responding to that train of thought, Browne asserted, "Did it seem harsh? 'Still' is the important word. 'Still wondering.' That album was an important time for me, to decide whether or not I wanted to keep doing this. I hate to always say this, but it was never the money. I have been to Nicaragua, and I have met people whose lives have been decimated by what the United States is doing there. And if I had one recurring thought during that time, it was, 'Maybe there's something that I could do.' "[9]

The cover of *Lives in the Balance* is an artistic rendering of a photograph of the Statue of Liberty, which in 1986 was surrounded in scaffolding. Lady Liberty was getting a face lift at the time, in preparation for her 100th birthday, hence the crisscrossing steel beams covering some of her face on this album cover. It was a symbolic way of saying in the photo that U.S. foreign policy, like the Statue of Liberty, needed a face lift.

In the album's liner notes, he dedicates the album to his sons, Ethan and Ryan. And then he adds special thanks to his girlfriend, Daryl Hannah. According to him at the time, "I'm very committed to working out my relationship with my girlfriend and the people I'm close to in my life, my kids."[10]

The reviews that *Lives in the Balance* garnered were decidedly on the negative side. But they ranged from barely positive, to blasé, to highly negative.

In the *Aquarian Weekly*, Lydia Carole DeFretos claimed, "Browne's new LP... is the record that the confused public needed a decade ago. But it is true that it's better late than never. Regardless of the calendar date, *Lives in the Balance* is both one of Browne's finest works and possibly the catalyst that this country needs to get off its collective ass. While every other artist around is jumping on the 'Ethiopia bandwagon,' leave it to Browne to pinpoint the troubles at home."[11]

Richard Harrington of the *Washington Post* seemed indifferent when he described *Lives in the Balance* as being "sharply etched political songs [that] question cultural imperialism, foreign policy and the current state of the American Dream."[12]

And in *Rolling Stone*, Jimmy Guterman was more confounded than judgmental when he found "Browne... attempting to channel his disillusionment toward finding some order in today's chaos.... He opens *Lives in the Balance* with 'For America,' both a prayer and a love song, which damns 'a generation's blank stare.' He doesn't find any answers—the LP closes with the bleak, dismembered chant, 'Time running out, time running out.' " The only really positive thing that this review pointed out was that "Browne's new music supports his lyrics instead of detracting from them."[13]

In the *All Music Guide to Rock*, William Ruhlmann succinctly states, "If Browne sounded more involved in his music than he had in some time, the specificity of its approach inevitably limited its appeal and its long-term significance."[14]

It was Joyce Millman of the *Village Voice* who focused on the album's true weak points to humorously proclaim, "Jackson Browne has righteous politics, and on his new album, *Lives in the Balance*, they're right in your face." Millman found it to be a statement against U.S. imperialism, highlighting Bruce Springsteen/ *Born in the USA*–styled patriotism. She found *Lives in the Balance* poised to deliver its message as a "ponderous, overblown editorial." While she surmised that some of his fans might be inspired to write protest letters to their congressmen, it would be "no thanks to the album's dishrag-limp rock. . . . *Lives in the Balance* is a well-intentioned but stifling lecture. . . . Alas, there's no fun allowed in Professor Browne's Poli Sci course this semester."[15]

That was really the problem here. It wasn't that Jackson's ideas were not valid or that his music didn't rock—because it truly did on this album. The real problem was that it simply wasn't fun to put an album on the stereo to listen to a political science lecture set to music.

There was also the problem that Browne's political statements were so heavy that the inclusion of "In the Shape of a Heart" and "Candy" made these songs come across like out-of-place filler. The appearance of this pair of tunes makes this album 25 percent rocking love songs, and 75 percent ponderous Central American politics. The by-product was an album that no one—except possibly Jackson himself—loved.

After years of keeping his press interviews to a minimum, Browne in 1986 and 1987 was very vocal. Suddenly, he was willing to speak to any publication or radio station that would listen. While his interviewers really longed to ask him rock star–based questions, there was only one thing that Jackson wanted to talk about during this period: his political beliefs.

Along the way, he took on the president, the CIA, and the U.S. government. Comparing himself to then President Reagan, Browne claimed, "Well, here's the difference. I write my material; Reagan doesn't. He reads his. That's also true of newscasters. I never really considered myself an entertainer. What's happening now is that people are finding their political feet in every walk of life. Ideas that might have been attributed to radical people in the '60s are now held by people of every walk of life: the idea of disarmament, the idea of non-intervention, issues about peace and the environment. People who don't think that 'entertainers' should have a voice in politics would just as soon leave war to the generals and politics to the 'professional' politicians. To me that's the opposite of democracy. A democracy implies that we have the participation of everybody on every level. I'm very pleased that on *Lives in the Balance* I was able to articulate ideas that I've held for a long time. You have to remind people: 'Look, this is the United States, remember? The thing we're fighting for? The freedom we're trying to preserve? I'm exercising it.' "[16]

> People who don't think that 'entertainers' should have a voice in politics would just as soon leave war to the generals and politics to the 'professional' politicians. To me that's the opposite of democracy.

Blasting the U.S. government, Jackson further expounded, "It would have been inconceivable 20 years ago that even radical people would understand, to the degree to which everybody understands now, what the C.I.A. has been up to. There were very few people who understood what happened in Central America. I think these subjects are more out in the open now. But it's not as if radical people are going to save the world. It's not as if I expect there to be a revolution in the United States."[18]

He also took on the whole irony of the electoral college system of voting for the president of the United States, "The biggest problem I have with electoral politics is that the whole premise is faulty. The idea that you're going to hire someone to take care of things for you—ideally it would be great. Everybody researches the issues and goes with the person who's going to carry out the policies as the voters think they should be carried out. But instead, people sell themselves in a cosmetic way, and people vote for them without finding out what they really represent or how they're going to pull these things off. And then they forget about it until the next time the elections come up."[19]

On June 15, 1986, Jackson Browne was one of the acts to lend his singing talents to a concert broadcast for the benefit of Amnesty International. Broadcast live from Giants Stadium in East Rutherford, New Jersey, on MTV, the show costarred Browne with the Police, U2, Bryan Adams, and Peter Gabriel.

When the *Lives in the Balance* album was released, it never cracked the Top 20 on either side of the Atlantic Ocean. In the United States it peaked at Number 23, and in the United Kingdom it got as high as Number 36. On July 8, 1986, it was certified "Gold" for sales in excess of 500,000 copies in the United States.

Of the three singles released from the album, "For America" made it to Number 30 in the United States. "In the Shape of a Heart," the album's one love song, stalled at Number 70 in the United States and made it to Number 66 in England. The title song "Lives in the Balance" never even made it onto the charts.

There was a great slogan that emblazoned T-shirts and posters in the 1960s: "Suppose they gave a war and nobody came." Well, "Suppose Jackson Browne recorded an antigovernment policy album and nobody bought it."

In January 1987, politically passionate Jackson made an unprecedented move. Despondent over the fact that his *Lives in the Balance* album had slid off the charts, he decided to take matters into his own hands by producing a video of the title track and to foot the bill himself. He also talked Asylum Records into servicing college radio stations with a special twelve-inch vinyl pressing of the song, with a letter composed by Browne himself.

> There was a great slogan that emblazoned T-shirts and posters in the 1960s: "Suppose they gave a war and nobody came." Well, "Suppose Jackson Browne recorded an antigovernment policy album and nobody bought it."

"I wanted to take one more shot at having this album heard," Jackson said at the time. This was a deeply personal project for him, and he was devoted to the cause he had adopted. "Because people are less aware of some of the subjects and think less about these things, to hear somebody speak so emphatically on the subject may make them uncomfortable. But in a way, that's what I intended to do."[20]

Part of the video was actual footage of the South American citizens who were the subject of this political album. "I want people to see the real faces of the Nicaraguans, the Nicaraguans who are mourning their dead. I think Americans should see those faces," Browne claimed.[21]

Since neither "In the Shape of a Heart" nor "For America" had become successful as singles, the record company was finished releasing seven-inch vinyl singles off of the album. Mike Bone, who was the senior vice president of marketing at Elektra/Asylum at the time, explained, "Basically, this album, as far as the active shelf life of the record, is pretty much over with.... The active period of the record has passed.... We did it because Jackson believed so strongly in this, and politically speaking he's hit the nail right on the head."[22]

Unfortunately, Jackson was not hitting the nail on the head with regard to reviving his *Lives in the Balance* album. Instead, he found himself beating a dead horse.

CHAPTER 12

World in Motion

IN THE LATE 1980S, JACKSON BROWNE found himself defending his political ideals, standing up for his musical choices, and still trying to make his opinions heard. There were several critics who now took regular potshots at his new image. He was accused of using his albums and concerts as a platform to shove his political views down people's throats. Because of this, his popularity waned and his record sales dropped.

Yet, he remained relentlessly devoted to the causes he held dear. He argued at the time, "I made an album [*Lives in the Balance*] and for almost the first time went around and did as much press as I could do. I wound up doing hundreds and hundreds of interviews on political subjects in a lot of rock publications and a lot of dailies, a lot of TV video shows or TV news programs. And I think that has an effect. I think if I were a person interested in these subjects and feeling that 'My God, doesn't anybody care what's going on?' and I heard a song like 'Lives in the Balance' coming over the radio, I'd be happy to hear it. I'd welcome it. I think a song can have a connecting effect. The effect is that it produces a dialogue. And there's not a lot of political dialogue on rock stations or on MTV."[1]

Then there was the whole wave of all-star charity events in the mid-1980s. It seemed that other singing stars were able to contribute their time and energy to these causes, and then return their focus to their careers in a "business as usual" fashion. Other stars simply moved on, but Jackson did not. He had only just begun to fight for newfound causes. He pondered during this era, "I think a lot has changed in the last couple of years because of the acceleration of events: Band Aid, Live Aid, 'Sun City.' There's an acceleration of events on the general topic of peace and the well-being of the planet—ending with the concerts of Amnesty International—where you actually have a chance to be in touch with the discrepancies that exist in our world view."[2]

In his concerts, he was often abandoning several of his greatest hits, in favor of performing more of his politically charged numbers. However, some of his older material did fit right into where he was at, attitude-wise. One of his older songs that seemed to work particularly well in concert with his new songs was his dramatic "Before the Deluge." According to him, "On the last tour I was on, that song and a song like 'For America' went well together. There are some songs I don't care to sing anymore, and that's probably because I'm not eighteen anymore."[3]

On September 30, 1987, Jackson was one of the celebrities to be part of a special all-star band to backup rock & roll legend Roy Orbison in the TV special *A Black and White Night*. The event was held at the Coconut Grove in the Ambassador Hotel in Hollywood, California.

The format of the show was to present Roy and his music. There was no talking. There were no on-camera tributes. What was presented was a seamless concert of all of Roy's greatest hits. His impressive backup band included Bruce Springsteen, Elvis Costello, Tom Waits, John David Souther, T-Bone Burnett, k. d. lang, Bonnie Raitt, Jennifer Warnes, and Jackson Browne.

It yielded not only a stunning TV special, but also a great video and album entitled *A Black and White Night Live* (1989). Among the incredible songs that Roy and his celebrity band performed included "Blue Bayou," "Only the Lonely," "In Dreams," "Dream Baby (How Long Must I Dream)," "Uptown," and "Oh, Pretty Woman."

On June 11, 1988, Jackson Browne was one of the stars to sing at Nelson Mandella's Seventieth Birthday Tribute. The massive concert was held at Wembley Stadium in London, England. The event was broadcast live around the world. Jackson had the distinction of being the only white American who was invited to perform that day.

When he returned to the United States, he launched a six-week concert tour. The profits from the tour were donated to the Christic Institute. A left-wing institute based in Washington, D.C., the Christic Institute was a nonprofit organization that was funding a lawsuit against twenty-nine people—many of them embroiled in the Iran-Contra scandal that was brewing at the time. Additional monies were donated to Nicaragua's Le Penca Project.

Jackson was donating his time and his music to the cause that he felt so compelled to support. The idea of having a high-profile spokesperson like him attached to their cause was calculated to make headines, and headlines it made.

During this tour were a pair of concerts at New York's Beacon Theater. According to Stephen Holden of the *New York Times*, "The evening's most audacious moment came when Mr. Browne sang his latest version of 'Cocaine Blues,' a traditional song he has been performing acoustically for many years with ad-libbed verses. Once a pied piper of chemical euphoria, Mr. Browne used the song to deliver sarcastically self-effacing confessions on the power of the drug to wilt the libido and to stimulate grandiose illusions of creativity. Turned inside out, it became a most effective anti-drug message."[4]

Stephen Williams of *Newsday* reported of the show, "Had Jackson Browne performed in England some years ago at the Globe Theater, the playwright Shakespeare might have been prompted to observe that '*all the world's a soap box*'.... When it comes to dealing with issues—drugs, Nicaragua, genocide, Vietnam—Browne plays second acoustic guitar to no one."[5]

Williams reported that in between numbers Jackson shamelessly lobbied for the Christic Institute and their defense of the Karen Silkwood case. According to the article, Browne also snidely spoke of "the Young Republicans or whoever they are." In doing so, he was referring to a group that was handing out literature with opposing political agendas outside the Beacon Theater. Among Browne's other onstage suggestions was that all of the audience members should return their Shell Oil credit cards as an effort to protest the oil company's policy of supplying fuel for the apartheid-addled South African government.

Anthony DeCurtis reported in *Rolling Stone* magazine, "In 1988, Browne, who is 40, did a six-week theater tour in support of the Christic Institute, a nonprofit organization whose lawsuit against a group of American covert operatives is currently on appeal. By and large, the audiences at those shows shared Browne's progressive views."[6]

Jackson acted surprised that in spite of the fact that he had very publicly

Jackson acted surprised that in spite of the fact that he had very publicly and verbally revealed some of the contradictory policies of the CIA and the U.S. government, that George H. W. Bush was elected as president of the United States in November 1988.

and verbally revealed some of the contradictory policies of the CIA and the U.S. government, that George H. W. Bush was elected as president of the United States in November 1988.

Amazed, Browne said, "I thought, 'Now that people can see that Reagan lied about the degree to which we were involved [in Nicaragua], they certainly won't vote for Bush.' I was *shocked* when Bush was elected. It completely turned my head around."[7]

Jackson observed during this period, "All of life is becoming more political and my writing reflects that. The way people conduct their lives now, everything is layered in politics and everybody has to be a kind of lawyer. We live in a time when everything has to be negotiated."[8]

On May 16, 1989, the RIAA officially certified as "Platinum" the albums *For Everyman* and *Late for the Sky*. At this point, he now had five albums that had been million sellers. However, it was his older albums that were selling much better than his latest pair.

"There are undoubtedly people who haven't really listened to my music since they were in school or something," Browne pondered. "Or, if they hear it now, they hear it on the radio. That's about people's lives changing. But what happened with me is that I changed in terms of what I wanted to talk about. I have less of a capacity to talk about internal things. As a result of my getting older, the world has become more interesting to me. There are a lot of great things at stake. I take things personally. People always used to ask me, 'Do you think you got involved in this nuclear-power issue because you have kids?' I don't think that's true at all, because the people who design these plants have kids. People who profit on nuclear weapons have kids. People who profit on nuclear weapons have children. I don't think it's a matter of that. In the course of events, a situation becomes very critical, and you do whatever you can. You respond with your heart, you respond with as much of your ability as you have to effect change."[9]

As a result of my getting older, the world has become more interesting to me. There are a lot of great things at stake. I take things personally.

More than anything else, he was amazed that more of his contemporaries didn't want to jump on his political bandwagon. "I think the real thing people are scared of is that their lives will change in such a way that they won't be fun anymore: 'I'm going to become completely immersed in this, and I won't be able to go enjoy myself or have a vacation and go where I want to go. I won't be able to ski.' I think you want to keep your sense of humor—I mean, it's possible to enjoy life and to want social justice. It's important; as a matter of fact, it's your duty to have fun, to enjoy life and to maintain a robust attitude toward it. But it does seem like an interruption by very real events—whether it's war or whether it's the shutdown of a factory," he claimed.[10]

In 1988 and 1989, Jackson was busy preparing his next album. Instead of using the unimpressive sales results of the *Lives in the Balance* album as a guide, his new album, *World in Motion*, was going to spread his political cause umbrella even wider.

According to him, "People began asking me early on what the record would be about, and it's hard to say while the process is going on, but it began to be about peace and what we think that is. Even the love songs—especially 'Anything Can Happen,' a song that's about belief in love and the idea that one day there will be peace, even if you're surround by wars."[11]

Released on June 6, 1989, Jackson's ninth album, *World in Motion*, was musically and stylistically fascinating. While it did contain a standard rock love song or two, the ten songs it represents are a clean slate on which Browne could express several different activist views of the state of planet Earth itself. In other words, he was hauling out his soapbox once again. This time around, he chose to produce the album with Craig Doerge, his current keyboard player.

It should also be noted that from this LP forward, Jackson's albums were no longer released under the moniker "Asylum Records." In the early 1980s, David Geffen began establishing his own label, Geffen Records, where he was able to lure such stars as Joni Mitchell, Neil Young, and Elton John. Jackson was to remain with Elektra Records, and from this point forward, for fourteen more years, it would be that label that would release his recordings.

The title track to *World in Motion*, which was written by Jackson and Craig Doerge, is really the liveliest and most succinct song on the album. It lyrically states how the United States is the land of plenty, while in some parts of that same country people are living in hunger and sleeping in doorways. "World in Motion" sets the tone of the album, whose themes are drawn from the front pages of the daily newspaper. A rhythmically rocking number, with background vocals by Bonnie Raitt, Jackson sounds very confident and connected with his musical message.

"Enough of the Night" examines the life of a girl who has lived her life in the fast lane. In high school she wasn't the "girl most likely to succeed"; rather, she was the one who wore blue leopard–patterned tights and was the most likely to excessively exceed. To emphasize his point that this girl has truly had enough of the night, the sound of squealing tires occasionally punctuates the track. And, what, Browne asks, has all this life in the fast lane gotten her?

"Chasing You into the Light" finds Jackson watching his girlfriend sleep on the bed next to him. She is having fitful dreams, but Browne is frustrated that he cannot seem to wake her up and reach her. In the song, he claims that he would like to rescue her, in the same way that she has emotionally rescued him. Presumably, this is about his on-again/off-again relationship with Daryl Hannah.

After two songs about relationships, Browne jumps back into the political science lectures. The song "How Long" asks the government how long it intends on spending millions of dollars on defense and weapons, when there are people in the world who are hungry. On this slow and purposeful song, Jackson's old pal David Lindley shows up for a nice lap steel guitar solo.

In the lilting ballad "Anything Can Happen," Browne pledges love to someone, with the disclaimer that any number of things can happen to negate one's dreams. Here, he tempers his words of love by lyrically wondering how people can devote their lives to making war.

Jackson gets more message oriented in "When the Stone Begins to Turn," which is about the jail term of Nelson Mandela. Here, he praises the work and the dreams of Dr. Martin Luther King and sings of how these freedoms that King dedicated his life's work to will one day also come to South Africa.

In "The Word Justice," which he wrote with Scott Thurston, Browne really goes after the U.S. government. He sings about the Iran-Contra arms scandal, the trial of Oliver North, the CIA's involvement in illegal Nicaraguan drug trafficking, and the ways in which the truth about what's really going on in Washington is often mangled—if it is revealed at all. He sings of the street gangs—the Crips and the Bloods—and the fact that "justice for all" only exists in theory.

"My Personal Revenge" was written by Tomás Borge and Louis Enrique

Mejía Godoy and translated into English by Jorge Calderón. To an acoustic track that has a Latin American feel, Browne interprets this song of wanting victory over government, so children can play freely in gardens, study in schools, and walk down a street free of beggars and homeless people.

He then interprets Little Steven Van Zandt's song/essay of what it is like to be actively involved in the political world. To a reggae beat in the song "I Am a Patriot," he claims that true patriots are not communists, capitalists, socialists, Democrats, or Republicans. They are those who believe in freedom for all.

The album ends with Browne's own composition, "Lights and Virtues." In it, he sings of having the courage to be alone in the quest for truth and justice. For an album with such fiery convictions in several of the songs, the last track is weak and slow musically. Whatever impact some of the songs might have made to the listener, the *World in Motion* album concludes limply. It is pleasant sounding, but comes across like "Jackson Browne Lite."

> To a reggae beat in the song "I Am a Patriot," he claims that true patriots are not communists, capitalists, socialists, Democrats, or Republicans. They are those who believe in freedom for all.

In the liner notes to *World in Motion*, Browne dedicated this album to his mother, Bea Koeppel. She had died of cancer the year before, and this was Jackson's way of publicly remembering her. His father also died in this same period. His family now consisted of his sister, Roberta (Berbie), his brother, Severin; his two sons; and his girlfriend, Daryl Hannah.

Keeping with the political content theme of the *World in Motion* album, the cover art reflected the dreary subject matter confronted in the music. A colored collage of tinted black-and-white images featured a dismal looking Jackson in one square, and the faces of starving children in other boxes. It did not make the package look like a cheery affair.

Jackson said in late 1989, "I'm more interested in the world at the moment. Being the object of a lot of attention keeps you from really getting to see very much but yourself. That's hard for me, because I've got other things that are much more interesting to me. I mean, I have a kid who's 15. I have a kid who's seven. I've got a relationship [with Daryl Hannah]. I've got what I think of as my family. In 'World in Motion' I say, 'You have a volunteer in me.' I really feel like I'm singing somebody else's song. I feel like I'm speaking not only for myself but for a lot of people who are very actively engaged in trying to bring about social change or just make a difference in the world."[12]

The reviews for *World in Motion* were mixed, if not decidedly negative. Ron Givens of *Stereo Review* claimed that while a cynic might say that Browne was stuck in the 1970s, he or she would be missing the point of his songwriting. Givens said, "As a romantic troubadour, Browne has few peers. On this record he portrays a man with an aging heart, one who's weary of the emotional fast lane, but not quite ready to exit.... Jackson Browne looks at life as a patriot, a social critic, a lover, a pal. He sings from his heart and soul. We are lucky to hear him."[13]

David Fricke of *Rolling Stone* said that *World in Motion* was "even more explicitly issue driven than its politically charged predecessor, *Lives in Balance*.... There are a million ways for music to say that people deserve better—better government, better life, better love. On *World in Motion*, Browne gets your attention by getting under your skin."[14]

In *All Music Guide to Rock*, William Ruhlmann takes the negative approach. He finds that *World in Motion* was comprised of "a repertoire best suited to an Amnesty International benefit.... War, homelessness, and Oliver North (though not by name) were condemned; freedom, truth, and Nelson Mandela were praised.... Except for the gloomy viewpoint, it was hard to recognize the Jackson Browne of his first few albums amid all the commentary.... [It was] disappointing."[15]

The *World in Motion* album peaked at a weak Number 45 in *Billboard* in the United States and failed to even make the charts in England. Neither of the singles, "Chasing You into the Light" and "World in Motion," made a dent in the charts. *World in Motion*, with Jackson's heavy-handed politics and a couple of love songs thrown in just in case, somehow missed touching any audience but his most die-hard supporters. He had hit the low point of his album sales. *World in Motion* was never to even achieve "Gold" status. Due to his political soapboxing, by the end of the 1980s he had effectively alienated the majority of his fans—in the millions.

Jackson kicked off the album's release with a series of concerts in the New York City area. On June 10 and 11, 1989, he played Radio City Music Hall. At this point in time, Jackson's between-song ramblings had been replaced with conviction-filled political speeches about his pet causes. Wayne Robins of *Newsday* claimed, "Browne has dedicated himself to issue-oriented music...."

While the [new] songs are more musically substantial . . . they're still more obvious, less insightful than Browne's best work. . . . The problem is not that Browne makes speeches, but that he doesn't often make good speeches. Rhetorically he's no Winston Churchill or Jesse Jackson. His political songs neither rouse the spirit, nor inspire the skeptical. So *World in Motion* was flat."[16]

And Steven Holden, reviewing the same show for the *New York Times*, found, "The incensed political feelings permeating Mr. Browne's new album gave Saturday's concert an edge of righteous indignation—a relatively new ingredient in his performances."[17]

On July 28, 1989, Jackson Browne began a sixteen-date concert tour of the United States. It kicked off at the Mud Island Amphitheatre in Memphis, Tennessee. The tour ended on August 27 in San Diego, California, where he headlined the Open Air Theater.

When he played at Bally's Grandstand under the Stars in Atlantic City, New Jersey, on this tour, he had a special guest star for his encore number. When he returned to the stage to sing "Stay," Bruce Springsteen joined him and made the song a duet.

One of the many benefit performances that he made that year included joining Neil Young and a host of other performers at the Paha Sapa Music Festival. Held on the Pine Ridge Reservation in South Dakota, the performance was to benefit the Oglala Lakota Sioux Indians.

By now, Jackson was becoming weary of defending his in-your-face political stance on his last two albums. He especially defended *Lives in the Balance*. He defiantly announced in 1989, "It sold more than *Late for the Sky*. I had a very strong feeling about those songs and about what got said on the record. I don't judge my work by what it sells. *Late for the Sky* INITIALLY sold about 380,000 copies, and constantly, and especially by the reviewers my work is compared to that time. I mean if [*Los Angeles Times* pop music writer] Robert Hillburn really wants to drive a stake in my heart, he'll say, 'Remember how beautiful that [*Late for the Sky*] was? Well, nothing since has been worth our listening to.'"[18]

He also started to be lampooned in the press by his peers as well. His un-

> By now, Jackson was becoming weary of defending his in-your-face political stance on his last two albums. He especially defended *Lives in the Balance*.

flinchingly serious mood was duly noted. In a 1989 *USA Today* story by Edna Gundersen, record producer Don Was (Weiss) made an amusing reference to the Jackson Browne school of pop music political activism. Don was one-half of the singing duo Was (Not Was). Their one big hit was the clever and catchy 1989 hit "Walk the Dinosaur." In the article, Don was quoted as saying of Was (Not Was), "We don't want to paint ourselves in any corner: Jackson Browne with a pointer showing you where the troops are in Nicaragua? No thanks."[19]

Fortunately, Jackson actually did have enough of a sense of humor about himself to find Don's sarcastic comment amusing. "Oh God. It's true that you can definitely go too far," he admitted. "The danger, of course, is that people will think they know what you're going to say before you say it and not bother to listen. 'Here he comes again. *Please* don't come with that shit, man. Can we *please* hear "Fountain of Sorrow"?' "[20] Unfortunately, that was the reality of the situation.

The album *World in Motion* earned the distinction of being the all-time poorest selling album of his career—to date. He had started the 1980s with a million-selling Number 1 album, and he finished 1989 with an album that failed to produce a single chart hit and never even went "Gold."

The question remained: Did Jackson ruin his career with activism? Obviously, the answer was yes. Browne claimed, "I've heard a number of people put forth the idea that my activism or my talking about political things in my music has resulted in less success, less sales at one time or another. It's a widely held idea that you're bothering people to talk about political things, that they'll be bothered, that we don't want to be preached at. That's nonsense, because people have always sung about what matters to them. But even if it were true, it wouldn't be a hard choice to make. It's more important to struggle for what you know is right and for what you feel to be valuable."[21]

> The question remained: Did Jackson ruin his career with activism? Obviously, the answer was yes.

He argued in his own defense, "The idea that entertainment should be separate from one's own aspirations and one's life goals, that's completely unlike what's happened for hundreds and hundreds of years. People have always sung about what's going on. People have always written plays and poems. It's just a very recent thing that in the United States, people in the entertainment industry and people in the advertising industry would like to make a separation."[22]

Interestingly enough, in 1989 Jackson's friend Bonnie Raitt scored the biggest selling album of her career, *Nick of Time*. She had been a well-respected and popular singer throughout the 1970s and 1980s, but never really scored that one big breakthrough album. However, with *Nick of Time*, her sound was crystalized, redefined, and became a huge hit. The man who was responsible for this new, refocused Bonnie, was producer Don Was. Observing this, Jackson would eventually enlist the services of Was for a couple of cuts on his next album.

On April 16, 1990, Jackson was in London to perform at a huge concert event: Nelson Mandela—An International Tribute for a Free South Africa. He sang two songs with singer Johnny Clegg in Wembley Stadium.

Tragically, on August 27, 1990, blues/rock guitar superstar Stevie Ray Vaughan was killed in a Bell 206 helicopter crash, following a concert at Alpine Valley Music Theatre in East Troy, Wisconsin. He had just finished an incredible on-stage jam with Eric Clapton, Robert Cray, Buddy Guy, Phil Palmer, and his brother, Jimmy Vaughan. Three days later, at Stevie Ray's funeral, Jackson, together with Stevie Wonder and Bonnie Raitt, sang "Amazing Grace." Stevie Ray was buried in Laurel Land Memorial Park in Dallas, Texas.

On October 12 and 13, Jackson was one of the stars of the huge Amnesty International benefit From Chile...An Embrace of Hope. It was held at the National Stadium in Santiago, Chile. Also on the bill were Sting, Peter Gabriel, Sinead O'Connor, and Crosby, Stills & Nash. And on October 26, Browne was one of the stars to sing at the fourth annual Bridge School benefit, which was organized by Neil Young. The event was held at the Shoreline Amphitheatre in Mountain View, California. Also performing that night were Elvis Costello, Edie Brickell, and Steve Miller.

Another fund-raising event was held to benefit the Christic Institute on November 16 and 17, 1990. Held at the Shrine Auditorium in Los Angeles, the two nights of concerts were all-acoustic evenings starring Jackson Browne, Bruce Springsteen, and Bonnie Raitt. The events raised $600,000. The funds were raised to financially back a lawsuit that accused the U.S. government of sanctioning arms sales and drug trafficking during the Iran-Contra scandal.

Jackson joined Bonnie Raitt on December 16, 1990, for a special concert in Sioux Falls, North Dakota. The event marked the 100th anniversary of the infamous massacre at Wounded Knee.

The year 1990 marked four decades of Elektra Records. To commemorate the event, the company put together a multiple CD album called *Rubaiyat:*

Elektra's 40th Anniversary. For the CD, Browne contributed the previously un-released song "First Girl I Loved."

On January 16, 1991, the Byrds were inducted into the Rock and Roll Hall of Fame. At the ceremony, which was held at the Waldorf Astoria Hotel in New York City, Jackson Browne and Don Henley got up on stage to join the Byrds for a version of their song "Feel a Whole Lot Better" during the annual after-induction jam session.

Browne was one of the performers at the Telluride Midsummer Music Festival on July 19, 1991. He performed at Town Park in Telluride, Colorado. He also appeared on two other albums that year. On the Chieftains' *The Bells of Dublin*, he is heard singing his composition "The Rebel Jesus" backed by the Irish group. On the Disney album *For Our Children*, he sang a duet version of the Beatles' song "Golden Slumbers" with Jennifer Warnes. This lullaby-like recording was later to appear on the 1999 Kid Rhino album *For Our Children 10*, commemorating ten years of the "For Our Children" group, which raised money for the AIDS Pediatric Foundation. To promote the *For Our Children* album, on August 14, 1991, Browne and Warnes made a guest appearance on *The Arsenio Hall Show*, singing their beautiful version of "Golden Slumbers."

The rest of 1991 was filled with charity appearances. On October 7, he sang on the bill of the *Ban the Dam Jam* show held at the Beacon Theater in New York City. Also on the bill that night were David Byrne, Bruce Cockburn, and the Indigo Girls. On the West Coast, on November 3, he sang the song "For a Dancer" at a memorial benefit for famed San Francisco concert promoter Bill Graham. The event was entitled Laughter, Love and Music: To Celebrate the Lives of Bill, Steve and Melissa, and it was held at the Golden Gate Park Polo Fields. The crowd that attended the event was estimated at 350,000.

On November 21, 1991, Browne lent his voice for the Second Annual Holly-wood Hunger Banquet for Oxfam America. The charity event, which cost $150 per ticket, was held at Sony Studios in Culver City, California. Also on the bill that night were Joni Mitchell, David Byrne, Al Jarreau, and Crosby, Stills & Nash. When guests arrived, they were given random meal tickets. The tickets divided the crowd into groups directly proportionate to the food distribution of the world. In that way, 15 percent of the guests were given a full multicourse meal, 25 percent were given a simple meal, and 60 percent were fed only rice and water.

When singer and keyboard player William "Smitty" Smith suffered a stroke and had no medical insurance, his buddies in the music business came together to stage a benefit concert to help offset his medical expenses. Jackson Browne was one of the singers to perform at the benefit concert Friends of Smitty on January 30, 1992. It was held at the Palace Theater in Hollywood, California. Also on the bill that night were Bonnie Raitt, Michael McDonald, and Rita Coolidge, Brenda Russell, and Mary Wilson of the Supremes—performing as an all-star female trio.

Browne was also one of the performers to star on the Lifetime Cable TV special *Free to Laugh*. The program, which was a benefit for Amnesty International, featured a blend of comedy and music.

When the Indigo Girls released their album *Rites of Passage*, it included a song they recorded with Browne, "Let It Be Me." To promote the album, on June 30, 1992, the duo appeared on *The Tonight Show*, and Jackson was on hand to sing the song with them.

By September 1992, Jackson Browne and Daryl Hannah's relationship was crumbling. As a couple, they had been running "hot" and "cold" for a while. During one of their spells of being apart in 1988, Hannah attended the wedding of director Herb Ross. It was Ross who had directed Hannah in the 1989 hit film *Steel Magnolias*.

Ross was marrying the sister of Jackie Kennedy Onassis, Lee Radziwill. Naturally, Jackie and her son, John F. Kennedy Jr., were in attendance. Daryl and John met at the wedding, and from that point forward remained friends who sometimes dated each other. There would be long periods of time when Daryl would go back to Browne, and in the interim, Kennedy was also dating Sarah Jessica Parker, model Julie Baker, and actress Christina Haag.

At this point, Jackson and Daryl had been sharing a 5,000-square-foot house in Santa Monica, California, valued at $2.5 million. In addition, she had her own apartment in New York City. So their relationship was decidedly "bi-coastal."

In September 1992, Jackson and Daryl had been quarreling. Reportedly, Daryl had flown out to the West Coast from New York to formally end their relationship and to gather some of her belongings. During

> At this point, Jackson and Daryl had been sharing a 5,000-square-foot house in Santa Monica, California, valued at $2.5 million.

the morning of September 23, the pair got involved in some sort of physical scuffle from which Hannah emerged bruised and allegedly "battered" and "abused."

People magazine reported, " 'It's awful,' says a close friend, given permission to speak to *People* by the normally press shy Hannah. According to the friend, Hannah suffered a black eye, a broken finger, swollen lips and body bruises at the hands of an out-of-control Browne. Says the source [of Hannah]: 'She's still in shock.' "[23]

According to Santa Monica police officer Sergeant Gary Gallinot, at 12:05 P.M. Jackson phoned the police with a complaint that "someone was ransacking his home." According to the police, when they arrived there—and unknown to them at the time—Hannah was hiding in the separate guest house on the property. Jackson had regained his composure by the time the cops got there and assured them that "everything is fine." Neither Sergeant Gallinot nor his partner filed a report, and they left the premises.[24]

When the police left, Daryl also left the property and contacted her sister, Page, who took her to have her injuries medically examined and treated by a doctor. That afternoon, Alan Nierob, a spokesperson for Daryl, delivered a press statement confirming, "She received serious injuries incurred during a domestic dispute with Browne for which she sought medical treatment."[25]

On hearing the news of Jackson and Daryl's physical scuffle, John F. Kennedy Jr. immediately flew out to California to come to her aid. She flew back to New York City with John, and in the ensuing days afterward, they were spotted together by the press. According to reports in the press, Daryl's hand was still wrapped up in a bandage, and she wore huge sunglasses to hide her blackened eye.

> On hearing the news of Jackson and Daryl's physical scuffle, John F. Kennedy Jr. immediately flew out to California to come to her aid.

Freaked out by the whole occurrence, Jackson Browne left town and headed to northern California. Neither Jackson nor Daryl spoke to the press, and neither of them filed police complaints against the other. This left the field wide open for speculation.

Smelling blood, *People* magazine jumped on the bandwagon, referring to the pair's roles in the altercation as "he the angry lover, she a battered victim."[26]

The die was cast. Since neither party was publicly speaking about the matter, it was their friends who were left to try to piece together the actual occurrence that morning of September 23.

Daryl's acquaintances came to her defense in the press. "This has happened before, but never this bad," said one of her "unnamed" friends to the press. And another claimed, "Who knows what caused it? Not even Daryl knows. He goes into blind rages and doesn't know what he does. He was trying to kick the door down." Still another friend of Hannah's asserted, "Everyone who know's her has been encouraging her to leave [Jackson]. He has an explosive personality."[27]

Sue Wexler, Daryl's mother, was quoted as saying of her daughter, "I saw her shortly after in the hospital. I saw the damage that was done to her. The doctor was very concerned. Jackson was a very, very good friend of mine, but when I saw Daryl, I just felt betrayed."[28]

"Jackson Browne has always been something of a dichotomy," says New York celebrity magazine feature writer Marcy MacDonald. "He has the image of being this big humanitarian, which is in direct contrast with his spousal abuse image. In my mind they are flip sides of the same coin. He is capable of great social deeds, and he is capable of having a volatile temper. In my mind, I am sure that he did what Daryl accused him of doing. All you had to do is look at Daryl Hannah's face to know that she was telling the truth."[29]

It was Browne's male friends who immediately came to his defense. "He is just not a violent guy. As far as I can tell, he was just trying to protect himself. *HE* was getting chased around by *HER*," claimed J. D. Souther.[30]

Don Henley insisted, "I would bet everything I own that Jackson did not batter Daryl."[31]

No matter how one sliced it, the ending of the affair of Jackson Browne and Daryl Hannah was definitely interesting and perplexing. Had one of them sued the other for battery or assault, the waters might have been clearer as to who was to blame. Was the blame for whatever it was that happened on September 23, 1992, equally shared between the two of them? Was Jackson capable of battering the one he loved? Did Daryl light into him like a she-cat, and did he merely defend himself? At the time, their individual silence left it to the press—and especially the tabloids—to sort it all out for them.

Not only was this an all-time low point in Jackson's recording career, but the explosive end to the whole Daryl Hannah affair did nothing positive for

> Not only was this an all-time low point in Jackson's recording career, but the explosive end to the whole Daryl Hannah affair did nothing positive for his public image.

his public image. How ironic it was indeed. On the one hand, here was Jackson ruining his album sales by loading them with songs about world peace, nuclear disarmament, and let's-love-each-other messages. And on the other hand, the public was reading about him in the headlines as *allegedly* being a misogynist and—even worse—a woman beater.

His silence in the press might have seemed a noble stance at the time. However, the whole affair seemed a bad career move for everyone concerned.

CHAPTER 13

I'm Alive

JACKSON BROWNE WAS REPORTEDLY STUNNED that the very private breakup with Daryl Hannah had ended up so badly and that it was so heavily covered by the press. When he had released his pair of political albums, *Lives in the Balance* and *World in Motion,* he had courted the media to spread his message. Now, he found that he was making headlines, but they were not the kind he wanted to create for himself.

Maintaining a press silence for much of the rest of the year, Jackson chose to remain quiet on the subject of his messy breakup until he was able to obtain some sort of perspective on it. Characteristic of his nature, he chose to put his thoughts and feelings into the songs he wrote for his next album to articulate his point of view and tell his side of the story. Until that was completed, he was not ready to speak to the press about what did or did not happen on September 23, 1992.

While the world was now burning to know the details of Browne's personal life, he quietly maintained a "business as usual" kind of stance and stayed away from interviewers. On October 10, 1992, Browne was one of the performers at the All Our Colors—The Good Road Concert held at the Shoreline Amphitheatre in Mountain View, California. Also on the bill that night were Santana, Steve Miller, and John Lee Hooker.

November 11 found him as one of the singing stars at a benefit concert to raise money for the victims of Hurricane Iniki, which had hit Hawaii. He joined Bonnie Raitt, Jimmy Buffett, and Crosby, Stills & Nash on stage for this worthy fund-raiser.

In January 1993, Jackson took part in a benefit at Universal Amphitheatre in

Universal City, California. This particular event raised monies for the Environ-mental Science and Engineering Program at the University of California, Los Angeles (UCLA).[1]

Concurrently, Jackson's contemporaries like Eric Clapton, Neil Young, and Rod Stewart were resinging their old hits on *Unplugged* albums. Instead, Browne was creating one of his most innovative new albums. For his next album, which he threw himself into in 1993, he was looking forward instead of backward.

Musically, he was stretching out a bit. Lately, he had been listening to what newcomers in the music business were producing. According to him at the time, "Ethan turned me on to Ice-T. He's speaking the truth from the point of view of an angry Black man. And I value that because, otherwise, who would tell me about this stuff? I wanna know. I say that for all of us white people who don't know whether you're smarter if you don't vote than if you do. He's doing brilliant stuff."[1]

It was in his *I'm Alive* album that Jackson chose to vent his frustration and anger. David Geffen explained, "It was a very difficult time [for Jackson]. When you're coming to the end of a relationship, it's one of the only things you can think about, isn't it?"[2]

Released on October 11, 1993, and coproduced by Jackson Browne and Scott Thurston, *I'm Alive* ranks up there with *Running on Empty* as being one of the strongest end-to-end thematic albums in Jackson's career. Every song on *Running on Empty* was about a rock & roll concert tour. Mirroring that con-cept, every song on *I'm Alive* is about the heartbreak and pain of Jackson's breakup with Daryl.

On the title track to the album, Jackson sings of looking around his world and seeing the lights alone. The dreams he had of spending his life with Daryl Hannah are shattered and gone. His lyrics speak of wanting to go somewhere where he doesn't have to hear her name or be re-minded that it is over. The painful con-clusion of their love affair is obviously a great loss to him. He is driving on California Highway 5, trying to get far enough away to escape his heartbroken memories.

> On the title track to the album, Jackson sings of looking around his world and seeing the lights alone. The dreams he had of spending his life with Daryl Hannah are shattered and gone.

"I'm Alive" is all about the pain of disappointment and how the pain lets him know that he is truly "alive." As he sings of being able to fill a swimming pool with his tears, it is clear that what has happened between him and Daryl was not what he wanted. This is a great rousing rock song about survival in the face of disappointment. The music is perfectly crackling and upbeat, making this an affirmation of emotional survival.

"My Problem Is You" is likewise about the pain of his breakup. However, this time he is waiting to be rescued from loneliness, knowing that she will never come to him again. This is a nice, multilayered ballad that shows off Browne's songwriting skills at their finest.

"Everywhere I Go" echos this sentiment, this time around to a medium-tempo and rhythmic reggae beat. Everywhere that Browne goes, he hears the heartbeat of his absent lover. In the middle of watching a football game, peering out at the sun, or standing in line in the grocery store, there is nowhere that he is not flooded with memories of her.

"I'll Do Anything" is all about begging the elusive woman of his dreams to come back to him. He professes how he wants her to return and he promises to make her dreams come true if she does. He longs to get her back again on this slow and beautiful ballad of emotional desperation. When she smiles, he hears angels sing. And he claims that he cannot bear the idea of someone else taking his place in her life.

In "Miles Away," Browne sings of the actual fight that caused the end of their affair. He tells of being in the bedroom, with his back against the wall. He claims that he doesn't want to fight with her when she is full of "rage" and is acting "mean and wild." Again, he looks at her and he can hear the sound of angels singing. However, he knows that in her mind it is already over, and her thoughts are "miles away."

"Too Many Angels," the most delicately crafted song on this album, takes the theme of angels for a third time. According to him, " 'Too Many Angels' is really a portrait of a person whose life is like a shattered life. A life that is sort of like two things at once—sort of a hounded person. A person who hears these angels singing, you know, and they come and go."[3] His friend, Jennifer Warnes, makes a vocal guest appearance on the background of this beautiful song.

When he used to walk on the beach, there would be two separate sets of footprints left in the sand. Now he is confused because when he looks at his path in the sand, there are now three sets of footprints. The new footprints obviously belong to the other man—in this case, John F. Kennedy Jr. "Take This Rain" tells this story in a song. Now, as the rain washes away the footprints in the sand, he realizes that he can finally start to love again, with a clean slate, just like the rain that has eradicated their footprints in the sand.

In "Two of Me, Two of You," Jackson sings of two people being in each of them—presumably him and Daryl. One version of him is rational and true, and the other is a "fool." That is the same of her, too. He prefers to believe that it is the foolish sides of them who have fought, and not the pure and rational people both he and his former lover are capable of being.

In "Sky Blue and Black," Jackson sings to his former lover that if she ever needs to be hugged or wants a shoulder to cry on, he is there for her. Sometimes the skies are blue, and sometimes they are black. At this point, he realizes that their love now seems doomed to end. It is a song of a resolve. (Or is there a tongue-in-cheek double meaning to the words "black and blue"?)

By the time that the last song on the album, "All Good Things," comes along, Jackson realizes that it's over. Like the old saying goes, "All good things must come to an end." Here is the resolve after the storm. He knows that Daryl Hannah has moved on with her life, and he sounds ready to do the same thing.

It is interesting to note that two of the most satisfying tracks on the album were coproduced by Don Was, Jackson Browne, and Scott Thurston. Don was in the studio to lend a hand on the songs "My Problem Is You" and "Too Many Angels."

With regard to the album, Jackson explained, "I'm doing what I always do, which is just talk about what happens in life. I mean, it's easier when the events of your life are completely unknown. Then it becomes harder the more people think they know what goes on in your life and imagine they know what the songs are about."[4]

> "I'm doing what I always do, which is just talk about what happens in life. I mean, it's easier when the events of your life are completely unknown. Then it becomes harder the more people think they know what goes on in your life and imagine they know what the songs are about."

He was satisfied at the time about the way the *I'm Alive* album turned out. He was full of emotions that he wanted to express at the time, and this set of ten recordings absorbed all of his feelings.

Also fitting was the black-and-white photograph by Bruce Weber on the cover of the album. Submerged in a pool of water up to his shoulders, Jackson appears to be emerging from the sea of despair, a sea in which he had been immersed when he wrote these ten highly autobiographical songs.

"It became really clear at a certain moment which songs I wanted to record," he claimed. "They're all songs about relationships. I suppose this album's more personal. It's very inside stuff. In that way, this is more like *Late for the Sky* than *Lives in the Balance*. The song 'Sky Blue and Black' on this album really reminds me of that time."[5]

When *I'm Alive* was released, critics were unanimously heralding it as a dramatic "comeback album" for Jackson Browne. He was able to look within himself and use these songs as an exercise of healing.

The critics instantly loved it. In *Rolling Stone*, reviewer Kara Manning proclaimed, "*I'm Alive* shudders with the pain of someone who's been soundly dumped. And Browne has gained a sense of gallows humor. Between despondent cries for reconciliation, the singer indulges in refreshingly silly self-deprecation...as *I'm Alive* moves on, Browne spirals more deeply into his agony. 'I'll Do Anything,' and 'Too Many Angels' and 'Take This Rain' vividly recall his earlier work. 'Sky Blue and Black,' shining with Browne's gentle piano and stream-of-consciousness regret, is one of his loveliest, saddest songs."[6]

Rob Tannenbaum of *GQ* magazine called *I'm Alive* "his best album since *Running on Empty*, Browne returns to personal lovelorn lyrics. Using jarringly simple language, Browne sketches the progress of emotions following the collapse of a relationship."[7]

In *Time*, Jay Cocks wrote, "*I'm Alive* is a duel between edgy resignation, of loving and hurtful recollection, and a cautionary wisdom that comes fresh from the skirmish on the front lines...the songs have the sting of oblique autobiography. This has been his way since his first album in 1971...but this time he has been undermined by the headlines....The album is one of the best and fiercest of a long career."[8]

In the *New York Times,* Stephen Holden wrote, "*I'm Alive* is a striking return to the kind of romantic subject matter that the Los Angeles singer and songwriter seemed to have abandoned after 1980 in favor of political songwriting. His finest album in nearly two decades, it has much in common with his 1974 masterpiece, *Late for the Sky*, whose songs also described the disintegration of a relationship....Mr. Browne speaks with the authority of someone who has risked a great deal to pursue a romantic ideal."[9]

Paul Evans of *Rolling Stone* cleverly claimed, "Putting Third World and rain forest politics on hold, Jackson Browne delivers a near-definitive collection of lost-love laments. Sinatra used to make brilliant records capturing a single mood; *I'm Alive* is that kind of tone poem, and its color is blue."[10]

Don Was, who coproduced two of the songs on the *I'm Alive* album, said of the recording's critical success, "I'm getting some feedback, along the lines of: 'Finally, it's a real Jackson Browne album, after a ten-year detour.' It's a great album, because he was truly passionate about what he was writing."[11]

The public seemed to agree as well: the side of Jackson Browne that everyone loved had officially returned. Released in October 1993, *I'm Alive* peaked at Number 35 in the United Kingdom and Number 40 in the United States. A steadily selling album, on December 6, 1995, it was certified "Gold" by the RIAA. Three singles were released off of it: "I'm Alive," "Sky Blue and Black," and "Everywhere I Go." The only song to make the charts was "Everywhere I Go," which spent a week at Number 67 in England. At this point in his career, his true genius was in albums like this one, and not in individual single hits.

Regarding the songs from the *I'm Alive* album that dealt with his breakup with Daryl, Don Was claimed, "He knew there was public interest in this, and he wanted to reply eloquently."[12]

Jackson said his dramatic breakup with Daryl Hannah ushered in "a change for the better." According to him, "The things I have to say to her have been said—in these songs."[13]

Finally, after the release of *I'm Alive,* he was able to speak in the press about the end of his ten-year affair with Daryl Hannah. Although it was good to hear him speaking about the "incident," he actually volunteered very little new information or details. "It's been hard to be sure," he said in late 1993. "What's very hard to live with, and could drive you around the bend, is when things are said about you that aren't true. I was accused of violence, and I deny it. What was described in the tabloids and in *People* magazine DID NOT happen. What *did* happen is not something I'm going to describe publicly.... I wanna tell people who read *People*, 'Get a life!' "[14]

If *People* magazine did get it wrong, then what actually did happen that fateful

> "I was accused of violence, and I deny it. What was described in the tabloids and in *People* magazine DID NOT happen. What *did* happen is not something I'm going to describe publicly.... I wanna tell people who read *People*, 'Get a life!' "

morning on September 23, 1992, between Daryl and Jackson? Browne was certainly not going to provide the specifics. According to him, "I'm not gonna say
what it was about, because it isn't anybody's business."[15]

However, he did point out, "Had I beaten her, would I have summoned the
police?"[16] Hmm, interesting point indeed.

But what about Daryl's black eye? Jackson only stated, "I realize that's very
damning. [I can't] describe publicly how that might have happened."

What about the "explosive personality" and his "blind rages"? Browne said,
"That's ridiculous. I mean, I have a temper like anybody. It bothers me that
that would be said. Because then anytime you're mad about anything...,"
then he suddenly stopped. Furthermore, he had to admit, "I realize to draw the
line [of explanation] there gives rise to a lot of questions."[17]

What did he think of the fact that the *I'm Alive* album was destined to be
perceived as a confession? "The thing is, there's nowhere to hide from that, and
it's...O.K. I'm not too worried about it," he stated.[18]

In 1983, Don Henley had released the song "Dirty Laundry," in which he
blasted the tabloid media over the way they had covered a certain incident
involving him. When a naked sixteen-year-old girl was discovered in Henley's
house, strung out on drugs, Don, too, had suddenly become the subject of
tabloid front-page news. The venomous song "Dirty Laundry" was his way
of getting back at the press. The single became a Number 3 hit, which de-
lighted Henley—as it fulfilled his plan to thumb his nose at the media.

Was Jackson planning on taking on *People* magazine and the tabloids by
writing a vengeful song? According to him, "I'm sure the [*I'm Alive*] album's
informed by that, but there's nothing retaliatory. I mean, Don always used to
write reviewers back, too. I actually had a song I was writing called 'People
Believe It,' in which the analogies were professional wrestling and the Reagan
and [George H.W.] Bush administrations. And I didn't finish that song for this
album, because along with all the other songs, it would seem like a defense. I
chose not to do that. As for the tabloid stuff, it's no secret that things are dis-
torted and exploited and lied about in those publications. For me to engage in
a defense would have been pretty futile."[19]

The interesting thing about Jackson's statements about his final argument
with Daryl was that he simply claimed it wasn't true. But he never said what
part of it was true and what wasn't true. Where did the black eye come from?
What really did happen? Neither one of them was talking.

With regard to the way this whole mess made him look in the press, he proclaimed, "I'm resigned to my perpetual status as a rock & roll villain."[20]

Well, apparently not everyone believed Jackson's side of the story. When Daryl Hannah appeared on the cover of *Harper's Bazaar* magazine in December 1993, writer Roy Blount Jr. came to her defense. "Why would anyone hit her?" he wrote. "I can't even imagine asking her about all those stories in the tabloids last year, about her old beau Jackson Browne getting violent with her, and Kennedy flying to her side."[21]

However, the most damning bit of press came when Joni Mitchell released her 1994 album *Turbulent Indigo*. On the album, she included the song "Not to Blame." In the song, Joni sings lyrics to the effect of: With all of your humanistic political causes, how does it feel to have your fist marks on the face of "the beauty" you supposedly love? In the song, Mitchell also indicts all of Jackson's male buddies who've rallied around him unquestioningly. She even goes so far as to paraphrase Don Henley's line in *People* magazine, where he said he would gamble his fame and fortune on a bet that Jackson was innocent. That was clearly the end of Joni's friendship with Jackson.

Although Mitchell reportedly sidestepped admission that the villain in the song was Jackson Browne, it certainly describes the "alleged" Hannah-Browne scuffle point for point. The song does move on to also confront battered women in general. However, the first thirteen lines of lyrics match the Browne story, which—as Joni sings—made headlines from "coast to coast."

A year later, Daryl was still with John F. Kennedy Jr. In an interesting career move, for her next film project she produced and starred in a made-for-TV remake of the 1950s' science-fiction kitsch classic *Attack of the 50 Ft. Woman*. Starring as Nancy, Hannah plays a woman who has a philandering husband. However, she seems to always keep her anger in check. When a flying saucer from outer space zaps her with a laser beam, her hormones go into overdrive and she grows to be fifty feet tall. Finally, midway through the movie she is pushed by her husband to the point where she must finally act out her rage. As the fifty-foot giantess, Nancy goes to kick her husband's ass. She announces to her psychiatrist, "I'm just looking for a little closure, that's all." In a fit of fury, fifty-foot Nancy is set on wrecking the whole town if necessary to find her husband. Was this Daryl's way of working through the anger she might be feeling toward Jackson?

At the same time that *I'm Alive* was in the stores, Daryl Hannah was seen kicking her man's ass in the vengeful *Attack of the 50 Ft. Woman*.

Meanwhile, Browne was as busy as ever with concert dates and promoting *I'm Alive*. With regard to his diminished record sales of late, Jackson claimed, "I've been accused of not wanting to sell records in the past. I mean, I'd like to sell a lot of records, but clearly it matters less to me whether my albums sell than whether or not I get to the heart of the matter."[22] Well, he clearly got to the heart of the matter this time around.

He was also winning plaudits from the critics, as he set off for a two-month concert tour of the United States, beginning in January 1994. On February 18, he was headlining the Paramount, which was the new name for the former Felt Forum at Madison Square Garden in New York City. Years ago, he was the opening act for the Eagles there. On this tour, he played the majority of the songs from the *I'm Alive* album, plus several of his classics like "Doctor My Eyes," "Late for the Sky," "Before the Deluge," "Sleep's Dark and Silent Gate," "The Pretender," "In the Shape of the Heart," and "These Days."

On May 24, as part of a promotion with Scholastic and Jackson's record company, Elektra Entertainment, he presented a plaque to Clarissa J. Markiewicz, a contest winner. Browne played a forty-five-minute concert for her. The presentation took place in Rochester, New York.

June 1994 found Browne on tour in Europe, where he headlined the Royal Albert Hall in London. He was the main stage performer at the Glastonbury Festival in Somerset, England. The following month he launched a tour of the United States. The opening night date was the Mann Music Center in Philadelphia, Pennsylvania. The popular *I'm Alive* tour concluded on August 30, when he performed in San Diego, California, at the Summer Pops Bowl.

While he was on the road to support his *I'm Alive* album, Jackson lent his voice to a couple of other albums. In 1994, he sang a duet on the song "Unloved" with Jann Arden on her album *Living Under June*. And in 1995, he rerecorded his composition "Rock Me on the Water" as a duet with country star Kathy Mattea on the album *Red Hot & Country*.

In August 1994, the Disney Channel presented a ninety-minute TV special starring Jackson Browne. As part of a series of musical specials Disney produced during this period, entitled *Going Home: Jackson Browne*, he is the subject of the entire fascinating hour and a half. *Going Home* blends interview footage, great upclose musical performances, and some rare vintage video of Browne and his musician buddies.

On camera, the troubadour is very relaxed and forthcoming about his long and varied career. Filmed during his *I'm Alive* era tours, the special presents Browne at his performing peak and shows what he is all about as a songwriter and entertainer.

One of the most interesting segments of the *Going Home* special shows the singer/songwriter in his massive workroom in his current house. Surrounded by mountains of cardboard boxes full of memorabilia, writing pads, file folders, and musical instruments, he speaks of his life and his creative process.

"I think this is Greg Copeland poetry," he says to the camera, as he is going through an old file folder. He reads a piece of the poetry aloud and then explains, "Greg Copeland is the guy who made me want to write songs. He and Steve Noonan were songwriting partners and they went to my high school, and they were my sister's friends, and they let me hang around. And, watching these guys write songs, is what made me want to write songs."[23] This introduction makes the perfect transition to segue into the song "These Days."

Going Home is filled with such charming moments. It also includes special interview segments with David Lindley, David Crosby, Don Henley, Graham Nash, and Jennifer Warnes. One of the rare performances that appears on this special entails Browne sitting down at the piano and performing the long-forgotten song "Birds of St. Marks," which is about Nico.

One of the best song performances on the special finds Jackson singing a version of his song "Lives in the Balance," with David Lindley sitting in, and Crosby and Nash singing the background vocals. There is also a nice segment of Browne working on the lyrics to "Too Many Angels."

Among the great vintage footage that *Going Home* includes is a clip of him in 1974 performing on stage with the Eagles singing "Your Bright Baby Blues," dressing room footage of Browne and Lindley singing "Take It Easy," and performance video from the 1979 MUSE concerts. Two of the rarest performances from this video are a pair of songs of protest: "Good Morning Little Mutant" and a great version of Bob Dylan's "All Along the Watchtower." Some of the footage was also shot at Abbey San Encino.

Released on video (and eventually DVD), this special stands as an incredible up close look at Jackson in his absolute prime. Although "World in Motion" and "Lives in the Balance" are two of the many songs he performs here, *Going Home: Jackson Browne* is totally entertaining and not heavy-handed. It does, however, lightly touch on his impassioned political views. A wonderfully conceived and produced video, it is heavy on song performances—twenty-three in all. *Going Home: Jackson Browne* is an excellent audio/visual "greatest hits" package.

Another documentary video from this era is *Nico: Icon*. Released in 1995, it includes new and vintage interviews with John Cale, Viva, Paul Morrissey, Jim Morrison, Lou Reed, Andy Warhol, and Jackson Browne. Although she had continued to pursue her avante-garde career, Nico was haunted by heroin addiction. Tragically, she died in Ibiza, Spain, in July 1988 of a brain hemorrhage. Since that time, she is now viewed as a legendary cult figure—especially among Andy Warhol devotees.

On September 2, 1995, Jackson was one of the many performers to perform at the Concert for the Rock and Roll Hall of Fame. Held at Cleveland Stadium in Cleveland, Ohio, the concert was also a huge simulcast TV special and ultimately a two-CD album. He sang "Songs of Freedom" and "Redemption Song." He also performed a duet with Melissa Etheridge on the song "Wake up Little Susie." The following year, his rendition of "Redemption Song" appeared on the resulting CD.

On October 7, he was in Sedona, Arizona, as one of the performers at the Sixth Annual Music Festival, which was a fund-raising event for the Native American Scholarship Fund. Whenever there was a cause that needed attention, Browne could always be counted on to lend his time and talent.

During this period, the most highly publicized charity event he was involved in took place on November 5, 1995, at Avery Fisher Hall in Lincoln Center, New York City. The money raised from that night and the resulting TV special, album, and video went to the Children's Defense League. It was a live all-star restaging of *The Wizard of Oz*, with Jewel as Dorothy, Roger Daltrey as the Tin Woodsman, Nathan Lane as the Cowardly Lion, and Jackson Browne as the Scarecrow.

After years and years of maintaining a career that cast him as the singer of serious songs about heartbreak, frustrating relationships, and political causes, this was a brilliant 180-degree turn for him. In years past, Jackson would never have considered a move this light hearted, and the outcome was delightful.

In addition to the four seekers of "a brain," "a heart," "courage," and "a home," the impressive cast included Natalie Cole as Glinda the Good Witch, Debra Winger as the Wicked Witch, Lucie Arnaz as Auntie Em, and Joel Grey as the Wizard. There were also special musical appearances by Phoebe Snow, Ronnie Spector, David Sanborn, Ry Cooder, and Dr. John.

Dressed in overalls and a straw hat, Jackson was great as the Scarecrow. His one solo number was "If I Only Had a Brain," which was one of the highlights of the evening. Browne was also one of the singers of the ensemble songs "We're Off to See the Wizard," "Lions, Tigers, and Bears," "If I Only Had the Nerve," the finale version of "Somewhere over the Rainbow," and several other bits of dialogue between the major songs. One of the most fun numbers he performed in as part of the ensemble—with Jewel, Lane, and Daltrey—was "The Jitterbug."

> Dressed in overalls and a straw hat, Jackson was great as the Scarecrow. His one solo number was "If I Only Had a Brain," which was one of the highlights of the evening.

"The Jitterbug" was in the original prerelease version of the 1939 film *The Wizard of Oz*. However, it was deleted because the film was running long. The footage is still missing, but rehearsal video and a rough mix of the audio presentation of the musical number still exist and are available on the DVD version of the film. This marked the first major presentation of that number in any context.

The concert was produced as a TV special for the TNT network, which broadcast on November 22, 1995. The following year both a video tape and an album version of this unique concert event were also released, under the name *The Wizard of Oz in Concert: Dreams Come True*.

Also in 1995, Jackson was one of the guest stars heard on Bonnie Raitt's live set, *Road Tested*. The album was taped in front of live audiences in July of that year, in Portland, Oregon, and in Oakland, California. On the album, Jackson can be heard singing a duet version of his song "My Opening Farewell" with Raitt. He then joined Bonnie, Bruce Hornsby, and Kim Wilson—of the Fabulous Thunderbirds—for an all-star quartet version of the John Prine song "Angel from Montgomery." These two guest appearances were also part of the Bonnie Raitt TV special that ran that year. The special became the DVD *Bonnie Raitt: Road Tested*, which was released in 2001.

Bonnie explained of Browne's appearance on her album and special, "Jackson was in the middle of making his [latest] record, so he flew up [to Oakland] the day before we shot and recorded, and we only had a couple of [rehearsals] with him. He has never sung his song in a different key and tried to sing a harmony part. He was a real champ to do it."[24]

Following his two controversial but unsuccessful political albums, it seemed that his altercation with Daryl Hannah made him take a good hard look at what he was doing with his life. With his *I'm Alive* album, he had returned to the kind of songwriting and perform- ing that originally drew audiences to him. Participating in *The Wizard of Oz* concert was a sign that he was feeling confident enough with his singing talent to stretch out and try new things. Not only was he "alive," but Jackson Browne was now back on top of his game. Again, it was time for him to move in a forward direction.

> Following his two controversial but unsuccessful political albums, it seemed that his altercation with Daryl Hannah made him take a good hard look at what he was doing with his life.

CHAPTER 14

Looking East

JACKSON STARTED OUT 1996 WITH THE RELEASE of his eleventh album, *Looking East*. This was a whole new and unique set of recordings for him. After years of operating mainly as a solo singer and songwriter, he turned this disc into a true band release.

He found that he was so in tune with the band he had toured with in 1994, that after he had released *I'm Alive*, he asked them to contribute their musical ideas to his writing. What he came up with was a much more varied-sounding album, both in style and subject matter. *Looking East* was to be Browne's musical vignette tour of Los Angeles. And, who better to assist him but his Los Angeles–based band?

In the late 1980s, Jackson had started writing songs with one of his bandmates for the *World in Motion* album, and he found that they had a great creative rapport together. According to Browne, "I made this record with a really good friend of mine and the co-producer I worked with on my last record—Scott Thurston. He's been in my band for years and we've worked together a lot."[1]

The next thing you know, he decided to let his whole band in on the writing process. In varying groupings, Jackson's writing partners on *Looking East* were Jeff Young, Kevin McCormick, Scott Thurston, Mark Goldenberg, Mauricio Lewak, Luis Conte, Jeff Cohen, Jorge Calderón, and Valerie Carter. Only two songs on the album were written by Jackson himself.

He describes the songs on *Looking East* as being "L.A.-centric. I'm not from middle America, I'm from L.A. I recognize that I don't have a middle American point of view, even though this place has the same social struggles that go on in the rest of the country. Now, the more serious problems that confront contemporary America are all pervasive. There are Crips and Bloods in small towns in Mississippi now."[2]

According to him, "Most of my songs have used metaphors to tell a story. Some have been about subjects that might take many pages to describe in detail. But when I write, I'm really trying to access something we already know.... The songs on this record are meant to be different components of a whole experience. No life is completely outward-looking and social in its focus."[3]

> "Most of my songs have used metaphors to tell a story. Some have been about subjects that might take many pages to describe in detail. But when I write, I'm really trying to access something we already know...."

Looking East was released on February 13, 1996. One of the most interesting aspects of this album was that he also acquiesced to turn over the role of producer to his band mates Scott Thurston and Kevin McCormick. The result was great, and the songs "The Barricades of Heaven" and "I'm the Cat" are two of the best and most appealing songs Jackson Browne has ever recorded.

The album gets off to a rocking start on the title cut. In the first lines of the song, Browne sings of standing with his feet in the waters of the Pacific Ocean, looking eastward, and essentially seeing the whole country of the United States from where he stands. It perfectly matches the album's cover photo: Browne facing east, as the sun goes down behind him in the watery West Coast horizon.

As he looks east, he seeks the meaning of it all. He sings that there is "power" everywhere and that there is also "hunger" everywhere. A rousing rocker, "Looking East" makes it clear that the politically questioning Jackson Browne is back in power here.

"The Barricades of Heaven" is simply beautiful. Recalling the power of "These Days," he looks back on his life, from the perspective of his forty-eighth year. He sings of his childhood and running around the beach cities—a backdrop where his teenage years were played out. He sings of being sixteen, playing in all those rock and folk clubs in California, and the dreams he had way back then. The pages are turning, turning on the calendar. As he taps into that same youthful sense of wonderment and possibility, he hopes it will never end. This song is catchy, lively, eclectic guitar–driven, and very successfully executed.

The same formula is used on "Some Bridges." Here he sings that some bridges are still standing and fulfilling their purpose of allowing journeys, while other bridges are broken and falling. He uses this as a simile for interpersonal relationships, between individuals and society in general. As he walks down the streets of Los Angeles, he spots kids who are destined for trouble, and other people who always do well—as though they have the Midas touch.

"Some Bridges" was reportedly partially inspired by a California high school choir with which Jackson had recently worked: the Hamilton High School Gospel Choir in Los Angeles. "I began to work with this choir nearly a year ago," he explained at the time. "They're starting out their lives in this school and they're approaching a world that is more difficult to succeed in every day. The bridge that I'm talking about is not only a bridge between people, but a bridge between people and where they want to go. The ladder by which some people can better themselves is being dismantled. When I'm saying 'some bridges are falling down, some bridges are still around,' I'm saying there's still an opportunity to make contact; there's something very precious at stake and it's not all gone yet."[4]

The Hamilton High School Gospel Choir would go on to record a live version of Jackson's song "World in Motion" with Browne. It was released on the Japanese edition of *Looking East* and on the B-side of the U.S. cassette single of "Some Bridges."

In the song "Information Wars," Jackson takes on the hypocrisy of the mass media that invades our minds twenty-four hours a day. He questions the sense of it all: people claiming they are helping the planet, while simultaneously raping Earth. Again, he tackles the corporate machinery, and again, he sees the ironies and finds no answers. He has the background singers wail out slogans like the "heartbeat" of America and "your true voice," making jarring use of Madison Avenue–styled slogans to sell poisonous ideas. It is Jackson Browne at his most musically cunning, brilliantly driving his point home.

> In the song "Information Wars," Jackson takes on the hypocrisy of the mass media that invades our minds twenty-four hours a day. He questions the sense of it all: people claiming they are helping the planet, while simultaneously raping Earth.

"I'm the Cat" really should have gone on to become as successful a single as

"Somebody's Baby" did in the early 1980s. It is that clever and catchy. Here, to a bubbly rock ballad beat, Jackson sings of being the hip "cat" someone needs in her life. He sounds playful, as he professes to be the "cat" who loves to give affection when he wants to and who also likes his time to roam alone. It is the perfect analogy for Browne, and it is a catchy, rhythmic delight.

"Culver Moon" is a stylish and fun homage to Los Angeles. He sings of many of Los Angeles's most blatant landmarks: it's the city where the Lakers are from, where huge posters of the busty Angelyne stare downward at you, and where the Chippendales strip for you. Reminiscent of Randy Newman's similar ode to that town, "L.A. (I Love It)," here, Jackson takes the Bruce Springsteen title "Cover Me" and blends it with Los Angeles's movie studios in Culver City to come up with "Culver Moon." According to Browne, 'It is a love song."[5] It is indeed hard not to love the silliness and blatantness of Los Angeles and this ode to it.

"Baby How Long" sounds suspiciously like a continuation of the themes from his *I'm Alive* album. In this bluesy, slow, and peculating number with twanging guitars, he accuses his former lover of having another man lined up all the time she was with him. It seems logical to assume that Daryl Hannah is the woman in this song. If you listen closely, you can hear Bonnie Raitt singing her heart out in the background. This is one of the pair of songs Browne penned solo on this LP.

The song "Nino" is Jackson Browne to a revved-up salsa beat. He proves that his biggest strongpoint in songwriting is viewing something and seeing the inspiration in it—much like a painter does.

This song took its inspiration from most of the members of the band with whom Jackson was playing and composing. "Nino" is an homage to his Cuban-born percussionist Luis Conte. Jackson explains, " 'Nino' is sort of a portrait of Luis, a kid away from his family who was thinking about home, having been transplanted into a completely unfamiliar environment. For me the song touches on a very simple and profound idea which is that we all carry the means to make ourselves happy, and the means to get where we want to go in life."[6]

According to him, "A lot of these songs were born out of spontaneous jamming and sound-checking, when a musician would start playing something interesting while he was checking his instrument."[7] To complete the Latin flavor of the music on "Nino," Jackson even sings eight lines of the chorus to this song in Spanish himself.

"Alive in the World" is the other song on the *Looking East* album that Jackson Browne wrote all by himself. And what a beautiful song it is. It is a thankful song, in which the troubadour captures that youthful wonderment that infused his early classic compositions. Here, he is older and wiser, and most of all, "alive in the world." This is one of the high points of the album.

The album ends on the light reggae number "It Is One." Pleasant sounding, it is also a bit of "Jackson Browne Lite." It is not a bad song, but it isn't lively enough to come across like a Jimmy Buffet–style reggae anthem, nor is it dramatic enough to emerge as memorable.

Guest appearances on the *Looking East* album include Bonnie Raitt, long-time buddy David Lindley, Vonda Shepard (of *Ally McBeal* fame), David Crosby, and a guest guitar appearance by Ry Cooder.

> "It's made it one of the most collaborative albums I've done," Jackson claims. "In the collaborative spirit of the record we included a number of friends and influences to complete the landscape."

"It's made it one of the most collaborative albums I've done," Jackson claims. "In the collaborative spirit of the record we included a number of friends and influences to complete the landscape."[8]

The reviews for *Looking East* were consistently strong. In *Entertainment Weekly*, Tony Scherman raved, "Browne's 11th album, is his first real attempt to fuse the personal and the political. . . . He wants to live in both, of course, and makes a tentative effort in 'Some Bridges,' locating his ruminating lover in class-divided L.A., not some Jacksonian inner landscape. 'Culver Moon' is Browne's breakthrough: musically raw, lyrically caustic, an ode to love and lust in a decomposing world. . . . The album's overall message is clear: He intends to keep growing. Without taking himself too seriously, either—'I'm the Cat,' which has no social agenda whatsoever, is Browne's most infectious tune since 'Somebody's Baby.' . . . In his last album, he had to tell us he was alive; here, he proves it."[9]

Stephen Holden wrote in the *New York Times*, "In 'Information Wars,' the most provocative cut on Jackson Browne's new album, *Looking East*, Mr. Browne, a 47-year-old Los Angeles singer and songwriter, mounts an attack on America's television culture that includes an ingenious collage of variations on familiar advertising slogans. Reiterated without their brand names, the slogans are turned against themselves in a way that reveals the Orwellian seductiveness of television."[10]

Although *Looking East* is an inconsistent album, it has several hidden gems like "I'm the Cat" and "The Barricades of Heaven." "Some Bridges" and "Alive in the World" are engaging as well. Unlike the *I'm Alive* album, which captured one mood brilliantly, this album is a bit all over the map, and in that way it failed to really capture a strong audience.

The *Looking East* album actually charted higher than *I'm Alive* had, peaking at Number 36 in the United States and Number 47 in England. The songs "Some Bridges" and "I'm the Cat" were released as singles, but neither charted.

Jackson spent much of 1996 on a highly varied concert tour of the United States and Europe. On June 18, he opened the nine-date British and Irish leg of his *Looking East* tour, commencing with an evening at the Colston Hall in Bristol, England. October 17 found him at a benefit concert at New York's City Center Theater. On the bill with Carly Simon, Lisa Loeb, Steve Earle, Bruce Cockburn, and NRBQ, Browne's performance helped raise money for the Rainforest Alliance. The concert was billed as "Smartsounds: Music for the Planet."

According to Jackson, while on tour his old material worked well with the songs from his *Looking East* album. "In the show now, 'Looking East' comes right after 'Rock Me on the Water,'" he claims. "It happened as an accident, but it's unmistakable for me in the course of doing a show what works, so there it stays. It's the album's title song, but I think it's one of the hardest songs for my audience to get into, and it's working. 'Rock Me on the Water' is about the '60s, the Watts riots and reading *Soul on Ice* and Bobby Seale's book. That whole idea of a city in flames and trying to find some sort of redemption in all of that has sort of come full circle with 'Looking East.' It has a political context but it's not a specific political problem; it's the social context for a song. I guess whether I was consciously avoiding it or not, I didn't want to write a song that was a list; I don't want to catalogue what's wrong with the world as much as refer to it and try to get to the heart of it. And so it winds up getting into spiritual territory, like 'Rock Me on the Water.' Because the world is the way it is because we're the way we are. I'm sitting here, and I know it's not the Great Satan, it's just the Great Fuck-up, the great snarl and tangle of commerce and people confusing commerce with progress, lifestyles with redemption."[11]

With regard to his songwriting, Jackson Browne claims, "I've been a compulsive sense-maker. I've always wanted to have an impact immediately, so the song could be consciously digested to engage the listener's attention. You get a lot the first time, but like with a book or the movie, just by nature of what music is, there's always something you don't get until later. The more somebody can affix their own experience and imagery to a song, the better experience it's gonna be for them."[12]

> "I've always believed that every aspect of life is worth writing about," Browne says.

He somehow remains consistently able to turn the several twists that his life makes into songs. He claims to enjoy the journey, as much as he enjoys the attainment of his goals. "I've always believed that every aspect of life is worth writing about," Browne says.[13]

For critics and fans alike, it seems that there are two different sides of Jackson. There is the sensitive, introspective side of him. And there is the deeply political side of him. Does he feel that there are two of him? "It's like Little Steven says, 'What's more personal than your political beliefs?'" he claims. "Personal and political aren't poles, they aren't on opposite sides of anything. But personal and public are. So when people write stuff like that, what they mean really is songs about love or personal experiences that are not on sociological themes go over here, everything else goes over there. It's an inadequate description. That whole discussion is really framed by the writer's own grasp of the world. One critic who didn't like 'Lives in the Balance' wasn't far off when he said that the song was more of a speech that needed to be made, so call it what you want."[14]

Indeed, his passion for inserting political messages in his songs is still very important to him. As he explains it, "I think the real question is whether or not the song succeeds. I don't have to look too far into that argument to see that what it means is A) they're not interested in hearing about this stuff, or B) they're not interested in hearing it from me. The politer version of that is, 'Why should we listen to a singer about nuclear power?' Or, 'Why should someone I'm used to hearing sing about love—tell us about human rights?' The answer to that is that, 'All those things are part of life, and my job is to write about life.'"[15]

What does he consider a successful socially conscious song? "There are a number of models for successful political songs," he says. "One of my favorites is Sting's 'They Dance Alone.' It's an appropriated image: What he did was come on a situation and transmitted this image of Chilean women dancing without their partners because they had 'disappeared.' It was illegal for them to demonstrate; they could've been shot. So they did the national dance without their husbands, and that was a statement that was impossible to ignore in that country. So Sting did those women, that country, the cause of human rights—a great service just by transmitting that image. So the criterion shouldn't be whether or not it's political; it should be whether or not it succeeds. Is [Billie Holiday's] 'Strange Fruit' less good because it's political?"[16]

"Strange Fruit" is one of the most fascinating and disturbing popular songs ever written. It is about the lynching of black men in the South. The allusive comparison of bodies swinging in the Southern trees to "strange fruit" is indeed an effective poetic image. It works in the same ways that Jackson's own songs do.

Throughout 1997, Jackson toured to promote his *Looking East* album. On July 26, 1997, he performed at the Cambridge Folk Festival in Cambridge, England. And on September 26, he made a rare TV show appearance on *Late Night with David Letterman*.

Jackson was also heard in 1997 on the album *Rock and Roll Doctor*. The album was a tribute to Browne's late buddy Lowell George, and the troubadour performed the song "I've Been the One." Other Lowell George classics on the album include "Cold Cold Cold" by Little Feat and Bonnie Raitt, "Roll um Easy" by John David Souther, "Sailin' Shoes" by Valerie Carter, "Long Distance Love" by Merry Clayton, and "Straight from the Heart" by Chris Hillman.

After twenty-five years of being a recording artist, on September 23, 1997, Elektra Records released the long-overdue Jackson Browne "greatest hits" album: *The Next Voice You Hear: The Best of Jackson Browne*. A single-disc set, it gathered together—in chronological order—thirteen of his chart hits and memorable album cuts, and added two new songs to it. "Doctor My Eyes," "These Days," "Fountain of Sorrow," "Late for the Sky," "The Pretender," and

"Running on Empty" were all gathered together on one album, at last. How-ever, there were several favorites from this era that did not make the cut, in-cluding the vital Jackson Browne gems "Take It Easy," "Rock Me on the Water," "For Everyman," and "Before the Deluge." As the biggest hit single of his entire career, finally "Somebody's Baby" makes an appearance on one of Browne's al-bums. The next six songs represent a good sampling of his later output, taking one cut from almost all of his albums, right up to—and including—*Looking East.* "Call It a Loan," "Tender Is the Night, "In the Shape of a Heart," "Lives in the Balance," "Sky Blue and Black," and "The Barricades of Heaven" bring this retrospective disc up to the present. The one album that was ignored was the disappointing *World in Motion.*

The two new cuts on the album are "The Rebel Jesus" and "The Next Voice You Hear." "The Rebel Jesus" was a song that he had recorded with the Irish group the Chieftains in 1991 on their album *The Bells of Dublin.* Here, he pre-sents his own version of the song, with David Lindley and several of his own current band members. The album finishes off with an excellent, hollow, and futuristic-sounding track, "The Next Voice You Hear." On it, Browne warns that "the next voice you hear" just may be the sound of your own lonely voice. Especially memorable is Jon Hassell's eerie trumpet playing, all muted as through a fog. And Jackson sounds very driven and attached to the message he is delivering. A fresh and memorable track, it is haunting and hypnotic and is totally worthy of being included on this well-received "greatest hits" package.

Easily, *The Next Voice You Hear* could have grown into a two-disc set. "Golden Slumbers" with Jennifer Warnes, the duet version of "My Opening Farewell" with Bonnie Raitt, and "Stay" with Bruce Springsteen would all be worthy special inclusions to this package. Likewise, some of his biggest hits singles were left out, including "Here Come Those Tears Again," "Boulevard," and "That Girl Could Sing."

The Next Voice You Hear peaked at Number 47 on the *Billboard* charts in the United States. It was also certified "Gold" for selling over a half-million copies. If someone wanted to own just a single Jackson Browne album, this would unarguably be it. It is a good mixture of all of his eras as a recording artist, a composer, and a performer.

Meanwhile, Browne's other albums continued to sell as well. On December 12, 1997, the RIAA certified the *Jackson Browne* (1972) album as having attained

"Platinum" or million-selling status. And that same day, *The Pretender* (1976) was certified as being "Double Platinum."

The release of one's "greatest hits" album is always a career move of reminiscing. As *The Next Voice You Hear* sold well in the stores, it was a time for Browne fans to be reminded of his songwriting strengths and for new listeners to gain a highly accessible view of his impressive career and his most masterfully unforgettable songs.

CHAPTER 15

The Naked Ride Home

JACKSON KEPT BUSY THROUGHOUT 1998 by performing for several charity events as well as by headlining a North American tour with Bonnie Raitt and Eric Clapton. From that point through the millennium, he continued to record and tour—both with his band and as a solo performer—alone on the naked stage. He continued to tackle new political issues with his music and to appear on the albums of several of his friends. And his own recording career was to grow and evolve.

He even started to be acknowledged for the merits of his vast creativity. Jackson was never one to pursue or seek out honors. Throughout his four decades as a recording artist, his career certainly never centered on any one major hit record or group of hits. However, viewed during the period of his fiftieth birthday, his accomplishments were certainly many. And finally he was about to be recognized for his talent by his peers.

On February 20 and 21, 1998, Jackson took part in a series of concerts as part of a memorial for singer Nicolette Larson. Larson had passed away on December 16, 1997, from a cerebral edema. As well as being an in-demand background singer, she is also known for her own solo hit "Lotta Love." After years of singing behind Linda Ronstadt, Emmylou Harris, Neil Young, the Doobie Brothers, Graham Nash, Rodney Crowell, and several others, in 1979 she released her own solo album, *Nicolette*. When "Lotta Love" hit Number 8 in the United States, she began a solo career.

Her live version of "Lotta Love," with the Doobie Brothers as her band, graces the *No Nukes* album. She followed that up with hits like "Rhumba Girl" and "Let Me Go Love," with Michael McDonald. In 1990, she married drummer Russell Kunkel, who has played with Jackson Browne on and off throughout the years.

The *Lotta Love* concerts in Nicolette's honor raised money for the UCLA Children's Hospital Foundation. Also on the bill with Jackson were Bonnie Raitt, Carole King, Rosemary Butler, and Crosby, Stills & Nash.

On March 17, 1998, the album *Where Have All the Flowers Gone: The Songs of Pete Seeger* was released. Included on it was the first studio-recorded duet that Jackson had done with Bonnie Raitt. Their cut on the album was a slowed down reggae version of the song "Kisses Sweeter Than Wine," which was one of the prime hits of the disc.

Talk about hootenanny night! The Pete Seeger tribute put Jackson on an album with several rock and folk singing greats, including Richie Havens, Judy Collins, Donovan, Odetta, Tom Paxton, the Weavers, Bruce Springsteen, John Gorka, Holly Near, Roger McGuinn of the Byrds, and Peter, Paul, and Mary.

He performed at the Sing out for Seva benefit concert on May 15, 1998, at the Berkeley Community Theater in San Francisco. The event was organized by 1960s rocker Wavy Gravy. And, on October 7, 1998, he performed an all-acoustic benefit to raise funds for the election campaign of Loretta Sanchez. The event was held at the Chapman University Auditorium in Orange, California.

Jackson Browne turned fifty on October 9, 1998. Although he thought about taking a month-long vacation to celebrate, he had other things to do. On October 18, he was one of the performers at the tribute for the late Beach Boy Carl Wilson. Carl had died on February 6, 1998, of lung cancer. The event was held at The Roxy, on Sunset Boulevard in Los Angeles.

In January 1999, when the Grammy Award nominations were announced, the Jackson Browne and Bonnie Raitt duet on "Kisses Sweeter Than Wine" was among the nominations for the category of Best Pop Collaboration with Vocals. Although they did not take home the award, it was to mark the one and only time he had come close to winning a Grammy Award. It is odd to think that with all of the great recordings he has produced, he has never received one of the trophies.

In 2000, Jackson Browne appeared on several other people's albums. The most dramatic one was his duet version of Bob Dylan's "My Back Pages" with Joan Osborne. It appeared on the soundtrack album from the film *Steal This Movie*. It was about Abby Hoffman and Jerry Rubin and the whole countercultural scene in the late 1960s. He also contributed a new version of his song of re-membrance "For a Dancer." It included harmony vocals by the band Venice, from the Venice album 2 *Meter Sessies*. And he recorded the song "A Man of Constant Sorrow" with Sharon Shannon and friends from her album *The Diamond Mountain Sessions*.

Catching Jackson live in concert during one of his dates in 2000, *Front Row News* reported that he was in great spirits on stage. "I probably wouldn't have written this song at the age I am now," he claimed as he went into the intro to the infamous masturbation ode, "Rosie." As the laughter in the audience died down, he said, "By the way, did I mention this song is not *about* me?"[1]

Giving an intro to "For a Dancer," he said of the late Scott Runyon, "This tune is about a friend of mine who was a very unusual guy. He was an ice skater, a tailor, a painter, and a dancer. He made his clothes, and even made his girlfriend's gown!"[2]

The song "Guantanamera" was recorded and released as a duet between Joan Baez and Jackson, and it appeared on the 2001 album *If I Had a Song: The Songs of Pete Seeger*.

Meanwhile, Jackson's own classic albums have continued to sell steadily throughout the years. On August 31, 2001, the RIAA certified the *Hold Out* (1980) album as "Double Platinum" in the United States. The same day, *Lawyers in Love* (1983) was certified "Platinum."

In February 2002, Browne was named as the fourth recipient of the John Steinbeck Award. The honor was bestowed on him during the centennial cele-bration of the famed native California writer's birth. The honor is presented to creative people whose works best exemplify the environmental and social val-ues of John Steinbeck. The previous recipients of this honor have included the acclaimed filmmaker John Sayles, the famed playwright Arthur Miller, and Jackson's rock musician buddy Bruce Springsteen.

"With this record, I began to not say anything to the band. I stopped leading and trying to make it go anywhere at all. Music is so much more a complete form of commun-ication than words. Words are so rudimentary."

It had been six years since his last full album of new material, when on September 24, 2002, Jackson Browne released his thir-teenth album. On *The Naked Ride Home*, Jackson claims that the recipe for success came from some "great accidents." He says, "With this record, I began to not say anything to the band. I stopped leading and trying to make it go anywhere at all. Music is so much more a complete form of communication than words. Words are so rudimentary."[3]

Handling the producing duties on this new album was Jackson and coproducer Kevin McCormick. He wrote four of the songs on his own, and the other five songs he wrote with the members of his newest band: Kevin McCormick, Mark Goldenberg, Mauricio Lewak, and Jeff Young.

The Naked Ride Home is one of Jackson's most eclectic albums. With a band new to his recordings, he sounds great here—and with a fine voice. The title track kicks off the album. A slow, rhythmic rocker, Jackson dares his girlfriend to take off her clothes and get in the car—just like the song title proclaims. He looks across the car to see his nude passenger, a girl who is unable to resist a reckless dare.

In "The Night Inside Me," Jackson thinks about what the darkness of night has meant to him through all of his life. When he was young, it freed him. To him, night represents both "promise and uncertainty."

One of the most curious but apt songs on the album is "Casino Nation." On the surface, it would seem that Jackson is using this song to express his feelings about how the once-noble North American Indian tribes have turned into twenty-first-century gambling casino owners, but that is only part of the picture on this song. He sings of the dichotomy of how the United States professes to embrace Jesus, while producing millions of lethal firearms. Rather cryptically, he sings of the modern age, of Ruby Ridge, and reality TV. Whatever it is he is trying to say with this song never quite crystalizes, and the song seems to ramble.

"For Taking the Trouble" has a nice, almost slow and jazzy feeling to it, while he sings with Bob Dylan–like talk-phrasing. He sings of a girl whom he obviously loves and wonders who she is loving now. The final stanza finds Browne mimicking the song "Iko Iko," as he sings about the girl's grandma. This song seems strangely undeveloped, and ultimately there is no hook to it.

More effective is the song "Never Stop." Here, he again sings to a lover, this time around he hopes she never stops loving him and being supportive of him. As slow and pensive as "For Taking the Trouble," "Never Stop" has more of a pleasant and bolstering tone to it.

Stepping into a bit of a blues beat, in "Walking Town" he sings of people driving around in their air conditioned cars, never really experiencing what the town is really all about, since they never walk through their town. Thematically, it covers the same idea that Ashford and Simpson addressed in their 1980s song "Nobody Walks in L.A." Here, Jackson seems to be walking around in circles, making observations about the streets and the rooftops of his "Walking Town" in little vignettes.

Jackson picks up the pace a bit for "About My Imagination." Lyrically, he sings about the acid trip he took as a teenager. For him, it was a time when he knew what life is all about. Now, he is not so sure. The most telling line in this song is one in which he proclaims that he wouldn't have a songwriting career without his vivid imagination. Finally, toward the end of this song the band cooks up a bit of a jam, and Jackson sings with more fire than he has on all of the songs that precede this one.

One of the most effective songs on this album is Jackson's nearly eight-minute-long salute to Italian filmmaker Sergio Leone. "Sergio Leone" evokes the sounds of the famed "spaghetti Westerns" of the 1960s. Browne sings how Leone came to America with his camera and proceeded to immortalize what he saw in the films he made. In this cinema homage to the filmmaker, he mentions Raoul Walsh, William Wyler, Howard Hawks, and John Ford and the inspiration Leone received from Akira Kurosawa and Sam Peckinpah. A slow and pensive song, "Sergio Leone" paints images with nice audio brushstrokes.

"Don't You Want to Be There" finds Jackson pondering death and heaven. He sings of hearing the trumpets of the angels playing. But is he glorifying death here or looking for answers to the myth of the existence of heaven? It is never really clear.

> "Don't You Want to Be There" finds Jackson pondering death and heaven. He sings of hearing the trumpets of the angels playing. But is he glorifying death here or looking for answers to the myth of the existence of heaven?

The ninth and last song on this album, "My Stunning Mystery Companion," is the one that makes the biggest musical impression here. It echoes the insightfulness and warmth of his earlier work. He finally picks up the pace a touch and sings of someone who has rescued him from his own life of being a solitary man. The person who is now in his life has somehow made his life seem worthwhile again. He sings of his expectations having been abandoned when a "stunning mystery companion" arrives in his life. Now, it seems, he is emotionally equipped to carry on.

On *The Naked Ride Home*, Jackson neither moves forward, nor backtracks. It is like a slow and thoughtful journal of impressions and ideas. Clearly, there was no intention at creating hit singles or chasing the elusive "hook" that exists in songs like "Somebody's Baby" or "Running on Empty." This is as close to a jazz/rock album as Browne has come. These are not tunes that you will find yourself humming once the album is over. It is an album full of artful rock, Jackson Browne style.

In its own defense, *The Naked Ride Home* isn't trying to be anything other than its own definition of style or content. Jackson wasn't trying to write a new chapter of *Late for the Sky* or *I'm Alive*. Here it is, take it or leave it. This is where Browne was at that moment in time.

In the *Music Box*, John Metzger glowingly wrote, "It's been a long time since Jackson Browne has released an album anywhere near as good as *The Naked Ride Home*. In fact, his latest release very well may prove to be the best of his career. That's saying something too ... *The Naked Ride Home* is such a pleasant surprise. For starters, it wraps Browne's eloquent lyrics in the same type of unfettered arrangements and organic melodies that made *Late for the Sky* and *For Everyman* such classics."[4]

> "It's been a long time since Jackson Browne has released an album anywhere near as good as *The Naked Ride Home*."

Holly George-Warren wasn't as dazzled in her review in *Entertainment Weekly*. According to her, "In the mid-'70s, Browne excelled at expressing innocence lost.... His first new CD in six years succeeds when he sticks to the earlier style—which has evolved into world-weary narration—but his message songs tend to meander. An intriguing oddity is the atmospheric paean to spaghetti-Western maestro Sergio Leone."[5]

Jackson made several appearances in the fall of 2002 to promote *The Naked Ride Home* album. On September 19, he was interviewed by British DJ Johnny Walker on BBC Radio 2. On October 9, he appeared in Austin, Texas, on an episode of the popular television show *Austin City Limits*.

Another radio program he appeared on was Scott Muni's show on the New York City station Q 104.3 (WAXQ). According to Muni's producer, Zach Martin, Jackson was in good spirits when he arrived at the studio. "He was very friendly. He was easy to get along with. He has a great sense of humor. I felt that he wasn't condescending at all. And, he didn't feel that anybody owed him anything, like: 'You should know who I am.' He was unassuming. That was the quality I got, 'unassuming.' "[6]

In the fall of 2002, it was announced that Jackson's singer/songwriter buddy Warren Zevon had been diagnosed with terminal lung cancer. On hearing this sad news, Browne said, "He is a standard-bearer; he's very adventurous and there's a confidence and power that translates to effectiveness. There's a literacy, not just of words but also an emotional literacy. The coin of that realm is honesty and vulnerability. But then, you know, there's a berserk quality to the whole thing when it's done."[7]

In November 2002, it was disclosed that a multimillion-dollar lawsuit was settled between songwriters Jackson Browne, J. D. Souther, and Jack Tempchin, and Warner Brothers Records. The album *The Eagles Greatest Hits*, which had been issued in 1976, hit Number 1, and had sold consistently ever since. In fact, it has sold a record shattering 27 million copies, and still stands as the best-selling album of all times in the United States. (Michael Jackson's *Thriller* holds the worldwide record.)

Browne, Souther, and Tempchin all contributed songs to that album, and they felt that Warner Brothers, which now controlled the albums, owed them back songwriting royalties. Apparently, this type of royalty is supposed to be adjusted for inflation, and it had not been. The trio of tunesmiths were seeking $10 million in royalties owed to them. Although the figure they ended up with was not disclosed, the courts ruled in their favor. In other words, Browne received a nice hefty check in 2002 for his contribution as one of the writers of the song "Take It Easy."

On May 11, 2003, Jackson was the musical guest on the animated TV show *The Simpsons*. Providing his voice to the animated version to himself, he was in the episode "Brake My Wife, Please."

Although the lawsuit against Warner Brothers Records drew headlines, nothing in Jackson's career that year could top the complaint that he filed against the Fox Television Network in 2003. In January 2003, TNT had broadcast the made-for-TV movie *America's Prince: The John F. Kennedy Jr. Story*. In the film, the romance between Daryl Hannah and Kennedy was

> Although the lawsuit against Warner Brothers Records drew headlines, nothing in Jackson's career that year could top the complaint that he filed against the Fox Television Network in 2003.

depicted. And, in two scenes, references were made to the effect that Kennedy had rescued Hannah from physical abuse at the hands of Jackson Browne.

Furthermore, he also filed a complaint against VH1, which was owned by Viacom. It seemed that they had broadcast a TV show called *When Cameras Cross the Line*. The show likewise made a similar assertion that Browne had physically beaten the actress.

The Associated Press ran a news item on July 18, 2003, announcing that VH1 agreed to delete the reference to abuse at the hands of Jackson on all future broadcasts of their program. They also issued a written apology to be broadcast whenever the show aired. And Fox agreed to amend the offending two scenes in the Kennedy movie.

Jackson Browne issued his own press statement claiming, "I never assaulted Daryl Hannah, and this fact was confirmed by the investigation conducted at the time by the Santa Monica Police Department. I am gratified that Fox agreed to take these steps."[8]

According to Donald Miller, his manager, "[Jackson] is appreciative that the producers moved so quickly to correct the program and apologize."[9]

Billboard magazine reported, "A written apology has been added to the beginning of the program. It states: 'In a previous version of this program, we incorrectly reported an alleged incident involving singer Jackson Browne and actress Daryl Hannah. Mr. Browne has always denied that such an incident occurred, and local authorities have reported to the media that based upon their investigation, the incident previously reported in our program did not occur. We have deleted that material from our program, and we apologize to Mr. Browne for its inclusion.'"[10]

The final Warren Zevon album, *Dirty Life and Times*, was released on August 26, 2003. Knowing that he was dying of cancer, all of his friends came out for one more studio appearance with him. The title track includes background voices by Billy Bob Thornton and Dwight Yoakam, with Ry Cooder on guitar and Don Henley on drums. "Disorder in the House" features a vocal and lead guitar by Bruce Springsteen. Jackson Browne, Billy Bob Thornton, and John Waite sing the chorus for Warren's chilling tongue-in-cheek cover of Bob Dylan's "Knockin' on Heaven's Door." Also on the album are Tom Petty and Emmylou Harris. Zevon died the following week, on September 7, 2003, and Jackson lost another dear friend.

On November 20, 2003, the Rock and Roll Hall of Fame officially announced its inductees for 2004. Topping the list was Jackson Browne. His fellow inductees included George Harrison, Prince, Bob Seger, Traffic, and ZZ Top. A musician or group becomes eligible for induction twenty-five years following the release of the musician's or group's first album. Then the Rock and Roll Hall of Fame Foundation's nominating committee selects five to seven nominees each year, and sends out ballots to an international panel of 1,000 rock critics, producers, and other insiders. The nominees that receive the highest number and more than 50 percent of the votes are inducted.

On January 24, 2004, Jackson Browne gave a surprise performance at *Sings Like Hell's 100th Show*. The event was part of a concert series held at the Lobero Theater in Santa Barbara, California. The presentation began with a fifteen-minute slide show that was narrated by Browne's old friend, photographer Henry Diltz. Browne then took the stage and performed "The Barricades of Heaven," "These Days," "My Stunning Mystery Companion," and "Lives in the Balance." Also on the bill that night were Peter Case, Dave Alvin, and Richard Thompson. As an encore, Jackson and Thompson performed "Carmelita" and "The Next Voice You Hear" together.

It was announced in February 2004 that Jackson had officially fulfilled his latest recording contract with Elektra Records. *Billboard* magazine reported that he was now shopping for a new label for his next album. According to Browne, "I've had conversations with a couple of different people, but it's still not time [to make a decision]. I have such difficulty talking to record companies before there's music to be played."[11]

According to *Billboard*, Browne was working on a series of his albums being released on audio DVD with bonus tracks, before dealing with a label switch. "The fact that I was basically on one label for my entire career used to be something I was proud about, but I don't necessarily think it's something [desirable]," he claimed. "There were times when you were about to release an album and then there would be some corporate shift and the five or six people you were working with were gone," he continued. "It would have been easier to go through the process of finding a new label each time."[12]

On February 8, 2004, Jackson Browne joined Emmylou Harris, Dwight Yoakam, Jorge Calderón, and Timothy B. Schmit of the Eagles in an all-star tribute to Warren Zevon. Warren's final album had been nominated for five different Grammy Awards, and he won one of them posthumously. Jackson was part of the all-star chorus that sang "Keep Me in Your Heart" live, with

Zevon's visual image on the huge video screens at the Staples Center and his voice singing the lead vocal, as though he were looking down from heaven.

Jackson's induction to the Nineteenth Annual Rock and Roll Hall of Fame was held at the Waldorf Astoria Hotel on March 15, 2004. It was an incredible all-star event, which reunited him with several longtime friends. It also formalized his stature as a true rock & roll legend.

The following day, Rhino Records released a deluxe two-disc retrospective of Jackson Browne's entire career as an Elektra recording star. By virtue of having a second disc to stretch out into, with thirty-two cuts *The Very Best of Jackson Browne* is actually a much fuller look at his scope as a singer and songwriter. His fourteenth American album contains vintage singles missing from *The Next Voice You Hear*, including "Rock Me on the Water," "Take It Easy," "My Red Neck Friend," "Stay," "Boulevard," "I'm Alive," and "The Night Inside Me." It also widens the spectrum with classic Browne album cuts including "For a Dancer," "The Load Out," "Lawless Avenues," and "Looking East."

> Jackson's induction to the Nineteenth Annual Rock and Roll Hall of Fame was held at the Waldorf Astoria Hotel on March 15, 2004. It was an incredible all-star event, which reunited him with several longtime friends.

In addition, on March 16, 2004, Elektra released a brand new audio DVD version of Jackson's album *Running on Empty*. In addition to delivering stunning multichannel stereo surround sound, the disc also featured two previously unreleased tracks: "Cocaine Again" and "Edwardsville Room 124." These songs were recorded during the original on-the-road *Running on Empty* recording sessions. "Cocaine Again" is actually an alternate version of the song "Cocaine," which had appeared on the original version of the album. The unique features of the DVD include full lyrics that can be projected on the TV screen and a photo montage of that fateful tour.

In the autumn of 2004 Jackson was heard on the album *Enjoy Every Sandwich: The Songs of Warren Zevon*. On it, he recorded Zevon's "Poor Poor Pitiful Me" with his lifelong friend Bonnie Raitt. This fitting tribute included performances by Don Henley, David Lindley, Bruce Springsteen, and Browne's idol Bob Dylan. Jackson also took part in the Vote for Change series of concerts.

CHAPTER 16

These Days

WHEN SOME PEOPLE GROW UP, THEY CHANGE as individuals. Tragedy in their lives can sour them and make them bitter. While attaining their life's goals, some creative people become so self-absorbed that they come across as pushy or spoiled. And others simply lose their drive and ideals along the way. Jackson Browne is someone that time has never changed. The causes that drove him as a young man are the same ones that motivate him now. He is someone who has been writing songs for over forty years now, and in many ways, nothing has changed about him.

On the other hand, he is someone who could never be channeled into any one genre or style. In fact, as soon as the public was able to peg him as being one thing, he'd already mutated into another area of musical expression. His sound may change from album to album, but the fact that he does things *his way* has never faltered.

Along the way, he was a singer of guitar-driven folk-oriented ballads, then he was a rocker, then he developed a slicker synthesizer sound, and then he devoted himself to songs of protest and political change. After *Running on Empty* became the biggest selling album of his career, he blatantly refused to cash in on it and do a *Running on Empty, Volume 2*. By the time *Hold Out* was released, he was already onto something else—in this case, synthesizer-accented 1980s music.

He surely is a big enough star to embark on a huge concert tour with massive projection screens and pyrotechnic lighting effects. However, you are more likely to see him doing an all-acoustic concert, either with a band or all by himself.

He is a star, but he has never gone off on a star trip. In fact, Jackson seems to find great amusement in the whole "celebrity" game. Although he is world famous, it was not fame itself that originally drew him into the music business. Explaining his own perspective, he claims, "The idea is not to hero-worship. For instance, if you've ever met Bob Dylan, you know that there's very little revealed anyway," he laughs. "You could say, 'I got to meet Bob Dylan,' or you could say, 'I *got* his music.'"[1]

According to him, "Our world is so bent on marketing celebrity, and some access you presume is real access. I guess you could call it death by envy."[2]

> "Our world is so bent on marketing celebrity, and some access you presume is real access. I guess you could call it death by envy."

With all of his dead-serious political causes, one might assume that he has no sense of humor whatsoever. However, nothing could be further from the truth. For instance, one of the television programs that amuses him the most lately is the cable show *MTV's Cribs*, in which rock stars show off their homes, as a surreal reality feature. Browne explains, "You let this camera in this rock star's home, and he's gonna show you his 'crib.' It's interesting to see what horrendous taste some of these people have in home furnishings. They may have all the money in the world, but you say to yourself, 'I can't believe the guy would live with that couch.'"[3]

Who are other singer/songwriters whom Jackson admires? According to him, "I think Rubén Blades is really incredible. He talks about subjects that have political implications, and he speaks about it completely from a human point of view. He portrays the life of a policeman—maybe a member of a death squad—waking up and talking to his wife and kissing his kids goodbye as he goes out to arrest someone. Songs like that are very provocative. A song like 'Russians' by Sting, goes really far, I think to raise questions. Questions like whether or not the Russians love their children. I mean, it's an *annoying* question. Of course they love their children. But the more you think about it, we act as if they don't."[4]

Listening to his songs like "Too Many Angels" and "Don't You Wanna Be There," one would surmise that he has strong ideas about faith and the afterlife. He claims, "I think that without justice you have a hard time leading any kind of a spiritual

> "I think that without justice you have a hard time leading any kind of a spiritual life. And I think recognizing other people's dilemmas is more important than reaching some sort of spiritual state."

life. And I think recognizing other people's dilemmas is more important than reaching some sort of spiritual state. My favorite slogan is 'If you want peace, fight for justice.' I kind of accept the idea of reincarnation. Only because it's inconceivable to me that we only get to be here once. It almost doesn't matter what you believe about what happens after death. I think the best values you can have are worthwhile regardless of whether they get you to heaven or not. Truth is its own reward, and justice is needed here on earth during our lives."[5]

He has very strong ideas about environmental conservation. "By the time I was a teenager, I felt it would be important to get a piece of land and do nothing with it. That's actually what I did. I have some land near Santa Barbara, which we've pretty much done nothing with except build a little place," he explains. "That house runs solely off the grid. It's powered by wind, and it's photovoltaic, and it's been that way for 20 years. A friend of mine saw this house—she referred to it as leaning up against the cheek of God. It is not a fancy house; the beauty of it is where it is and its integration with the outdoors. There's a diesel backup system that runs off propane. When I say off the grid, I mean electricity, because I still use propane. I've got a couple of ranch vehicles that run on propane, and the propane is delivered to the ranch. These cars didn't get more than 8 or 10 miles per gallon. It was a drag to drive 20 miles to get them filled, and you'd get back and they'd be half empty. So I started running them off propane, which is much better for emissions. It's something like 80 percent cleaner."[6]

Success in an artistic field has to do with what your goals are, and how well you achieve them. Along those lines, author and media manipulator Angela Bowie claims, "Every generation redefines activism. Protest songs have gone from the likes of Woody Guthrie, to Pete Seeger, to Joan Baez, to Donovan, to Tim Buckley, to Al Stewart. In my mind, Jackson Browne has more in common with those visionaries than he does Bruce Springsteen and John Cougar Mellencamp."[7]

For Bowie, "People who can sing about disappointment, love, death, social ramifications—anything serious they really get caught up in it. If they are good at distilling emotions that we can all identify with—like Jackson does—it is wonderful. Whenever I see Joan Baez on television, or on the radio, I stop to see what her message is or her cause is this time around. It is always something worthy of considering, whether I wholly agree or not. Jackson Browne has this quality as well. I always want to find out, 'What is the message this time around?'"[8]

Contemplating Jackson's ability to draw audiences to his songs and messages, Bowie finds that "in my opinion, Browne has the same ability to zero in on a cause that needs the spotlight shone upon it, and he does, because he is driven. The truly fascinating thing about him is that each of his songs is actually the synopsis for a screenplay."[9]

He is the type of person who does not think of himself as a big self-promoter. Radio producer Zach Martin claims, "He's not a very assuming person. That's part of his charm as I found him. He didn't feel like anybody owed him anything. He just produced what he wanted to—what he felt was good work in his life, and let it stand on its own. Which, a lot of people aren't brave enough to do. They second guess themselves, or they're afraid to be on their own, or that they need somebody else to be successful. But what I respect about him is he stood on his own, and made some political decisions that you think—hindsight being twenty-twenty—wasn't worth the aggravation in exchange for it."[10]

On the subject of Jackson Browne diving into the middle of politically charged issues, Zach says, "I think he does it because he likes to do it, and he likes the 'art' portion of it. He is probably not a great business person. Which is okay, because we are not all designed to be that way. And, if he was designed to be that way, it would lessen his effectiveness on what he does and what he offers. Now, when you take him—and his complete body of work—you will find: 'I know that song. I've heard that song before.' "[11]

What Zach most admires about Browne is his musical taste and talent, "He's got a great voice that doesn't need a lot of processing and makeup. He doesn't need overproduction to make it sound slick and enjoyable to listen to. And then, on top of everything else, what really makes him who he is, and spectacular in his own right, is his lyrics. His way that he can take a topic and put it together lyrically. I admire that."[12]

Jackson himself has said, "I think a career is all about taking chances."[13]

Along these lines, Martin proclaims, "Some of his political decisions that got him in trouble, to me that symbolizes courage. Whether you disagree or agree with somebody, that they were able to do that and stand by that decision, and accept the consequences of that decision, I have an enormous amount of respect for them making that decision. He really is underappreciated for his contribution to rock music—as a lyricist, as a performer, as a musician."[14]

Randy Jones, the original cowboy in the Village People, claims, "It wasn't until I saw Jackson Browne in concert in Manhattan that I really 'got' him as a performer. I have always loved the song 'Somebody's Baby,' but when you listen closely to his music, you find that every song tells a story. In my mind, he is rock music's best storyteller."[15]

And according to his dear friend Bonnie Raitt, "I don't think there's anybody that writes about matters of the heart in such a poignant way as Jackson. There's something about it—especially when he's singing his own songs—the way he plays his own piano, the way he plays guitar and sings, it's just a total 'soul mate' for me. I just found something so truthful and heartbreaking at the same time."[16]

> According to his dear friend Bonnie Raitt, "I don't think there's anybody that writes about matters of the heart in such a poignant way as Jackson."

But then Jackson Browne isn't someone who has made his decisions around what he thought people would think about him. "In the end, what people think about you is their business," he says. "I don't believe you can control how people feel about you—I mean, it's too much work. You have to take the trouble to try not to be misunderstood. Other than that, I think that how people see that has as much to do with how they are as the way I am. Most people encourage me. I think it's just natural to want to give something back to people if you feel grateful that you're in a position to communicate."[17]

He has no intention of just being labeled a "political songwriter." That in itself is too limiting. "I think most people write a political song because the subject has touched them in some way. If they become known as 'political songwriters,' it's really a way of categorizing them," he says.[18]

Nor has he ever succumbed to the temptation to lend his music, his voice, or his talent to any means of advertising. As he explains it, "I haven't let any of my songs be licensed. If I needed the money, I'd certainly do it. What happens, though, is if you license a song for an ad, you change what it is. There's a generation coming up that associates 'I Heard It Through the Grapevine' with [a TV commercial for] raisins."[19]

After all these years, Browne still feels that rock & roll music is truly a live and vital means of expression. "I think that rock & roll is one of the main communications mediums," he says. "It's one that people really care about and are attuned to a lot more than the six o'clock news. Fundamentally, people are smart. They know that there's a lot more to the news than what this smiling idiot on the TV is telling them. So rock & roll is a much more viable way of communicating concerns and needs."[20]

How does Jackson Browne feel about his career in the music business? "More than a career, I feel that I've got a function. I see things in a much more holistic way. Some people bake the bread, and some people write the songs."[21]

Jackson Browne's success has never been measured in a single Top 10 hit or any one million-selling album. It has to do with expressing his heart. He is a poet who happens to write lyrics to songs he sings. He

> "More than a career, I feel that I've got a function. I see things in a much more holistic way. Some people bake the bread, and some people write the songs."

never set out to be a rock star. In fact, there have been times that he made decisions within his career to make sure he never chased fame for the sake of fame. But nonetheless, fame has found him.

In a seascape filled with instant stars and flash-in-the-pan talents, Jackson Browne is an artist for life. Like the captain of a ship, he plots his own course. If another "Gold" or "Platinum" record crosses his path, that would be great. If it doesn't, he will just continue to do what he has always done: Turn his deepest feelings and insights into lyrically poetic music that touches people in deeply emotional ways. In a world of talent-free "pretenders," Jackson Browne is the real item—a sensitive singer and songwriter whose talent transcends time and trends. That's what makes Jackson Browne rock & roll's most beloved and timeless troubadour.

Sources

Prologue: Twenty-first Century Everyman

1. Author's notes, Palace Theater, Stamford, Connecticut, October 30, 2003.
2. Jay Cocks, "Jackson's Day in Court," *Time*, September 12, 1983.
3. Rob Tannenbaum, "The Return of The Pretender," *GQ*, November 1993.
4. Joe Smith, *Off the Record: An Oral History of Popular Music*, edited by Mitchell Fink, Warner Books, 1988.
5. Eric Alterman, "Rockin' in the Free World," *The Nation*, November 11, 2002.
6. Anthony DeCurtis, "Jackson Browne," *Rolling Stone*, October 15, 1992.

1: Clyde Jackson Browne

1. Wayne Hoffman, "Jackson Browne Q&A," *Nature Conservancy*, 2003.
2. Rich Wiseman, *Jackson Browne: The Story of a Hold Out*, Doubleday/Dolphin Books, 1982.
3. Jay Cocks, "Jackson's Day in Court," by *Time*, September 12, 1983.
4. Rob Tannenbaum, "The Return of The Pretender," *GQ*, November 1993.
5. Wiseman, *Jackson Browne*.
6. *Jackson Browne: Going Home*, Video, Pioneer Video, 2001, originally broadcast on the Disney Channel, August 1994.
7. Hoffman, "Jackson Browne Q&A."
8. Tannenbaum, "Return of The Pretender."
9. Cameron Crowe, "A Child's Garden of Jackson Browne," *Rolling Stone*, May 23, 1974.
10. Crowe, "Child's Garden of Jackson Browne."
11. Wiseman, *Jackson Browne*.
12. Crowe, "Child's Garden of Jackson Browne."

13. Tannenbaum, "Return of The Pretender."

14. Steve Pond, "Jackson Browne Adapts," *Rolling Stone*, September 15, 1983.

15. Anthony DeCurtis, "Jackson Browne," *Rolling Stone*, October 15, 1992.

16. Josh Mills, "Jackson Browne," *New York Sunday News*, October 5, 1975.

17. Anthony DeCurtis, "Jackson Browne," *Rolling Stone*, November 5–December 10, 1987.

18. Gene Santoro, "Jackson Browne," *The Nation*, May 13, 1996.

19. Crowe, "Child's Garden of Jackson Browne."

20. Jenny Eliscu, "Jackson Browne: The Music Q+A," *Rolling Stone*, November 14, 2002.

2: The Balladeer

1. *The Best of the Byrds: Greatest Hits, Volume II*, liner notes by Allee Willis, Columbia Records, 1972.

2. Rich Wiseman, *Jackson Browne: The Story of a Hold Out*, Doubleday/Dolphin Books, 1982.

3. Jenny Eliscu, "Jackson Browne: The Music Q+A," *Rolling Stone*, November 14, 2002.

4. Eliscu, "Jackson Browne."

5. Joe Smith, *Off the Record: An Oral History of Popular Music*, edited by Mitchell Fink, Warner Books, 1988.

6. Wiseman, *Jackson Browne*.

7. Wiseman, *Jackson Browne*.

8. Wiseman, *Jackson Browne*.

9. Wiseman, *Jackson Browne*.

10. Wiseman, *Jackson Browne*.

11. Rob Tannenbaum, "The Return of The Pretender," *GQ*, November 1993.

12. Smith, *Off the Record*.

13. Smith, *Off the Record*.

14. Smith, *Off the Record*.

15. Cameron Crowe, "A Child's Garden of Jackson Browne," *Rolling Stone*, May 23, 1974.

16. Smith, *Off the Record*.

17. Wiseman, *Jackson Browne*.

18. Smith, *Off the Record*.

19. Smith, *Off the Record*.

20. *Jackson Browne: Going Home*, Video, Pioneer Video, originally broadcast on the Disney Channel, August 1994.

21. Crowe, "Child's Garden of Jackson Browne."

22. Smith, *Off the Record*.

23. David Resin, "Jackson Browne: '... Such a Clever Innocence,'" *Crawdaddy*, January 1974.

24. Eliscu, "Jackson Browne."

25. Smith, *Off the Record*.

26. Eliscu, "Jackson Browne."

27. Crowe, "Child's Garden of Jackson Browne."

28. Richard Meltzer, "Jackson Browne" profile, *Rolling Stone*, June 22, 1972.

29. Crowe, "Child's Garden of Jackson Browne."

30. Crowe, "Child's Garden of Jackson Browne."

31. Wiseman, *Jackson Browne*.

32. Crowe, "Child's Garden of Jackson Browne."

33. Smith, *Off the Record*.

34. Micky Dolenz and Mark Bego, *I'm a Believer: My Life of Monkees, Music and Madness*, Cooper Square Press, 2004.

35. Wiseman, *Jackson Browne*.

36. Jackson Browne, interview by Tom Nolan, *Cheetah*, January 1968.

37. Browne, interview.

38. Browne, interview.

39. *Rolling Stone*, "John J. Rock" column, 1968.

40. Smith, *Off the Record*.

41. Wiseman, *Jackson Browne*.

42. Jean Valley, John Skow, Edward J. Boyer, and David DeVoss, "Linda Ronstadt: Torchy Rock/Linda down the Wind," *Time*, February 28, 1977.

43. Valley et al., "Linda Ronstadt."

44. Eliscu, "Jackson Browne."

45. Tannenbaum, "Return of The Pretender."

46. Crowe, "Child's Garden of Jackson Browne."

47. David Crosby and Carl Gottlieb, *Long Time Gone: The Autobiography of David Crosby*, Doubleday, 1988.

48. Jac Holzman and Gavan Daws, *Follow the Music*, First Media Group, 1998.

49. Holzman and Daws, *Follow the Music*.

50. Wiseman, *Jackson Browne*.

51. Wiseman, *Jackson Browne*.

52. Crowe, "Child's Garden of Jackson Browne."

53. Smith, *Off the Record*.

54. Holzman and Daws, *Follow the Music*.

55. Holzman and Daws, *Follow the Music*.

56. Crowe, "Child's Garden of Jackson Browne."

57. Wiseman, *Jackson Browne*.

58. Wiseman, *Jackson Browne*.

59. Gene Santoro, "Jackson Browne," *The Nation*, May 13, 1996.

60. Smith, *Off the Record*.

61. Smith, *Off the Record*.

3: Saturate Before Using

1. Anthony DeCurtis, "Jackson Browne," *Rolling Stone*, November 5–December 10, 1987.

2. *Lillian Roxon's Rock Encyclopedia*, Tempo Books, Grosset and Dunlap Publishers, 1969.

3. Ian Halperin, *Fire and Rain: The James Taylor Story*, Mainstream Publishing, 2001.

4. Cameron Crowe, "A Child's Garden of Jackson Browne," *Rolling Stone*, May 23, 1974.

5. Jenny Eliscu, "Jackson Browne: The Music Q+A," *Rolling Stone*, November 14, 2002.

6. Crowe, "Child's Garden of Jackson Browne."

7. Rich Wiseman, *Jackson Browne: The Story of a Hold Out*, Doubleday/Dolphin Books, 1982.

8. Mark Bego, *Linda Ronstadt: It's So Easy*, Eakin Press, 1990.

9. Bego, *Linda Ronstadt*.

10. Bego, *Linda Ronstadt*.

11. David Crosby interview by Ben Fong-Torres, *Rolling Stone*, 1970.

12. Wiseman, *Jackson Browne*.

13. Crowe, "Child's Garden of Jackson Browne."

14. Crowe, "Child's Garden of Jackson Browne."

15. Tom King, *The Operator: David Geffen Builds, Buys, and Sells the New Hollywood*, Random House, 2000.

16. King, *Operator*.

17. Michele Kort, *Soul Picnic: The Music and Passion of Laura Nyro*, Thomas Dunn Books, 2002.

18. Robert Hillburn, *Los Angeles Times*, 1970.

19. Susan Mittelkauf, telephone interview by author, February, 4, 2004.

20. Mike Jahn, "Fillmore Bow Made by Jackson Browne," *New York Times*, December 25, 1970.

21. Jackson Browne on stage at The Jabberwocky, Syracuse, New York, 1970.

22. Browne on stage at The Jabberwocky.

23. Browne on stage at The Jabberwocky.

24. Browne on stage at The Jabberwocky.

25. Kort, *Soul Picnic*.

26. Rob Tannenbaum, "The Return of The Pretender," *GQ*, November 1993.

27. Anthony Bozza, "Track X Track," *Rolling Stone*, February 19, 1998.

28. Wiseman, *Jackson Browne*.

29. King, *Operator*.

30. David Crosby and Carl Gottlieb, *Long Time Gone: The Autobiography of David Crosby*, Doubleday, 1988.

31. Irwin, "Jackson Browne."

32. *Jackson Browne: Going Home*, Video, Pioneer Video, originally broadcast on the Disney Channel, August 1994.

33. *Jackson Browne: Going Home*.

34. *Jackson Browne: Going Home*.

35. *Jackson Browne: Going Home*.

36. *Jackson Browne: Going Home*.

37. *Jackson Browne: Going Home*.

38. *Rolling Stone* ad for *Jackson Browne*, January 17, 1972.

39. *Jackson Browne: Going Home*.

40. Alex Ward, "Jackson Browne," *Washington Post*, September 7, 1972.

41. Bud Scoppa, review of *Jackson Browne*, *Rolling Stone*, March 2, 1972.

42. *Billboard*, review of *Jackson Browne*, 1972.

43. Crosby and Gottlieb, *Long Time Gone*.

4: For Everyman

1. Peter Herbst, "Jackson Browne," *The Boston Phoenix*, 1972.

2. Jackson Browne on stage at Stony Brook, New York, 1972.

3. Browne on stage at Stony Brook.

4. Rich Wiseman, *Jackson Browne: The Story of a Hold Out*, Doubleday/Dolphin Books, 1982.

5. Wiseman, *Jackson Browne*.

6. Wiseman, *Jackson Browne*.

7. Tom King, *The Operator: David Geffen Builds, Buys, and Sells the New Hollywood*, Random House, 2000.

8. Cameron Crowe, "A Child's Garden of Jackson Browne," *Rolling Stone*, May 23, 1974.

9. Richard Meltzer, "Jackson Browne" profile, *Rolling Stone*, June 22, 1972.

10. Wiseman, *Jackson Browne*.

11. Wiseman, *Jackson Browne*.

12. Wiseman, *Jackson Browne*.

13. Lynne Van Maitre, "Jackson Browne," *Chicago Tribune*, 1973.

14. Wiseman, *Jackson Browne*.

15. Nat Freedland, "Jackson Browne," *Cashbox*, 1973.

16. Crowe, "Child's Garden of Jackson Browne."

17. Crowe, "Child's Garden of Jackson Browne."

18. Crowe, "Child's Garden of Jackson Browne."

19. Bud Scoppa, "New Faces," *Senior Scholastic*, August 7, 1973.

20. Scoppa, "New Faces."

21. Anthony Bozza, "Track X Track," *Rolling Stone*, February 19, 1998.

22. Wiseman, *Jackson Browne*.

23. Crowe, "Child's Garden of Jackson Browne."

24. Janet Maslin, "Jackson Browne," *New Times*, November 30, 1973.

25. Janet Maslin, review of *For Everyman*, *Rolling Stone*, 1973.

26. John Rockwell, review of *Jackson Browne*, *New York Times*, October 12, 1973.

27. Anthony De Curtis, "*Rolling Stone* Hall of Fame: Jackson Browne *For Everyman*," *Rolling Stone*, February 19, 1998.

28. David Crosby, interview by Ben Fong-Torres, *Rolling Stone*, 1974.

29. Wiseman, *Jackson Browne*.

30. David Resin, "Jackson Browne: '...Such a Clever Innocence,'" *Crawdaddy*, January 1974.

31. Resin, "Jackson Browne."

32. Crowe, "Child's Garden of Jackson Browne."

5: Late for the Sky

1. Cameron Crowe, "A Child's Garden of Jackson Browne," *Rolling Stone*, May 23, 1974.

2. Crowe, "Child's Garden of Jackson Browne."

3. Lynne Van Maitre, "Jackson Browne," *Chicago Tribune*, 1973.

4. David Resin, "Jackson Browne: '...Such a Clever Innocence,'" *Crawdaddy*, January 1974.

5. Crowe, "Child's Garden of Jackson Browne."

6. Rich Wiseman, *Jackson Browne: The Story of a Hold Out*, Doubleday/Dolphin Books, 1982.

7. Wiseman, *Jackson Browne*.

8. Wiseman, *Jackson Browne*.

9. Wiseman, *Jackson Browne*.

10. Anthony Bozza, "Track X Track," *Rolling Stone*, February 19, 1998.

11. Anthony DeCurtis, "Jackson Browne," *Rolling Stone*, November 5–December 10, 1987.

12. *Late for the Sky*, liner notes by Jackson Browne, Asylum Records, 1974.

13. Stephen Holden, review of *Late for the Sky*, *Rolling Stone*, 1974.

14. James Wolcott, "Jackson Browne: In the Pouring Rain," *Village Voice*, November 14, 1974.

15. David Spiwak, review of *Late for the Sky*, *Crawdaddy*, 1974.

16. Robert Martin, "Jackson Browne," *Toronto Globe and Mail*, quoted in *Current Biography*, October 1989.

17. Crowe, "Child's Garden of Jackson Browne."

18. Stephen Holden, "Jackson Browne: Lord Byron as L.A. Dude," *Village Voice*, November 22, 1976.

19. Wiseman, *Jackson Browne*.

6: The Pretender

1. Rich Wiseman, *Jackson Browne: The Story of a Hold Out*, Doubleday/Dolphin Books, 1982.

2. Rob Tannenbaum, "The Return of The Pretender," *GQ*, November 1993.

3. Anthony DeCurtis, "Jackson Browne," *Rolling Stone*, November 5–December 10, 1987.

4. Joe Smith, *Off the Record: An Oral History of Popular Music*, edited by Mitchell Fink, Warner Books, 1988.

5. "Jackson Browne," interview by Peter Frame, John Tobler and Paul Kendall, *Zigzag*, 1976.

6. Stephen Holden, "Jackson Browne: Lord Byron as L.A. Dude," *Village Voice*, November 22, 1976.

7. Jan DeKnock, "Jackson Browne," *Chicago Tribune*, September 4, 1983.

8. Janet Maslin, "Jackson Browne Changes His Tune to Showmanship," *New York Times*, Janet Maslin, February 19, 1978.

9. David Marsh, review of *The Pretender*, *Rolling Stone*, January 27, 1977.

10. Larry Roher, review of *The Pretender*, *Washington Post*, November 24, 1976.

11. Anthony DeCurtis, "As Jackson Browne's 'World' Turns," *Rolling Stone*, October 5, 1989.

12. Holden, "Jackson Browne."

13. Holden, "Jackson Browne."

14. Browne, interview.

7: Running on Empty

1. Paul Nelson, "Jackson Browne: On Love, Marriage and the Girl in His Songs," *Rolling Stone*, August 7, 1980.
2. Steve Pond, "Jackson Browne Adapts," *Rolling Stone*, September 15, 1983.
3. Nelson, "Jackson Browne: On Love."
4. Nelson, "Jackson Browne: On Love."
5. Rich Wiseman, *Jackson Browne: The Story of a Hold Out*, Doubleday/Dolphin Books, 1982.
6. Paul Nelson, "Jackson Browne," *Rolling Stone*, March 9, 1978.
7. David Lindley, interview by Dan Forte, *Guitar Player*, 1978.
8. Wesley Strick, "Jackson Browne Thrives on the Endless Road," *Circus*, 1978.
9. Strick, "Jackson Browne Thrives on the Endless Road."
10. Gene Santoro, "Jackson Browne," *The Nation*, May 13, 1996.
11. Anthony Bozza, "Track X Track," *Rolling Stone*, February 19, 1998.
12. Pond, "Jackson Browne Adapts."
13. Pond, "Jackson Browne Adapts."
14. *Running on Empty*, liner notes, Elektra/Asylum Records, 1977.
15. Strick, "Jackson Browne Thrives on the Endless Road."
16. Anthony DeCurtis, "As Jackson Browne's 'World' Turns," *Rolling Stone*, October 5, 1989.
17. Janet Maslin, "Jackson Browne Changes His Tune to Showmanship," *New York Times*, February 19, 1978.
18. Paul Nelson, "A Ticket to Ride," *Rolling Stone*, March 9, 1978.
19. *Billboard*, review of *Running on Empty*, December 24, 1977.
20. Carl Arrington, review of *Running on Empty*, *New York Post*, January 13, 1978.

8: The MUSE Concerts

1. Daisann McLane, "Tribute to Lowell George Draws 20,000," *Rolling Stone*, September 20, 1979.
2. McLane, "Tribute to Lowell George Draws 20,000."
3. *No Nukes*, the official program magazine from the MUSE concerts, 1979.
4. *Dinah!* TV show hosted by Dinah Shore, July 30, 1979.
5. *Dinah!* TV show.
6. *Dinah!* TV show.
7. *No Nukes*, the official program magazine.
8. Daisann McLane, "M.U.S.E.: Rock Politics Comes of Age," *Rolling Stone*, November 15, 1979.

9. McLane, "M.U.S.E."

10. *No Nukes*, the official program magazine.

11. Author's notes, the MUSE concert of September 19, 1979, Madison Square Garden, New York.

12. Steve Pond, "Jackson Browne Adapts," *Rolling Stone*, September 15, 1983.

13. McLane, "M.U.S.E."

14. McLane, "M.U.S.E."

15. *No Nukes*, the official program magazine.

16. Press release, sent out by Elektra/Asylum Records to journalists along with the *No Nukes* album, December 1979.

17. *No Nukes*, the official program magazine.

18. Anthony DeCurtis, "Jackson Browne," *Rolling Stone*, November 5–December 10, 1987.

9: Hold Out

1. Paul Nelson, "Jackson Browne: On Love, Marriage and the Girl in His Songs," *Rolling Stone*, August 7, 1980.

2. Nelson, "Jackson Browne."

3. Nelson, "Jackson Browne."

4. Nelson, "Jackson Browne."

5. Nelson, "Jackson Browne."

6. Nelson, "Jackson Browne."

7. Nelson, "Jackson Browne."

8. Nelson, "Jackson Browne."

9. Nelson, "Jackson Browne."

10. Nelson, "Jackson Browne."

11. Nelson, "Jackson Browne."

12. Nelson, "Jackson Browne."

13. Nelson, "Jackson Browne."

14. Nelson, "Jackson Browne."

15. *Hold Out*, liner notes by Jackson Browne, Asylum Records, 1980.

16. Nelson, "Jackson Browne."

17. Nelson, "Jackson Browne."

18. Nelson, "Jackson Browne."

19. Nelson, "Jackson Browne."

20. Lydia Carole DeFretos, "A Profile of Jackson Browne: After Compromise, the Welcome Return of the Common Man," *The Aquarian*, March 12, 1986.

21. Vladimir Bogdanov, Chris Woodstra, and Stephen Thomas Erlewine, eds. *All Music Guide to Rock,* 3rd ed., Backbeat Books, 2002.

22. Jackson Browne, interview regarding *No Nukes* by Peter Gordon, *Thirsty Ear,* 1980.

23. Janet Maslin, review of *No Nukes, Rolling Stone,* 1980.

24. Leonard Maltin, *1998 Movie and Video Guide,* Signet Books, 1997.

25. Robert Palmer, "Rock: Jackson Browne Plays on L.I.," *New York Times,* July 21, 1980.

26. Palmer, "Rock."

27. Nelson, "Jackson Browne."

28. Nelson, "Jackson Browne."

29. David Crosby and Carl Gottlieb, *Long Time Gone: The Autobiography of David Crosby,* Doubleday, 1988.

30. Jackson Browne on stage at Survival Sunday, the Hollywood Bowl, June 1981.

31. Browne on stage at Survival Sunday.

32. Robert Blake and Jackson Browne at the press conference held by the Abalone Alliance at the Greater Los Angeles Press Club, August 1981.

33. Gene Santoro, "Jackson Browne," *The Nation,* May 13, 1996.

34. Steve Pond, "Jackson Browne Adapts," *Rolling Stone,* September 15, 1983.

35. Pond, "Jackson Browne Adapts."

36. Pond, "Jackson Browne Adapts."

37. Pond, "Jackson Browne Adapts."

38. Crosby and Gottlieb, *Long Time Gone.*

39. Anthony DeCurtis, "Jackson Browne," *Rolling Stone,* November 5–December 10, 1987.

40. Don Shewey, "Licks: All You Need Is Love," *Village Voice,* June 22, 1982.

41. Pond, "Jackson Browne Adapts."

10: Lawyers in Love

1. Steve Pond, "Jackson Browne Adapts," *Rolling Stone,* September 15, 1983.

2. Pond, "Jackson Browne Adapts."

3. Pond, "Jackson Browne Adapts."

4. Jay Cocks, "Jackson's Day in Court," by *Time,* September 12, 1983.

5. "Jackson Browne Interview" by Elektra Records, sent out as a press release to accompany the *Looking East* album, 1996.

6. Pond, "Jackson Browne Adapts."

7. Pond, "Jackson Browne Adapts."

8. Cocks, "Jackson's Day in Court."

9. Cocks, "Jackson's Day in Court."

10. Pond, "Jackson Browne Adapts."

11. *Lawyers in Love*, liner notes by Jackson Browne, Elektra/Asylum Records, 1983.

12. Cocks, "Jackson's Day in Court."

13. Lydia Carole DeFretos, "A Profile of Jackson Browne: After Compromise, the Welcome Return of the Common Man," *The Aquarian*, March 12, 1986.

14. Michael Hill, "Everyman for Himself," *Village Voice*, August 16, 1983.

15. Vladimir Bogdanov, Chris Woodstra, and Stephen Thomas Erlewine, eds. *All Music Guide to Rock*, 3rd ed., Backbeat Books, 2002.

16. Pond, "Jackson Browne Adapts."

17. Pond, "Jackson Browne Adapts."

18. Pond, "Jackson Browne Adapts."

19. Pond, "Jackson Browne Adapts."

20. Pond, "Jackson Browne Adapts."

21. Pond, "Jackson Browne Adapts."

22. Pond, "Jackson Browne Adapts."

23. Anthony DeCurtis, "Jackson Browne," *Rolling Stone*, November 5–December 10, 1987.

11: Lives in the Balance

1. Anthony DeCurtis, "Jackson Browne," *Rolling Stone*, November 5–December 10, 1987.

2. DeCurtis, "Jackson Browne."

3. "Jackson Browne," *Current Biography*, October 1989.

4. DeCurtis, "Jackson Browne."

5. Eric Alterman, "Rockin' in the Free World," *The Nation*, November 11, 2002.

6. Alterman, "Rockin' in the Free World."

7. DeCurtis, "Jackson Browne."

8. "Jackson Browne," *Current Biography*.

9. Anthony DeCurtis, "As Jackson Browne's 'World' Turns," *Rolling Stone*, October 5, 1989.

10. DeCurtis, "Jackson Browne."

11. Lydia Carole DeFretos, "A Profile of Jackson Browne: After Compromise, the Welcome Return of the Common Man," *The Aquarian*, March 12, 1986.

12. Richard Harrington, review of *Lives in the Balance*, *The Washington Post*, 1986.

13. Jimmy Guterman, "Jackson Browne Gets out of His Head," *Rolling Stone*, April 10, 1986.

14. Vladimir Bogdanov, Chris Woodstra, and Stephen Thomas Erlewine, eds. *All Music Guide to Rock*, 3rd ed., Backbeat Books, 2002.

15. Joyce Millman, "Jackson Browne: Blandinista!" *Village Voice*, April 29, 1986.

16. Joe Smith, *Off the Record: An Oral History of Popular Music*, edited by Mitchell Fink, Warner Books, 1988.

17. Anthony DeCurtis, "Jackson Browne," *Rolling Stone*, October 15, 1992.

18. DeCurtis, "Jackson Browne," November 5–December 10, 1987.

19. DeCurtis, "Jackson Browne," November 5–December 10, 1987.

20. Anthony DeCurtis, "Video Vérité: Jackson Browne Makes His Point about U.S. Policy in Central America," *Rolling Stone*, January 29, 1987.

21. DeCurtis, "Video Vérité."

22. DeCurtis, "Video Vérite."

12: World in Motion

1. Anthony DeCurtis, "Jackson Browne," *Rolling Stone*, November 5–December 10, 1987.

2. DeCurtis, "Jackson Browne."

3. DeCurtis, "Jackson Browne."

4. Stephen Holden, "Old and New by Jackson Browne," *New York Times*, October 9, 1988.

5. Stephen Williams, "Browne's Soap-Box Circuit," *Newsday*, October 7, 1988.

6. Anthony DeCurtis, "As Jackson Browne's 'World' Turns," *Rolling Stone*, October 5, 1989.

7. Rob Tannenbaum, "The Return of The Pretender," *GQ*, November 1993.

8. Stephen Holden, "The Pop Life" column, *New York Times*, October 5, 1988.

9. DeCurtis, "Jackson Browne."

10. DeCurtis, "Jackson Browne."

11. DeCurtis, "As Jackson Browne's 'World' Turns."

12. DeCurtis, "As Jackson Browne's 'World' Turns."

13. Ron Givens, review of *World in Motion*, *Stereo Review*, October 1989.

14. David Fricke, review of *World in Motion*, *Rolling Stone*, 1989.

15. Vladimir Bogdanov, Chris Woodstra, and Stephen Thomas Erlewine, eds. *All Music Guide to Rock,* 3rd ed., Backbeat Books, 2002.

16. Wayne Robins, "Jackson Browne from the Pulpit," *Newsday*, June 12, 1989.

17. Stephen Holden, "Speeches and Reflections from Jackson Browne," *New York Times*, June 12, 1989.

18. DeCurtis, "As Jackson Browne's 'World' Turns."

19. Don Was (Weiss), interview by Edna Gundersen, *USA Today*, 1989.

20. DeCurtis, "As Jackson Browne's 'World' Turns."

21. Wayne Hoffman, "Jackson Browne Q&A," *Nature Conservancy*, 2003.

22. Hoffman, "Jackson Browne Q&A."
23. Karen S. Schneider, Tom Cunneff, Lorenzo Benet, Vicki Sheff, and Allison Lynn, "White Knight," *People*, October 19, 1992.
24. Schneider et al., "White Knight."
25. Schneider et al., "White Knight."
26. Schneider et al., "White Knight."
27. Schneider et al., "White Knight."
28. Elizabeth Gleick, Tom Cunneff, Barbara Sandler, Allison Lynn, and Mary Huznec, "Two of a Kind," *People*, August 16, 1993.
29. Marcy MacDonald, telephone interview by author February 4, 2004.
30. Schneider et al., "White Knight."
31. Schneider et al., "White Knight."

13: I'm Alive

1. Rob Tannenbaum, "The Return of The Pretender," *GQ*, November 1993.
2. Tannenbaum, "Return of The Pretender."
3. *Jackson Browne: Going Home*, Video, Pioneer Video, 2001, originally broadcast on the Disney Channel, August 1994.
4. David Wild, "A Life in Balance: Jackson Browne Gets Serious about Love," *Rolling Stone*, October 14, 1993.
5. Wild, "Life in Balance."
6. Kara Manning, review of *I'm Alive*, *Rolling Stone*, November 11, 1993.
7. Tannenbaum, "Return of The Pretender."
8. Jay Cocks, "Songs of an Open Heart," *Time*, December 13, 1993.
9. Stephen Holden, review of *I'm Alive*, *The New York Times*, November 14, 1993.
10. Paul Evans, review of *I'm Alive*, *Rolling Stone*, 1993.
11. Tannenbaum, "Return of The Pretender."
12. Tannenbaum, "Return of The Pretender."
13. Tannenbaum, "Return of The Pretender."
14. Tannenbaum, "Return of The Pretender."
15. Tannenbaum, "Return of The Pretender."
16. Tannenbaum, "Return of The Pretender."
17. Tannenbaum, "Return of The Pretender."
18. Wild, "Life in Balance."
19. Wild, "Life in Balance."
20. Tannenbaum, "Return of The Pretender."
21. Stephen Holden, review of *Looking East*, *New York Times*, February 13, 1996.

22. Wild, "Life in Balance."

23. *Jackson Browne: Going Home.*

24. Mark Bego, *Bonnie Raitt: Still in the Nick of Time,* Cooper Square Press, 2003.

14: Looking East

1. *Jackson Browne: Going Home*, Video, Pioneer Video, 2001, originally broadcast on the Disney Channel, August 1994.

2. "Jackson Browne Interview" by Elektra Records, sent out as a press release to accompany the *Looking East* album, 1996.

3. "Jackson Browne Interview."

4. "Jackson Browne Interview."

5. "Jackson Browne Interview."

6. "Jackson Browne Interview."

7. "Jackson Browne Interview."

8. "Jackson Browne Interview."

9. Tony Scherman, review of *Looking East*, *Entertainment Weekly*, February 16, 1996.

10. Stephen Holden, review of *Looking East*, *New York Times*, February 13, 1996.

11. Gene Santoro, "Jackson Browne," *The Nation*, May 13, 1996.

12. Santoro, "Jackson Browne."

13. "Jackson Browne Interview."

14. Santoro, "Jackson Browne."

15. Santoro, "Jackson Browne."

16. Santoro, "Jackson Browne."

15: The Naked Ride Home

1. Ralph Bowling and Rick Bowen, "Jackson Browne: Bare-to-the-Bone Stage Delivers Big," *Front Row News*, June 30, 2000.

2. Bowling and Bowen, "Jackson Browne."

3. Jenny Eliscu, "Jackson Browne: The Music Q+A," *Rolling Stone*, November 14, 2002.

4. John Metzger, review of *The Naked Ride Home*, *Music Box*, September 23, 2002.

5. Holly George-Warren, review of *The Naked Ride Home*, *Entertainment Weekly*, October 4, 2002.

6. Zach Martin, telephone interview by author, January 13, 2004.

7. Press release quoted on the Unofficial Jackson Browne Website, September 2002.

8. Associated Press, newswire release about the resolve of Jackson Browne's complaint with Fox-TV, July 18, 2003.
9. Associated Press newswire release.
10. Associated Press newswire release.
11. Melinda Newman, "Browne, Smith Sever Ties with Old Labels," *Billboard* online, January 29, 2004.
12. Newman, "Browne, Smith Sever Ties with Old Labels."

16: These Days

1. Jenny Eliscu, "Jackson Browne: The Music Q+A," *Rolling Stone*, November 14, 2002.
2. Eliscu, "Jackson Browne."
3. Eliscu, "Jackson Browne."
4. Anthony DeCurtis, "Jackson Browne," *Rolling Stone*, November 5–December 10, 1987.
5. DeCurtis, "Jackson Browne."
6. Wayne Hoffman, "Jackson Browne Q&A," *Nature Conservancy*, 2003.
7. Angela Bowie, interview by author, Tucson, Arizona, January 28, 2004.
8. Bowie, interview.
9. Bowie, interview.
10. Zach Martin, telephone interview by author, January 13, 2004.
11. Martin, interview.
12. Martin, interview.
13. *Jackson Browne: Going Home*, Video, Pioneer Video, 2001, originally broadcast on the Disney Channel, August 1994.
14. Martin, interview.
15. Randy Jones, interview by author, February 11, 2004.
16. *Jackson Browne: Going Home.*
17. DeCurtis, "Jackson Browne."
18. Anthony DeCurtis, "Jackson Browne," *Rolling Stone*, October 15, 1992.
19. Jackson Browne, "The Big Poetry Powwow: interview with Poet David St. John," *Interview*, March 1999.
20. DeCurtis, "Jackson Browne," November 5–December 10, 1987.
21. Anthony DeCurtis, "As Jackson Browne's 'World' Turns," *Rolling Stone*, October 5, 1989.

Bibliography

Bego, Mark. *Bonnie Raitt: Still in the Nick of Time*. Cooper Square Press, 2003.

———. *Linda Ronstadt: It's So Easy*. Eakin Press, 1990.

Bogdanov, Vladimir, Chris Woodstra, and Stephen Thomas Erlewine, eds. *All Music Guide to Rock*, 3rd ed. Backbeat Books, 2002.

Crosby, David, and Carl Gottlieb. *Long Time Gone: The Autobiography of David Crosby*. Doubleday, 1988.

Dafydd, Rees, and Luke Crampton. *Rock Stars Encyclopedia*, DK Publishing, 1999.

Dolenz, Micky, and Mark Bego. *I'm a Believer: My Life of Monkees, Music and Madness*. Hyperion, 1993.

Halperin, Ian. *Fire and Rain: The James Taylor Story*. Mainstream Publishing, 2001.

Holzman, Jac and Gavan Daws. *Follow the Music*, First Media Group, 1998.

King, Tom. *The Operator: David Geffen Builds, Buys, and Sells the New Hollywood*, Random House, 2000.

Kort, Michele. *Soul Picnic: The Music and Passion of Laura Nyro*. Thomas Dunn Books, 2002.

Lillian Roxon's Rock Encyclopedia. Tempo Books, Grosset and Dunlap Publishers, 1969.

Maltin, Leonard. *1998 Movie and Video Guide*, Signet Books, 1997.

Smith, Joe. *Off the Record: An Oral History of Popular Music*. Edited by Mitchell Fink. Warner Books, 1988.

Tobler, John. *This Day in Rock*. Carol and Graff Books, 1993.

Whitburn Joel. *Billboard Book of Top 40 Albums*. Billboard Publications, 1995.

———. *Top Pop, 1955–1982*, Record Research, 1983.

———. *Top Pop Albums, 1955–1985*. Record Research, 1985.

Wiseman, Rich. *Jackson Browne: The Story of a Hold Out*. Doubleday/Dolphin Books, 1982.

Discography

Albums

On this list, the term "Gold" refers to sales in excess of 500,000 copies in the United States, "Platinum" refers to sales in excess of 1 million copies in the United States, and "Double Platinum" refers to sales of 2 million copies in the United States. Likewise, "Quintuple Platinum" refers to 5 million copies, and "Septuple Platinum" refers to 7 million copies sold, also in the United States. The abbreviation RIAA stands for Record Industry Association of America. For albums sold exclusively in foreign markets, see the list of "Rare and Foreign Albums" following this initial list.

1. *Jackson Browne*

Released January 2, 1972, Elektra/Asylum Records
Produced by Richard Sanford Orshoff
RIAA Certified "Gold" November 16, 1976/"Platinum" December 12, 1997

1. "Jamaica Say You Will" (3:23)
   (Jackson Browne)

2. "A Child in These Hills" (3:57)
   (Jackson Browne)

3. "Song for Adam" (5:22)
   (Jackson Browne)

4. "Doctor My Eyes" (3:11)
   (Jackson Browne)

5. "From Silver Lake" (3:49)
   (Jackson Browne)

6. "Something Fine" (3:47)
   (Jackson Browne)

7. "Under the Falling Sky" (4:08)
   (Jackson Browne)

8. "Looking into You" (4:20)
   (Jackson Browne)

9. "Rock Me on the Water" (4:13)
   (Jackson Browne)

10. "My Opening Farewell" (4:45)
    (Jackson Browne)

2. *For Everyman*

Released October 15, 1973, Elektra/Asylum Records
Produced by Jackson Browne
RIAA Certified "Gold" October 8, 1975/"Platinum" May 16, 1989

1. "Take It Easy" (3:39)
   (Glenn Frey and Jackson Browne)

2. "Our Lady of the Well" (3:51)
   (Jackson Browne)

3. "Colors of the Sun" (4:26)
   (Jackson Browne)

4. "I Thought I Was a Child" (3:43)
   (Jackson Browne)

5. "These Days" (4:41)
   (Jackson Browne)

6. "Red Neck Friend" (3:56)
   (Jackson Browne)

7. "The Times You've Come" (3:39)
   (Jackson Browne)

8. "Ready or Not" (3:33)
   (Jackson Browne)

9. "Sing My Songs to Me" (3:25)
   (Jackson Browne)

10. "For Everyman" (6:20)
    (Jackson Browne)

3. *Late for the Sky*

Released September 19, 1974, Elektra/Asylum Records
Produced by Jackson Browne and Al Schmitt
RIAA Certified "Gold" December 24, 1974/"Platinum" May 16, 1989
Note: This album is also available as a 24K gold CD

1. "Late for the Sky" (5:36)
   (Jackson Browne)

2. "Fountain of Sorrow (6:42)
   (Jackson Browne)

3. "Farther On" (5:17)
   (Jackson Browne)

4. "The Late Show" (5:09)
   (Jackson Browne)

5. "The Road and the Sky" (3:04)
   (Jackson Browne)

6. "For a Dancer" (4:42)
   (Jackson Browne)

7. "Walking Slow" (3:50)
   (Jackson Browne)

8. "Before the Deluge" (6:18)
   (Jackson Browne)

4. *The Pretender*

Released November 10, 1976, Elektra/Asylum Records
Produced by Jon Landau

RIAA Certified "Gold" November 15, 1976/"Platinum" April 12, 1977/"Double Platinum" December 12, 1997

Note: This album is also available as a 24K *gold* CD

1. "The Fuse" (5:47)
    (Jackson Browne)

2. "Your Bright Baby Blues" (6:01)
    (Jackson Browne)

3. "Linda Paloma" (4:05)
    (Jackson Browne)

4. "Here Come Those Tears Again" (3:35)
    (Jackson Browne and Nancy Farnsworth)

5. "The Only Child" (3:40)
    (Jackson Browne)

6. "Daddy's Tune" (3:34)
    (Jackson Browne)

7. "Sleep's Dark and Silent Gate" (2:35)
    (Jackson Browne)

8. "The Pretender" (5:50)
    (Jackson Browne)

5. *Running on Empty*

Released December 6, 1977, Elektra/Asylum Records
Produced by Jackson Browne
RIAA Certified "Gold" December 28, 1977/"Platinum" August 25, 1978/"Quintuple Platinum" December 12, 1997/"Septuple Platinum" September 6, 2001

1. "Running on Empty" (5:20)
    (Jackson Browne)

2. "The Road" (4:50)
    (Danny O'Keefe)

3. "Rosie" (3:37)
    (Jackson Browne and Donald Miller)

4. "You Love the Thunder" (3:52)
   (Jackson Browne)

5. "Cocaine" (4:55)
   (Rev. Gary Davis, additional lyrics by Jackson Browne and Glenn Frey)

6. "Shaky Town" (3:36)
   (Danny Kortchmar)

7. "Love Needs a Heart" (3:28)
   (Lowell George, Valerie Carter, and Jackson Browne)

8. "Nothing but Time" (3:05)
   (Jackson Browne and Howard Burke)

9. "The Load Out" (5:38)
   (Jackson Browne and Bryan Garofalo)

10. "Stay" (3:28)
    (Maurice Williams)

6. *Hold Out*

Released June 27, 1980, Elektra/Asylum Records
Produced by Jackson Browne and Greg Ladanyi
RIAA Certified "Gold" September 15, 1980/"Platinum" September 15,
1980/"Double Platinum" August 31, 2001

1. "Disco Apocalypse" (5:08)
   (Jackson Browne)

2. "Hold Out" (5:37)
   (Jackson Browne)

3. "That Girl Could Sing" (4:34)
   (Jackson Browne)

4. "Boulevard" (3:15)
   (Jackson Browne)

5. "Of Missing Persons" (6:31)
   (Jackson Browne)

6. "Call It a Loan" (4:35)
   (David Lindley and Jackson Browne)

7. "Hold on Hold Out" (8:08)
   (Craig Doerge and Jackson Browne)

7. *Lawyers in Love*

Released August 1, 1983, Elektra/Asylum Records
Produced by Jackson Browne and Greg Ladanyi
RIAA Certified "Gold" November 8, 1983/"Platinum" August 31, 2001

1. "Lawyers in Love" (4:18)
   (Jackson Browne)

2. "On the Day" (3:56)
   (Jackson Browne)

3. "Cut It Away" (4:45)
   (Jackson Browne)

4. "Downtown" (4:37)
   (Jackson Browne)

5. "Tender is the Night" (4:50)
   (Russell Kunkel, Danny Kortchmar, and Jackson Browne)

6. "Knock on Any Door" (3:39)
   (Danny Kortchmar, Craig Doerge, and Jackson Browne)

7. "Say It Isn't True" (5:20)
   (Jackson Browne)

8. "For a Rocker" (4:05)
   (Jackson Browne)

8. *Lives in the Balance*

Released February 19, 1986, Elektra/Asylum Records
Produced by Jackson Browne
RIAA Certified "Gold" July 8, 1986

1. "For America" (5:10)
   (Jackson Browne)

2. "Soldier of Plenty" (4:34)
   (Jackson Browne)

3. "In the Shape of a Heart" (5:39)
   (Jackson Browne)

4. "Candy" (4:10)
   (Greg Copeland and Wally Stocker)

5. "Lawless Avenues" (5:37)
   (Jorge Calderón and Jackson Browne)

6. "Lives in the Balance" (4:12)
   (Jackson Browne)

7. "Till I Go Down" (4:20)
   (Jackson Browne)

8. "Black and White" (5:11)
   (Jackson Browne)

9. *World in Motion*

Released June 6, 1989, Elektra/Asylum Records
Produced by Scott Thurston and Jackson Browne

1. "World in Motion" (4:24)
   (Jackson Browne and Craig Doerge)

2. "Enough of the Night" (4:54)
   (Jackson Browne)

3. "Chasing You into the Light" (4:16)
   (Jackson Browne)

4. "How Long" (6:10)
   (Jackson Browne)

5. "Anything Can Happen" (5:05)
   (Jackson Browne)

6. "When the Stone Begins to Turn" (4:48)
   (Jackson Browne)

7. "The Word Justice" (4:18)
   (Jackson Browne and Scott Thurston)

8. "My Personal Revenge (4:02)
(Tomás Borge and Louis Enrique Mejía Godoy; English translation by Jorge Calderón)

9. "I Am a Patriot" (4:02)
(Little Steven Van Zandt)

10. "Lights and Virtues" (4:53)
(Jackson Browne)

10. *I'm Alive*

Released October 11, 1993, Elektra Records
Produced by Jackson Browne and Scott Thurston
RIAA Certified "Gold" December 6, 1995

1. "I'm Alive" (5:01)
(Jackson Browne)

2. "My Problem Is You" (4:40)
(Jackson Browne)

3. "Everywhere I Go" (4:36)
(Jackson Browne)

4. "I'll Do Anything" (4:31)
(Jackson Browne)

5. "Miles Away" (3:52)
(Jackson Browne)

6. "Too Many Angels" (6:04)
(Jackson Browne)

7. "Take This Rain" (4:49)
(Jackson Browne)

8. "Two of Me, Two of You" (2:56)
(Jackson Browne)

9. "Sky Blue and Black" (6:06)
(Jackson Browne)

10. "All Good Things" (4:28)
    (Jackson Browne)

11. *Looking East*

Released February 13, 1996, Elektra Records
Produced by Scott Thurston and Kevin McCormick
Note: In the United States there is a Special Edition Enhanced CD version of
Looking East. The Japanese edition of *Looking East* includes a bonus track:
"World in Motion" recorded live in Los Angeles with the Hamilton High School
Gospel Choir.

1. "Looking East" (4:56)
   (Jackson Browne, Jeff Young, Kevin McCormick, Scott Thurston, Mark
   Goldenberg, Mauricio Lewak, and Luis Conte)

2. "The Barricades of Heaven" (5:41)
   (Jackson Browne, Young, McCormick, Thurston, Goldenberg, Lewak, and
   Conte)

3. "Some Bridges" (4:51)
   (Jackson Browne, Young, McCormick, Thurston, Goldenberg, Lewak, and
   Conte)

4. "Information Wars" (5:14)
   (Jackson Browne, Jeff Cohen, Young, McCormick, Thurston, Goldenberg,
   Lewak, and Conte)

5. "I'm the Cat" (3:54)
   (Jackson Browne, Young, McCormick, Thurston, Goldenberg, Lewak, and
   Conte)

6. "Culver Moon" (5:45)
   (Jackson Browne, Young, McCormick, Thurston, Goldenberg, Lewak, and
   Conte)

7. "Baby How Long" (5:04)
   (Jackson Browne)

8. "Nino" (5:12)
   (Jackson Browne, Jorge Calderón, Young, McCormick, Thurston,
   Goldenberg, Lewak, Conte, and Valerie Carter)

9. "Alive in the World" (4:50)
   (Jackson Browne)

10. "It Is One" (4:56)
    (Jackson Browne, Young, McCormick, Thurston, Goldenberg, Lewak, Conte, and Carter)

12. *The Next Voice You Hear: The Best of Jackson Browne*

Released September 23, 1997, Elektra Records
Producers: Various
RIAA Certified "Gold" September 16, 2002

1. "Doctor My Eyes" (3:20)
   (Jackson Browne)

2. "These Days" (4:39)
   (Jackson Browne)

3. "Fountain of Sorrow" (6:53)
   (Jackson Browne)

4. "Late for the Sky" (5:38)
   (Jackson Browne)

5. "The Pretender" (5:53)
   (Jackson Browne)

6. "Running on Empty" (4:55)
   (Jackson Browne)

7. "Call It a Loan" (4:48)
   (Jackson Browne and David Lindley)

8. "Somebody's Baby" (4:22)
   (Jackson Browne and Danny Kortchmar)

9. "Tender Is the Night" (4:54)
   (Jackson Browne, Russell Kunkel, and Danny Kortchmar)

10. "In the Shape of a Heart" (5:42)
    (Jackson Browne)

11. "Lives in the Balance" (4:16)
    (Jackson Browne)

12. "Sky Blue and Black" (6:07)
    (Jackson Browne)

13. "The Barricades of Heaven" (5:43)
    (Jackson Browne, Jeff Young, Kevin McCormick, Scott Thurston, Mark Goldenberg, Mauricio Lewak, and Luis Conte)

14. "The Rebel Jesus" (4:39)
    (Jackson Browne)

15. "The Next Voice You Hear" (4:49)
    (Jackson Browne)

13. *The Naked Ride Home*

Released September 24, 2002, Elektra Records
Produced by Jackson Browne & Kevin McCormick

1. "The Naked Ride Home" (5:56)
   (Jackson Browne)

2. "The Night Inside Me" (4:38)
   (Jackson Browne, Kevin McCormick, Mark Goldenberg, Mauricio Lewak, and Jeff Young)

3. "Casino Nation" (6:56)
   (Jackson Browne, McCormick, Goldenberg, Lewak, and Young)

4. "For Taking the Trouble" (4:24)
   (Jackson Browne)

5. "Never Stop" (4:56)
   (Jackson Browne, McCormick, Goldenberg, Lewak, and Young)

6. "Walking Town" (6:20)
   (Jackson Browne, McCormick, Goldenberg, Lewak, and Young)

7. "About My Imagination" (6:09)
   (Jackson Browne, McCormick, Goldenberg, Lewak, and Young)

8. "Sergio Leone" (7:57)
   (Jackson Browne, McCormick, Goldenberg, Lewak, and Young)

8. "Don't You Want to Be There" (7:34)
   (Jackson Browne)

9. "My Stunning Mystery Companion" (4:51)
   (Jackson Browne)

14. *The Very Best of Jackson Browne*

Released March 16, 2004, Rhino Records
Producers: Various

DISC ONE:

1. "Doctor My Eyes"
   (Jackson Browne)

2. "Rock Me on the Water"
   (Jackson Browne)

3. "Jamaica Say You Will"
   (Jackson Browne)

4. "Take It Easy"
   (Glenn Frey and Jackson Browne)

5. "These Days"
   (Jackson Browne)

6. "For Everyman"
   (Jackson Browne)

7. "Red Neck Friend"
   (Jackson Browne)

8. "Fountain of Sorrow"
   (Jackson Browne)

9. "For a Dancer"
   (Jackson Browne)

10. "Late for the Sky"
    (Jackson Browne)

11 "Before the Deluge"
   (Jackson Browne)

12. "Your Bright Baby Blues"
    (Jackson Browne)

13. "The Pretender"
    (Jackson Browne)

14. "Here Come Those Tears Again"
    (Jackson Browne and Nancy Farnsworth)

15. "The Load Out"
    (Jackson Browne and Bryan Garofalo)

16. "Stay"
    (Maurice Williams)

DISC TWO:

1. "Running on Empty"
   (Jackson Browne)

2. "You Love the Thunder"
   (Jackson Browne)

3. "That Girl Could Sing"
   (Jackson Browne)

4. "Boulevard"
   (Jackson Browne)

5. "Somebody's Baby"
   (Jackson Browne and Danny Kortchmar)

6. "Tender Is the Night"
   (Russell Kunkel, Danny Kortchmar and Jackson Browne)

7. "In the Shape of a Heart"
   (Jackson Browne)

8. "Lawless Avenues"
   (Jorge Calderón and Jackson Browne)

9. "Lives in the Balance"
   (Jackson Browne)

10. "I Am a Patriot"
    (Little Steven Van Zandt)

11. "Sky Blue and Black"
(Jackson Browne)

12. "I'm Alive"
(Jackson Browne)

13. "The Barricades of Heaven"
(Jackson Browne, Jeff Young, Kevin McCormick, Scott Thurston, Mark Goldenberg, Mauricio Lewak, and Luis Conte)

14. "Looking East"
(Jackson Browne, Jeff Young, Kevin McCormick, Scott Thurston, Mark Goldenberg, Mauricio Lewak, and Luis Conte)

15. "The Naked Ride Home"
(Jackson Browne)

16. "The Night Inside Me"
(Jackson Browne, Kevin McCormick, Mark Goldenberg, Mauricio Lewak, and Jeff Young)

Rare & Foreign Albums

1. *Retrospective*

Released 1993, Elektra Records
Note: This album was distributed as a promotional release to radio stations in the United States.

1. "Doctor My Eyes" (3:11)
(Jackson Browne)

1. "Take It Easy" (3:39)
(Glenn Frey and Jackson Browne)

2. "These Days" (4:41)
(Jackson Browne)

3. "For a Dancer" (4:42)
(Jackson Browne)

4. "The Pretender" (5:50)
(Jackson Browne)

5. "Running on Empty" (5:20)
    (Jackson Browne)

6. "That Girl Could Sing" (4:34)
    (Jackson Browne)

7. "Somebody's Baby" (4:01)
    (Jackson Browne and Danny Kortchmar)

8. "Tender Is the Night" (4:50)
    (Russell Kunkel, Danny Kortchmar, and Jackson Browne)

9. "In the Shape of a Heart" (5:39)
    (Jackson Browne)

10. "I Am a Patriot" (4:02)
    (Little Steven Van Zandt)

11. "Late for the Sky" (5:09)
    (Jackson Browne)

2. Best of . . . Live

Released 1996 and 1998, Elektra Records
Note: This was released as an exclusive Australian tour souvenir in 1996, and then it was released again as an exclusive Japanese tour souvenir in 1998

1. "Doctor My Eyes"
    (Recorded live in Oakland, California, March 3, 1996)

2. "My Problem Is You"
    (Recorded live in Houston, Texas, August 20, 1994)

3. "In the Shape of a Heart"
    (Recorded live in Oslo, Norway, July 2, 1996)

4. "Take It Easy"
    (Recorded live in Dallas, Texas, August 19, 1994)

5. "For a Dancer"
    (Recorded live in Oslo, Norway, July 2, 1996)

6. "The Pretender"
    (Recorded live in Belfast, Ireland, June 19, 1996)

7. "Running on Empty"
   (Recorded live in Oakland, California, March 1, 1996)

8. "The Load Out"
   (Recorded live in Glasgow, Scotland, July 14, 1996)

9. "Stay"
   (Recorded live in Glasgow, Scotland, July 14, 1996)

10. "Somebody's Baby"
    (Recorded live in Glasgow, Scotland, July 13, 1996)

11. "Before the Deluge"
    (Recorded live in Glasgow, Scotland, July 13, 1996)

3. *Best of ... Live/The Next Voice You Hear: The Best of Jackson Browne*

Released in Japan, May 20, 2003, Elektra Records
Note: This is a two CD set released in Japan only. It combines the previous "live" album with a slightly different version of Jackson's *Best of* album. "Stay" and "Lawyers in Love" are added and "Sky Blue and Black" is dropped, in comparison to the U.S. version of the album. This two-disc set is available worldwide via the Internet.

DISC ONE:

1. "Doctor My Eyes"
   (Recorded live in Oakland, California, March 3, 1996)

2. "My Problem Is You"
   (Recorded live in Houston, Texas, August 20, 1994)

3. "In the Shape of a Heart"
   (Recorded live in Oslo, Norway, July 2, 1996)

4. "Take It Easy"
   (Recorded live in Dallas, Texas, August 19, 1994)

5. "For a Dancer"
   (Recorded live in Oslo, Norway, July 2, 1996)

6. "The Pretender"
   (Recorded live in Belfast, Ireland, June 19, 1996)

7. "Running on Empty"
    (Recorded live in Oakland, California, March 1, 1996)

8. "The Load Out"
    (Recorded live in Glasgow, Scotland, July 14, 1996)

9. "Stay"
    (Recorded live in Glasgow, Scotland, July 14, 1996)

10. "Somebody's Baby"
    (Recorded live in Glasgow, Scotland, July 13, 1996)

11. "Before the Deluge"
    (Recorded live in Glasgow, Scotland, July 13, 1996)

DISC TWO:

1. "Doctor My Eyes" (3:20)
    (Jackson Browne)

2. "These Days" (4:39)
    (Jackson Browne)

3. "Fountain of Sorrow" (6:53)
    (Jackson Browne)

4. "Late for the Sky" (5:38)
    (Jackson Browne)

5. "The Pretender" (5:53)
    (Jackson Browne)

6. "Running on Empty" (4:55)
    (Jackson Browne)

7. "Stay" (3:28)
    (Maurice Williams)

8. "Call It a Loan" (4:48)
    (Jackson Browne and David Lindley)

9. "Somebody's Baby" (4:22)
    (Jackson Browne and Danny Kortchmar)

10. "Tender Is the Night" (4:54)
    (Jackson Browne, Russell Kunkel, and Danny Kortchmar)

11. "Lawyers in Love" (4:18)
    (Jackson Browne)

12. "In the Shape of a Heart" (5:42)
    (Jackson Browne)

13. "Lives in the Balance" (4:16)
    (Jackson Browne)

14. "The Barricades of Heaven" (5:43)
    (Jackson Browne, Jeff Young, Kevin McCormick, Scott Thurston, Mark Goldenberg, Mauricio Lewak, and Luis Conte)

15. "The Rebel Jesus" (4:39)
    (Jackson Browne)

16. "The Next Voice You Hear" (4:49)
    (Jackson Browne)

Appearances on Other Albums, Singles, and Videos

1. "Fool Yourself," "Run Like a Thief," "I'm Blowing Way," and "Your Sweet and Shiny Eyes"
   (Singing background vocals on the Bonnie Raitt album *Home Plate*, 1975)

2. "Crow on the Cradle"
   (Live duet with Graham Nash from the *No Nukes* soundtrack, 1979)

3. "Before the Deluge"
   (Live from the *No Nukes* soundtrack, 1979)

4. "Stay"
   (Live duet with Bruce Springsteen featuring the E Street Band and Rosemary Butler, from the *No Nukes* soundtrack, 1979)

5. "Get Together" by Jesse Colin Young
   [Jackson Browne is in the chorus along with Graham Nash and Rosemary Butler]
   (Live from the *No Nukes* soundtrack, 1979)

6. "Power" by the Doobie Brothers and James Taylor
   [Jackson Browne is in the chorus along with Carly Simon, Nicolette Larson, John Hall, Graham Nash, and Rosemary Butler]
   (Live from the *No Nukes* soundtrack, 1979)

7. "Takin' It to the Streets" by the Doobie Brothers and James Taylor
   [Jackson Browne is in the chorus along with Carly Simon, Nicolette Larson, John
   Hall, Graham Nash, and Rosemary Butler]
   (Live from the *No Nukes* soundtrack, 1979)

8. "For Everyman"
   (Live with David Lindley on the charity album *Bread and Roses Festival of
   Acoustic Music, Vol. 1,* 1979)

9. "You're a Friend of Mine"
   (Duet with Clarence Clemons on his album *Hero,* 1985)

10. "Sun City"
    [The title song includes solo lines and chorus appearances by Afrika Bambaataa,
    Ray Barretto, Stiv Bator, Pat Benatar, Big Youth, Ruben Blades, Kurtis Blow, Bono,
    Duke Bootee, Jackson Browne, Ron Carter, Clarence Clemons, Jimmy Cliff, George
    Clinton, Miles Davis, Will Downing, Bob Dylan, the Fat Boys, Peter Gabriel, Peter
    Garrett, Bob Geldof, Daryl Hall, Herbie Hancock, Nona Hendryx, Linton Kwesi
    Johnson, Stanley Jordan, Kashif, Eddie Kendricks, Little Steven Van Zandt, Darlene
    Love, Malopoets, Grandmaster Melle Mel, Michael Monroe, John Oates, Sonny
    Okosuns, Bonnie Raitt, Joey Ramone, Lou Reed, David Ruffin, Run-DMC, Scorpio,
    Gil Scott-Heron, Shankar, Bruce Springsteen, Zak Starkey, Ringo Starr, Tina B,
    Pete Townshend, Via Afrika, Tony Williams, Peter Wolf, and Bobby Womack]
    (single and album out of the 1980s megastar charity album mold, 1985)

11. "You Are a Friend of Mine"
    (Duet with Clarence Clemons on his album, *Hero,* 1985)

12. "Voice of America"
    (B-side of the "In the Shape of a Heart" single, 1986)

13. "For Everyman"
    (Live acoustic on the Amnesty International album *The Secret Policeman's Third
    Ball,* 1987)

14. "El Salvador"
    (Duet with Joan Baez on her album *Speaking of Dreams,* 1989)

15. "Only the Lonely," "In Dreams," "Dream Baby," "Leah," "Move On down the
    Line," "Crying," "Mean Woman Blues," "Running Scared," "Blue Bayou," "Candy
    Man," "Uptown," "Ooby Dooby," "The Comedians," "(All I Can Do Is) Dream
    You," "It's Over," "Oh Pretty Woman"

(Background vocals along with Bonnie Raitt, k. d. lang, Jennifer Warnes, Steven Soles and John David Souther, all behind Roy Orbison, on Orbison's album and TV special *Black and White Night Live*, 1989)

16. "First Girl I Loved"
   (On the album *Rubaiyat: Elektra's 40th Anniversary*, 1990)

17. "The Rebel Jesus"
   (Backed by the Chieftains on their album *The Bells of Dublin*, 1991)

18. "Golden Slumbers"
   (Duet with Jennifer Warnes on the Disney album *For Our Children*, 1991, and on the Kid Rhino album *For Our Children 10*, 1999)

19. "Let It Be Me"
   (Sung with the Indigo Girls on their album *Rites of Passage*, 1992)

20. "Unloved"
   (Duet with Jann Arden on her album *Living Under June*, 1994)

21. "Rock Me on the Water"
   (Duet with Kathy Mattea on the album *Red Hot & Country*, 1994)

22. "Doctor My Eyes"
   (Remixed and remastered for the *My Girl 2* soundtrack, 1994)

23. "Sky Blue and Black"
   (Live at the Royal Albert Hall, London, from the CD-single of "Sky Blue and Black," 1994)

24. "I'm Alive"
   (Live in Hamburg, Germany, October 28, 1993, bonus track on one of the CD-single versions of "Everywhere I Go," 1994)

25. "The Pretender"
   (Live in Hamburg, Germany, October 28, 1993, bonus track on one of the CD-single versions of "Everywhere I Go," 1994)

26. "Birds of St. Marks"
   (Included on the *Jackson Browne: Going Home*, 1994 TV special, video, and DVD)

27. "Running on Empty"
   (Live in Hamburg, Germany, October 28, 1993, bonus track on one of the CD-single versions of "Everywhere I Go," 1994)

28. "Late for the Sky"
    (Live session from radio station KCRW's *Rare on Air: Volume 2*, 1995)

29. "Let It Be Me"
    (Duet with Timothy B. Schmidt on the soundtrack *Bye Bye, Love*, 1995)

30. "My Problem Is You"
    (Backed by Luis Conte and his band from his album *The Road*, 1995)

31. "My Opening Farewell"
    (Duet with Bonnie Raitt on her album *Road Tested*, 1995)

32. "Angel from Montgomery"
    (With Bonnie Raitt, Bruce Hornsby, and Kim Wilson on Raitt's *Road Tested*
    album, 1995)

33. "Redemption Song"
    (Live in Cleveland, Ohio, from *The Concert for the Rock and Roll Hall of Fame*
    album, 1996)

34. "If I Only Had a Brain"
    (Live from the *Wizard of Oz in Concert: Dreams Come True* benefit soundtrack,
    1996)

35. "We're Off to See the Wizard"
    (Live duet with Jewel from *Wizard of Oz in Concert: Dreams Come True* benefit
    soundtrack, 1996)

36. "Lions and Tigers and Bears"
    (Live with Jewel, Jackson Browne, and Roger Daltrey from *Wizard of Oz in
    Concert: Dreams Come True* benefit soundtrack, 1996)

37. "We're Off to See the Wizard" Version 2
    (Live with Jewel, Jackson Browne, and Roger Daltrey from *Wizard of Oz in
    Concert: Dreams Come True* benefit soundtrack, 1996)

38. "If I Only Had the Nerve"
    (Live with Nathan Lane, Jewel, Jackson Browne, and Roger Daltrey from *Wizard
    of Oz in Concert: Dreams Come True* benefit soundtrack, 1996)

39. "We're Off to See the Wizard" Version 3
    (Live with Jewel, Jackson Browne, Roger Daltrey, Nathan Lane from *Wizard of Oz
    in Concert: Dreams Come True* benefit soundtrack, 1996)

40. "The Jitterbug"
    (Live with Jewel, Jackson Browne, Roger Daltrey, and Nathan Lane from *Wizard of Oz in Concert: Dreams Come True* benefit soundtrack, 1996)

41. "Over the Rainbow"
    (Live with Jackson Browne with full company from *Wizard of Oz In Concert: Dreams Come True* benefit soundtrack, 1996)

42. "Before the Deluge"
    (Live in Dublin, Ireland, June 27, 1994, bonus track on the CD-single of "I'm the Cat," 1996)

43. "Soldier of Plenty"
    (Live in London, England, June 12, 1994, bonus track on the CD-single of "I'm the Cat," 1996)

44. "In the Shape of a Heart"
    (Live in Osaka, Japan, April 22, 1994, bonus track on the CD-single of "I'm the Cat," 1996)

45. "World in Motion"
    (Live in Los Angeles with the Hamilton High School Gospel Choir; bonus track on the Japanese edition of "Looking East," 1996)

46. "I've Been the One"
    (From the Lowell George tribute album *Rock and Roll Doctor*, 1997)

47. "Kisses Sweeter Than Wine"
    (Duet with Bonnie Raitt from the Pete Seeger tribute CD *Where Have All the Flowers Gone*, 1998)

48. "My Back Pages"
    (Duet with Joan Osborne on the Bob Dylan song from the *Steal This Movie* soundtrack, 2000)

49. "For a Dancer"
    (With harmony vocals by the band Venice on the Venice album *2 Meter Sessies*, 2000)

50. "A Man of Constant Sorrow"
    (Backed by Sharon Shannon and friends on her album *The Diamond Mountain Sessions*, 2000)

51. "Guantanamera"
    (Duet with Joan Baez on the album *If I Had a Song: The Songs of Pete Seeger*, 2001)

52. "Knockin' on Heaven's Door"
    (With Billy Bob Thornton and John Waite, from the Warren Zevon album *Dirty Life and Times*, 2003)

53. "Poor Poor Pitiful Me"
    (Duet with Bonnie Raitt on the album *Enjoy Every Sandwich: The Songs of Warren Zevon*, 2004)

Singles

"Doctor My Eyes" (1972)

"Rock Me on the Water" (1972)

"My Red Neck Friend" (1973)

"Ready or Not"/"Take it Easy" (1974)

"Walking Slow" (1974)

"Fountain of Sorrow" (1975)

"Here Come Those Tears Again" (1977)

"The Pretender" (1977)

"Running on Empty" (1978)

"Stay" (1978)

"Boulevard" (1980)

"That Girl Could Sing" (1980)

"Somebody's Baby" (1982)

"Lawyers in Love" (1983)

"Tender Is the Night" (1983)

"For the Rocker" (1983)

"Sun City" (1985) [with several other artists]

"You're a Friend of Mine" (1986) [with Clarence Clemons]

"In the Shape of a Heart" (1986)

"Lives in Balance" (1986)

"For America" (1986)

"Chasing You into the Light" (1989)

"World in Motion" (1989)

"I'm Alive" (1993)

"Sky Blue and Black" (1994)

"Everywhere I Go" (1994)

"Some Bridges" (1996)

"I'm the Cat" (1996)

"The Night Inside Me" (2002)

Jackson Browne
On Video Cassette and DVD

1. *No Nukes* (1980)/Video only
2. *Roy Orbison: A Black and White Night Live* (1999)/DVD and video
3. *Jackson Browne: Coming Home* (1994)/ DVD and video
4. *Nico: Icon* (1995)/DVD and video
5. *Wizard of Oz in Concert: Dreams Come True* (1996)/Video only
6. *Bonnie Raitt: Road Tested* (2001)/DVD and video
7. *Under the Covers* (2002)/DVD

Jackson Browne
Songs Recorded by Other Artists

"Before the Deluge"

Blue Heaven, *After the Deluge: A Tribute to Jackson Browne* (Charma, 1977)
Joan Baez, *Honest Lullaby* (Portrait, 1979)
Christy Moore, *King Puck* (EMI 2001)

"Cast Off All My Fears"

Hour Glass, *Hour Glass* (Liberty, 1967)

"Colors of the Sun"

Tom Rush, *Tom Rush* (Columbia, 1972)
Bonnie Koloc, *You're Gonna Love Yourself in the Morning* (Ovation, 1974)

"Doctor My Eyes"

The Jackson Five, *Lookin' through the Windows* (Motown, 1972)
—A Top 10 single in Great Britain
Mary Travers, *All My Choices* (Warner Brothers, 1973)

"Doolin-Dalton" (written with Glenn Frey, J. D. Souther, and Don Henley)

The Eagles, *Desperado* (Asylum, 1973)

"Fairest of Seasons" (written with Greg Copeland)

Nico, *Chelsea Girl* (Verve, 1967)

"For a Dancer"

Prelude, *Owl Creek Incident* (Pye, 1975)
Linda Ronstadt and Emmylou Harris, *Western Wall: The Tucson Sessions* (Elektra/Asylum 1999)

"Fountain of Sorrow"

Joan Baez, *Diamonds and Rust* (A&M, 1975)

"From Silver Lake"

Hedge and Donna, *Hedge and Donna 2* (Capitol, 1968)

"Gone to Sorrow"

Ashes Featuring Pat Taylor, *Ashes Featuring Pat Taylor* (Vault, 1970)

"Holding"

The Nitty Gritty Dirt Band, *The Nitty Gritty Dirt Band* (Liberty, 1966)
Blue Heaven, *After the Deluge: A Tribute to Jackson Browne* (Charma, 1977)

"I Thought I Was a Child"

Bonnie Raitt, *Takin' My Time* (Warner Brothers, 1973)

"It's Been Raining Here in Long Beach"

The Nitty Gritty Dirt Band, *Ricochet* (Liberty, 1967)

"Jamaica Say You Will"

The Nitty Gritty Dirt Band, *All the Good Times* (United Artists, 1971)
The Byrds, *Byrd Manix* (Columbia, 1971)

Tom Rush, *Merrimac Country* (Columbia, 1972)
Bonnie Koloc, *Hold on to Me* (Ovation, 1972)
Sugarblue, *Sugarblue* (Warner Brothers, 1972)
Joe Cocker, *Joe Cocker* (A&M, 1972)

"James Dean" (written with Glenn Frey, J. D. Souther, and Don Henley)

The Eagles, *On the Border* (Asylum, 1979)

"Late for the Sky"

Mae McKenna, *Everything That Touches Me* (Transatlantic-U.K., 1976)
Blue Heaven, *After the Deluge: A Tribute to Jackson Browne* (Charma, 1977)

"Love Needs a Heart" (written with Lowell George and Valerie Carter)

The Harptones, *Love Needs* (Ambient Sound, 1982)

"Mae Jean Goes to Hollywood"

Johnny Darrel, *California Stop-Over* (United Artists, 1969)

"Melissa"

The Nitty Gritty Dirt Band, *The Nitty Gritty Dirt Band* (Liberty, 1966)

"My Opening Farewell"

Michael Johnson, *There Is a Breeze* (ATCO, 1973)
Bonnie Raitt, *Sweet Forgiveness* (Warner Brothers, 1977)
Blue Heaven, *After the Deluge: A Tribute to Jackson Browne* (Charma, 1977)
Bonnie Raitt, *Road Tested* (Capitol, 1995)
—Performed with Jackson Browne

"Nightingale"

The Eagles, *The Eagles* (Asylum, 1972)

"Our Lady of the Well"

Johnny Rivers, *Home Grown* (United Artists, 1971)

"The Painter"

Steve Noonan, *Steve Noonan* (Elektra, 1968)
Blue Heaven, *After the Deluge: A Tribute to Jackson Browne* (Charma, 1977)

"The Pretender"

Gary U. S. Bonds, *Dedication* (EMI, 1981)

"Rock Me on the Water"

Johnny Rivers, *Home Gown* (United Artists, 1971)
Linda Ronstadt, *Linda Ronstadt* (Capitol, 1971)
Eugene Wallace, *Book of Fool* (EMI, 1974)

"Shadow Dream Song"

The Nitty Gritty Dirt Band, *Ricochet* (Liberty, 1967)
Steve Noonan, *Steve Noonan* (Elektra, 1968)
Tom Rush, *The Circle Game* (Elektra, 1968)
Blue Heaven, *After the Deluge: A Tribute to Jackson Browne* (Charma, 1977)

"She's a Flying Thing"

Steve Noonan, *Steve Noonan* (Elektra, 1968)
Blue Heaven, *After the Deluge: A Tribute to Jackson Browne* (Charma, 1977)

"Sleep's Dark and Silent Gate"

Bonnie Raitt, *The Glow* (Warner Brothers, 1979)

"Something Fine"

Dianne Davidson, *Mountain Mama* (Janus, 1972)
Leo Sayer, *Leo Sayer* (Warner Brothers, 1978)

"Somewhere There's a Feather"

Nico, *Chelsea Girl* (Verve, 1967)
Blue Heaven, *After the Deluge: A Tribute to Jackson Browne* (Charma, 1977)

"Song for Adam"

Dianne Davidson, *Mountain Mama* (Janus, 1972)
Kiki Dee, *Loving and Free* (MCA, 1973)
Larry Norman, *Streams of White Light in Darkened Corners* (AB, 1974)

"Take It Easy" (written with Glenn Frey)

The Eagles, *The Eagles* (Asylum, 1972)
Johnny Rivers, *Rockin' Rivers* (United Artists, 1974)

"Tenderness on the Block" (with Warren Zevon)

Warren Zevon, *Excitable Boy* (Asylum, 1978)

"There Came a Question"

Hedge and Donna, *All the Friendly Colours* (Capitol, 1969)

"These Days"

Nico, *Chelsea Girl* (Verve, 1967)
The Nitty Gritty Dirt Band, *Rare Junk* (Liberty, 1967)
Johnny Darrel, *California Stop-Over* (United Artists, 1969)
Gator Creek, *Gator Creek* (Mercury, 1970)
Tom Rush, *Tom Rush* (Columbia, 1972)
Jennifer Warren [Warnes], *Jennifer* (Reprise, 1972)
Ian Matthews, *Valley Hi* (Elektra, 1973)
Gregg Allman, *Laid Back* (Capricorn, 1973)
Terry Melcher, *Terry Melcher* (Reprise, 1974)
Cher, *Stars* (Warner Brothers, 1975)
Mae McKenna, *Everything That Touches Me* (Transatlantic/U.K. 1976)

"Trusting Is a Hard Thing" (written with Steve Noonan)

Steve Noonan, *Steve Noonan* (Elektra, 1968)

"Tumble Down"

Steve Noonan, *Steve Noonan* (Elektra, 1968)

"Under the Falling Sky"

Bonnie Raitt, *Give It Up* (Warner Brothers, 1972)
Bonnie Raitt, *The Bonnie Raitt Collection* (Warner Brothers, 1990)

"You Love the Thunder"

Hank Williams Jr. (Warner Brothers, 1978)
—Released as a single

About the Author

MARK BEGO is the author of several best-selling books on rock & roll and show business. With over forty-five books published and over 10 million books in print, he is acknowledged as the best-selling biographer in the rock and pop music field. His biographies include the life stories of some of the biggest stars of rock, soul, pop, and country. His first Top 10 *New York Times* best seller was *Michael!* about Michael Jackson (1984). Since that time, he has written *Cher!* (2001), *Rock Hudson: Public and Private* (1986), *Aretha Franklin: Queen of Soul* (1989), *Jewel* (1998), *Madonna: Blonde Ambition* (2000), *Bette Midler: Still Divine* (2002), *Bonnie Raitt: Still in the Nick of Time* (2003), and *Tina Turner: Break Every Rule* (2003).

In the 1990s, Bego branched out into country music books, writing *Country Hunks* (1994), *Country Gals* (1995), *I Fall to Pieces: The Music and the Life of Patsy Cline* (1995), *Alan Jackson: Gone Country* (1996), *George Strait: The Story of Country's Living Legend* (1997), *LeAnn Rimes* (1998), and *Vince Gill* (2000).

Bego has coauthored books with several rock stars including *Martha Reeves: Dancing in the Street, Confessions of a Motown Diva*, which spent five weeks on the *Chicago Tribune* best-seller list in 1994. He worked with Micky Dolenz of the Monkees (*I'm a Believer*, 1993 and 2004), Jimmy Greenspoon of Three Dog Night (*One Is the Loneliest Number*, 1991), and Mary Wilson (*Dreamgirl: My Life As a Supreme*, 2000).

His writing has also been featured in several record albums and CDs. In 1982, he wrote the interior notes to the Columbia House five-record boxed set *The Motown Collection*. His liner notes can also be found in the CD collection *Mary Wilson: I Am Changing* (2000).

In 1998, Mark wrote books about three of the hottest leading men in late

1990s cinema. His *Leonardo DiCaprio: Romantic Hero* spent six weeks on the *New York Times* best-seller list. He followed it up with *Matt Damon: Chasing a Dream* and *Will Smith: The Freshest Prince*. He has also written *The Linda Gray Story* (1988) and *Julia Roberts: America's Sweetheart* (2003).

In 1998, Melitta Coffee launched *Mark Bego: Romantic Hero Blend* coffee as part of their Celebrity Series. He is currently developing his book *Rock & Roll Almanac* (1995) into a television series. He divides his time between New York City, Los Angeles, and Tucson, Arizona. Visit his website at www. markbego.com.